Key Performance Indicators for Government and Non Profit Agencies

Key Performance Indicators for Government and Non Profit Agencies

Implementing Winning KPIs

DAVID PARMENTER

WILEY

John Wiley & Sons, Inc.

Published by John Wiley & Sons, Inc., Hoboken, New Jersey.
Published simultaneously in Canada.

For general information on our other products and services or for technical support, please contact our Customer Care Department within the United States at (800) 762-2974, outside the United States at (317) 572-3993 or fax (317) 572-4002.

Wiley also publishes its books in a variety of electronic formats. Some content that appears in print may not be available in electronic books. For more information about Wiley products, visit our web site at www.wiley.com.

Library of Congress Cataloging-in-Publication Data:

Parmenter, David.
   Key performance indicators for government and non profit agencies : implementing winning KPIs / David Parmenter. – 1
      p. cm.
   Includes index.
   ISBN 978-0-470-94454-7 (cloth); ISBN 978-1-118-22146-4 (ebk);
   ISBN 978-1-118-23530-0 (ebk); ISBN 978-1-118-26004-3 (ebk)
 1. Performance technology.   2. Performance standards.   3. Organizational effectiveness.   4. Nonprofit organizations–Management.   5. Administrative agencies–Management.   I. Title.
   HF5549.5.P37P373 2012
   658.4′013–dc23

                                                                    2012004859

Printed in the United States of America

10 9 8 7 6 5 4 3 2 1

To Jeremy Hope, a guru, mentor, and friend. His thinking has been an inspiration to me and I am sure, in years to come, his work will sit alongside the great work of the giant paradigm shifters: Peter Drucker, Jim Collins, Tom Peters & Robert Waterman, Gary Hamel, and Jack Welch.

Contents

Preface

Performance measurement is failing organizations worldwide, whether they are multinationals, government departments, or non profit agencies. The measures that have been adopted were dreamed up without any linkage to the critical success factors of the organizations. Often these measures are monthly or quarterly. Management reviews them and says, "That was a good quarter" or "That was a bad month."

Performance measures should help your organization align daily activities to strategic objectives. This book has been written to assist government and non profit agencies with developing, implementing, and using winning key performance indicators (KPIs)—those performance measures that will make a profound difference.

Companion to the KPI Book

This book is designed to help those project managers who are about to embark on a KPI project. It is designed to be a companion work to my earlier book, *Key Performance Indicators: Developing, Implementing, and Using Winning KPIs*, 2nd edition (John Wiley & Sons 2010). This book includes my latest research, new material developed to help convey the "winning KPI methodology," while at the same time focusing specifically on government and non profit agency examples and case studies.

The new content includes:

- The myths of performance measurement.
- The importance of understanding the behavioral side of performance measurement.
- Revitalizing performance management including reference to the work of the Paradigm Shifters (Drucker, Collins, Welch, Hamel, Peters and Waterman, and others).
- The reasons that the traditional balanced-scorecard approach has failed.
- More examples to aid with finding your critical success factors.
- Case studies for government and non profit agencies.
- Relevant government and non profit agency performance measures.

To implement winning KPIs into a government or non profit agency you will thus need both of my books on KPIs. I expect many readers of this book will already have the KPI book, so repetition would not have been appreciated. To the new readers, who may be disappointed, I offer a number of the relevant templates electronically through my web site for no fee.

This small investment by the reader has saved me from repeating the material from the earlier work so I can focus more on bigger picture issues listed above.

As a companion book to the KPI book it contains my latest thinking and private sector readers who have already read my KPI book will find much of this book useful particularly Chapters 1 to 5, 10, and 13, and Appendixes A, B, D, G, and H.

Embarking on a KPI/Balanced-Scorecard Project

The goal of this book is to help minimize the risks that working on a KPI/balanced-scorecard project encompasses. It is designed for the project team, senior management, external project facilitators, and team coordinators whose are responsible for steering such a project to success. The roles they play could leave a great legacy in the organization for years to come, or could amount to nothing by implementing the many performance measurement initiatives that have failed. It is my wish that the material in this book, along with the workshops I deliver around the world, will increase your likelihood of success. In order for both you and your project to succeed, I suggest that you:

- Read Chapters 1, 2, 3, and 6 carefully, a couple of times.
- Visit my web site, www.davidparmenter.com, for other useful information.
- Read the remaining chapters.
- Begin Step 1 in Chapter 9 by setting up the focus group one-day workshop.
- Listen to my webcasts, which can be accessed via www.davidparmenter.com.
- Seek an outside facilitator who will help guide/mentor you in the early weeks of the project.
- Begin the KPI project team-building exercises, and undertake any training to plug skill gaps identified in the KPI project team.

This book is also aimed at providing a foundation for the balanced-scorecard platform. As mentioned in Appendix H, I believe the balanced scorecard will be with us for centuries to come; we just need to make it work better. I see my methodology as underpinning the work of Kaplan and Norton rather than undermining it.

Letter to the Chief Executive Officer

Due to the workload of chief executive officers (CEOs), few will have the time to read much of this book. I have thus written a letter to the CEO of your organization to help explain his or her involvement. It is important that the CEO knows:

- The content of Chapters 1 through 8.
- The seven characteristics of KPIs.
- The difference between success factors and critical success factors.
- The extent of his or her involvement, and the risks the project faces if the CEO does not actively support the KPI team.
- The content of webcasts that cover implementing winning KPIs, which can be accessed via www.davidparmenter.com.

David Parmenter
Writer, Speaker, Facilitator
Helping organizations measure, report, and improve performance
PO Box 10686, Wellington, New Zealand
(+ 64 4) 499 0007 parmenter@waymark.co.nz
www.davidparmenter.com

April 30, 2012

Dear CEO,

Re: **Invitation to put winning key performance indicators in your organization**

I would like to introduce you to a process that will have a major impact on your organization. It will link you and your organization's staff to the key activities in the organization that have the most impact on the bottom line. If implemented successfully, it will have a profound impact, enabling you to leave a major legacy.

(continued)

(Continued)

I would like to wager that you have not carried out an exercise to distinguish those critical success factors from the many success factors you and your senior management team talk about on a regular basis. I would also point out that much of the reporting you receive, whether it is financial or on performance measures, does not aid your daily decision-making process. I know this because much of the information you receive is monthly, data received well after the horse has bolted.

I recommend that you read the following chapters of this book:

Chapter 1. Background—the importance of understanding the dark side of measures.
Chapter 2. Myths of Performance Measurement—the reasons why performance measures may not be working in your organization.
Chapter 3. Revitalizing Performance Management—this will assist you in adopting a more holistic and modern approach to enhancing performance based on the leading thinkers of our time.
Chapter 4. Measurement Leadership Has to Come from the Chief Executive Officer—outlines your role and the must-read list of books that will make a difference to you.
Chapter 5. Strategy and Its Relevance to Performance Measures—having a balanced strategy that is clear and precise.
Chapter 6. The Great KPI Misunderstanding—explains the background to a new way of looking at KPIs, considered by many to be a breakthrough in understanding KPIs.
Chapter 7. Finding Your Organization's Critical Success Factors—this could be a major legacy at your organization.
Chapter 8. Foundation Stones for Implementing Key Performance Indicators—explains why so many initiatives fail.

Armed with this information, I trust that you will support the winning KPI project with commitment and enthusiasm. By the time you read this letter, this work will have received international acceptance. My KPI book *Key Performance Indicators: Developing, Implementing, and Using Winning KPIs*, 2nd edition (John Wiley & Sons, 2010) is already one of the bestsellers in performance measurement.

I ask that you spare 15 minutes of your time and listen to my webcast on "The Late Planes in the Sky KPI" (www.davidparmenter.com). It will clearly illustrate to you what a KPI is and that nearly all of your KPIs do not operate in the way this measure does.

I am hopeful that this book, with the support material available on my website (www.davidparmenter.com), will help you and your organization achieve a significant improvement in performance. I look forward to hearing about your progress.

Kind regards,
David Parmenter
parmenter@waymark.co.nz

Who Should Read What

This book is a resource for anyone in the organization involved with the development and use of KPIs. It is desirable that all KPI project team members, the external project facilitator, team coordinators, and local facilitators (if required) have their own book to ensure all follow the same plan. Team members are expected to take the book with them when meeting staff and management, as they will be able to clarify issues by using examples from the book. (Note that this book is copyrighted, so it is a breach of the copyright to photocopy sections for distribution.)

	Overview	Board	CEO and Senior Management Team	KPI Project Team, External Facilitator	Team Coordinators
Chapter 1	Background	√	√	√	√
Chapter 2	Myths of Performance Measurement	√	√	√	√
Chapter 3	Revitalizing Performance Management	√	√	√	√
Chapter 4	Measurement Leadership Has to Come from the Chief Executive Officer	√	√	√	√
Chapter 5	Strategy and Its Relevance to Performance Measures		√	√	√

	Overview	Board	CEO and Senior Management Team	KPI Project Team, External Facilitator	Team Coordinators
Chapter 6	The Great KPI Misunderstanding		√	√	
Chapter 7	Finding Your Organization's Critical Success Factors		√	√	
Chapter 8	Foundation Stones for Implementing Key Performance Indicators		√	√	
Chapter 9	Implementing the 12-Step Process			√	√
Chapter 10	Determining the Measures			√	
Chapter 11	Case Studies			√	
Chapter 12	Selling Change		√	√	
Chapter 13	Common Critical Success Factors and Their Likely Measures for Government and Non Profit Agencies			√	√
Chapter 14	Reporting Performance Measures	√	√	√	√
Epilogue	Resources			√	√
Appendix A	The Foundation Stones of Performance-Related Pay Schemes		√		
Appendix B	Effective Recruiting— Getting the Right People on the Bus		√	√	√
Appendix C	The Public Sector Can Abandon the Flawed Budget Process		√		
Appendix D	Jack Welch's Strategy Slides	√	√	√	
Appendix E	Suggested Success Factors for Government and Non Profit Agencies		√	√	

	Overview	Board	CEO and Senior Management Team	KPI Project Team, External Facilitator	Team Coordinators
Appendix F	List of Performance Measures Suitable for Government and Non Profit Agencies			√	
Appendix G	Presenting the Critical Success Factors to the Board/Government Official	√	√		
Appendix H	Main Differences between the Balanced-Scorecard and Winning-KPIs Methodologies	√	√	√	

What about Us (The Private Sector)?

This book is a companion to my previous work and, therefore, is valid for those readers who are based in the private sector. This book would never have been written if it were not for the insatiable demand within government and non profit agencies for this information. It will shed more light on the KPIs and will assist with your implementation of winning KPIs and the balanced scorecard, no matter what part of the private sector you are in.

As mentioned, private sector readers who have already read my KPI book will still find much of this book useful, particularly Chapters 1 to 5, 10, and 13, and Appendixes A, B, D, G, and H.

Electronic Media Available

To support you implementing the strategies and better practices in this book, the following electronic media are available (some for a small fee):

- Webcasts and recorded presentations (see www.davidparmenter .com/webcasts). Some of these are free to everyone and some are accessed via a third party for a fee.
- I have placed some complementary electronic media on my web site (www.davidparmenter.com) that will be helpful to readers. The web site will refer to a word from a specific page in this book which you need to use as a password.
- All of the checklists and agendas and most of the report formats can be purchased from www.davidparmenter.com using a PayPal link on the site.

Acknowledgments

I would like to acknowledge the commitment and dedication of Waymark Solutions staff members who helped me complete this project (Louis and Jennifer). I thank my wife, Jennifer, who has been so understanding during my absences from family life when I was buried in my office finishing off another chapter.

I want to thank Sheck Cho for his encouragement to write this book.

To all the other people who have been an influence in my life, I say thank you for providing me the launching pad for the journey I am now on.

PART I

Setting the Scene

CHAPTER 1

Background

I am often asked "Are KPIs as relevant for government and non profit agencies as they obviously are for the private sector?" My answer is always an unequivocal yes. I would even go on to say that KPIs could have a more profound impact in government and non profit agencies as resources are scarcer and staff can easily be diverted away from what is important by the politics inherent in such institutions.

Are Agencies Really Non Profit Agencies?

I was asked by a member of my golf club not to refer to government and non profit agencies as not-for-profit or non profit agencies because it sent the wrong message. It certainly does. These agencies delivering services around the world are running their organization utilizing all the best management practices they can muster.

A surplus or profit should never be considered wrong in these entities as surpluses are an essential part of an agency's longevity. These surpluses or profits are required for:

- Funding years when uncertain revenue will be less than necessary.
- Reinvesting in fixed assets because depreciation will never be enough to fund replacement assets.
- Funding of new initiatives that will make a breakthrough in performance management, which will lead to further efficiencies.

Thus, for all those working in government and non profit agencies, no offense is meant by the title of this book. Bear in mind that we had to pick a title that was brief and commonly understood.

Measurement in Government and Non Profit Agencies

For measurement to work in government and non profit agencies, there has to be a radical change in the way performance management and measurement is approached and addressed.

Without tackling the common flaws in performance measurement, without a sound understanding of the great management thinkers of the last 60 years, and without a sound grip of the performance management foundation stones, key performance indicators (KPIs) will simply flounder. Hence, I have decided to discuss these three issues before I venture into the detail of KPIs and how they can make a difference to the operations of government and non profit agencies.

Government and non profit agencies were among the first to embrace the balanced scorecard. Part of the reason for this, I believe, is that management in these two sectors keep abreast with current trends more than their counterparts in the private sector. They are, thus, more aware of the changes in business thinking.

Measurement is just as important in government and non profit agencies, as the scarcity of both people and financing means any wastage is more acute. In addition, the impact of better alignment to the organization's strategy and critical success factors will benefit many.

Unintended Behavior: The Dark Side of Measures

Measurement initiatives are often cobbled together without the knowledge of the organization's critical success factors and without an understanding of the behavioral consequences of a measure. As is mentioned in Chapter 2, it is a myth of performance measurement that most measures lead to better performance.

Every performance measure has a dark side, a negative consequence. The key is to understand it. Well over half the measures in an organization may be encouraging unintended behavior. This book will repeatedly drive home the importance of understanding this dark side and selecting fewer measures, as well as selecting those with a minimal negative consequence.

How performance measures can go wrong can be illustrated by two examples.

Example: City Train Service

A classic example is provided by a city train service that had an on-time measure with some draconian penalties targeted at the train drivers. The train drivers who were behind schedule learned simply to stop at the top end of each station, triggering the green light at the other end of the platform, and then to continue the journey without the delay of letting passengers on or off. After a few stations, a driver was back on time, but the customers, both on the train and on the platform, were not so happy.

Management needed to realize that late trains are not caused by train drivers, just as late planes are not caused by pilots. The only way these skilled people would cause a problem would be either arriving late for work or taking an extended lunch when they are meant to be on duty. Management should have been focusing on controllable events that led to late trains, such as the timeliness of investigating signal faults reported by drivers, preventative maintenance on critical equipment that is running behind schedule, and so on.

Example: Accident and Emergency Department

Managers at a hospital in the United Kingdom were concerned about the time it was taking to treat patients in the accident and emergency department. They decided to measure the time from patient registration to being seen by a house doctor. Staff realized that they could not stop patients registering with minor sports injuries but they could delay the registration of patients in ambulances as they were receiving good care from the paramedics.

The nursing staff thus began asking the paramedics to leave their patients in the ambulance until a house doctor was ready to see them, thus improving the "average time it took to treat patients." Each day there would be a parking lot full of ambulances and some circling the hospital. This created a major problem for the ambulance service, which was unable to deliver an efficient emergency service.

Management should have been focusing on the timeliness of treatment of critical patients, and, thus, they only needed to measure the time from registration to consultation of these critical patients. Nurses would have thus treated patients in ambulances as a priority, the very thing they were doing before the measure came into being.

To avoid putting in a measure that will not work you need to:

- Set up a trained team who approve all measures. This team should be trained in all aspects of performance management and measurement that is discussed in this book and in others such as Dean Spitzer's *Transforming Performance Measurement*.[1] If you want chaos, allow teams and managers to invent their own measures. In that case, you may as well close this book now as it will make little impact.
- Ensure that you are measuring something that matters. The key here is to understand the critical success factors. In the hospital situation, it was

the treatment of critical patients, hence we measure the timely treatment of these patients. In the train example, the critical success factor was the timely maintenance and timely rectification of signal failures. The measures that would assist with timely trains would include:

- Signal failures not rectified within xx minutes of being reported. These failures should be reported promptly to the CEO, who will make the phone call to the appropriate manager (receiving these calls on a regular basis would be career-limiting).
- Planned maintenance that has not been implemented should be reported to the senior management team on a weekly basis, keeping the focus on completion.

■ Consult with staff so that you have some idea of the possible unintended consequences of the measure. You have to ask staff "If we measure xxxx, what action will you take?"

■ Pilot the performance measure to enhance its chance of success. Putting measures in without this piloting is simply being naive.

There needs to be a new approach to measurement—one that is done by staff who have been suitably trained, an approach that is consultative, promotes partnership between staff and management, and finally achieves behavioral alignment to the organization's critical success factors and strategic direction.

Balanced Scorecards within Government and Non Profit Agencies

The groundbreaking work of Kaplan and Norton[2] brought to management's attention the fact that performance needed to be measured in a more holistic way. Kaplan and Norton suggested four perspectives in which to review performance: financial, customer, internal process, and learning and growth.

Right from the start, the government and non profit agencies were quick to see the benefits of a balanced-scorecard approach, and many initiated projects. Unfortunately many of these initiatives have failed for reasons set out in Chapter 2, Myths of Performance Measurement. It is my fervent hope that this book will kick-start the enthusiasm to restart, reinvigorate, or start for the first time reporting performance in a balanced way.

Checklist: Where Are You in Your Journey with Performance Measures?

The checklist in Exhibit 1.1 is designed to assess your progress with performance measures.

EXHIBIT 1.1   Assessing Your Progress with Performance Measures Checklist

	Is it covered?
Knowledge of the critical success factors	
1. Senior management have a common understanding of the organization's success factors	☐ Yes ☐ No
2. The organization has identified the critical success factors	☐ Yes ☐ No
3. The critical success factors have been communicated to all staff and are used on a daily basis to focus priorities	☐ Yes ☐ No
Balanced scorecard implementation	
4. We have established our balanced-scorecard perspectives	☐ Yes ☐ No
5. The project was largely run by in-house resources with some outside advisory assistance	☐ Yes ☐ No
6. Measures have been ascertained by teams so there is balance between the scorecard perspectives	☐ Yes ☐ No
7. Measures have be derived from brainstorming the identified critical success factors	☐ Yes ☐ No
8. Measures have been segregated into different types so that only measures with specified criteria are called KPIs	☐ Yes ☐ No
9. There is a sound understanding about performance measurement, KPIs, critical success factors within the senior management team	☐ Yes ☐ No
How KPIs are operating	
10. All measures are carefully monitored to ensure they promote appropriate behavior	☐ Yes ☐ No
11. Teams monitor their performance measures	☐ Yes ☐ No
12. Senior management review performance measures more frequently than monthly	☐ Yes ☐ No
13. The CEO is daily focusing on the KPIs and contacting the appropriate people to rectify identified issues	☐ Yes ☐ No
14. There are less than 10 KPIs in the organization and these are monitored frequently 24/7, daily, or weekly	☐ Yes ☐ No
15. KPIs are not linked to pay, they are seen as "tickets to the game"	☐ Yes ☐ No

Your score:

Under 5: Need to read

Between 5 to 10: This book will assist you with improvements

Over 10: You should have written the book

Major Benefits of Performance Measures

The major benefits of performance measures can be grouped and discussed under these three headings:

- The alignment and linking daily actions to the critical success factors of the organization.
- Improving performance.
- Creating wider ownership, empowerment, and fulfillment.

Alignment and Linking Daily Actions to the Critical Success Factors of the Organization

As Exhibit 1.2 shows, even though an organization has a strategy, teams are often working in directions very different from the intended course.

Performance measures should have been carefully developed from the organization's critical success factors. The critical success factors will help staff align their daily activities with the organization's critical success factors as shown in Exhibit 1.3. This behavioral alignment is often the missing link between good and great organizations.

In his book, *Transforming Performance Measurement*,[3] Spitzer points out that one of the most important roles of management is to communicate expectations to the workforce. He goes on to say *people will do what management inspects (measures), not necessarily what management expects.* Thus, we need to put in place the right measures.

KPIs are the only things that truly link day-to-day performance in the workplace to the organization's strategic objectives. Some people think that because the annual planning process comes from a medium-term view (called the development plan in Exhibit 1.4), which in turn is linked to

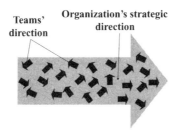

EXHIBIT 1.2   Discord with Strategy

Source: David Parmenter, *Winning CFOs: Implementing and Applying Better Practices*, Copyright © 2011 by David Parmenter. Reprinted with permission of John Wiley & Sons, Inc.

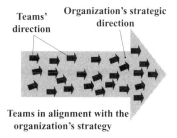

EXHIBIT 1.3 Alignment with Strategy

Source: David Parmenter, *Winning CFOs: Implementing and Applying Better Practices*, Copyright © 2011 by David Parmenter. Reprinted with permission of John Wiley & Sons, Inc.

the strategic plan, strategy is linked to day-to-day activities. It looks good on paper but never works in practice. Strategy is broad and wide ranging, whereas the annual-planning process is a dysfunctional silo-based process.

Improving Performance

Performance measures can and should have a profound impact on performance. Measurement:

- Tends to make things happen, it helps people see progress and motivates action.
- Increases visibility of a more balanced performance and focuses attention on what matters.

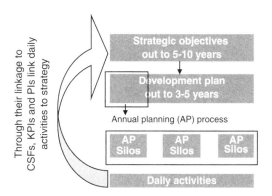

EXHIBIT 1.4 Linkage of KPIs to Strategic Objectives

Source: David Parmenter, *Key Performance Indicators: Developing, Implementing, and Using Winning KPIs*, 2nd ed. Copyright © 2010 by David Parmenter. Reprinted with permission of John Wiley & Sons, Inc.

- Increases objectivity—Spitzer points out that staff actually like measuring and even like being measured, but they do not like being judged subjectively.
- Improves your understanding, your decision making, and execution—Spitzer points out that you will not be able to consistently execute well without measurement. Measurement can improve your business intuition and significantly increase your "decision-making batting average."
- Improves consistency of performance—Spitzer points out that outstanding success is about consistent success over the long term.
- Facilitates feedback on how things are going, thereby providing early warning signals to management. Spitzer points out that without good measurement your organization is flying blind.
- Enables you to manage the future. By measuring future events, you can ensure they happen (e.g., a CEO should look weekly at the list of celebrations, or recognitions, scheduled for the next two weeks. This would ensure success is celebrated in the organization.).

Creating Wider Ownership, Empowerment, and Fulfillment

Peter Drucker[4] talked about leadership being very much like an orchestra conductor. Giving the general direction and the timing and leaving the execution to the experts (the players). Performance measures communicate what needs to be done and help staff understand what is required. They enable leaders to give the general direction and let the staff make the daily decisions to ensure progress is made appropriately.

This shift to training, and trusting staff to make the right calls is very much the Toyota way. Any incorrect decision is seen as a fault in training rather than with the individual.

The delegation of authority to the front line is one of the main foundation stones of KPIs (see Chapter 8). This issue was discussed at great length in *In Search of Excellence*.[5]

I have yet to meet a human being who desires failure or finds failure rewarding. Where measures are appropriately set, staff will be motivated to succeed. Peters and Waterman refer to studies which have shown that performance will improve when more attention is paid to what staff are doing. In one behaviorist study, staff productivity rose when the lighting was improved; it then rose again when they dimmed the lighting!

Notes

1. Dean R. Spitzer, *Transforming Performance Measurement: Rethinking the Way We Measure and Drive Organizational Success* (New York: AMACOM, 2007).

2. Robert S. Kaplan and David P. Norton, *The Balanced Scorecard: Translating Strategy into Action* (Cambridge, MA: Harvard Business Press, 1996).

3. Spitzer, *Transforming Performance Measurement*.

4. Elizabeth Haas Edersheim, *The Definitive Drucker: Challengers for Tomorrow's Executives—Final Advice from the Father of Modern Management* (New York: McGraw-Hill, 2006).

5. Thomas J. Peters and Robert H. Waterman, *In Search of Excellence: Lessons from America's Best Run Companies* (New York: Harper & Row, 1982).

CHAPTER 2

Myths of Performance Measurement

B efore we can enter into the discussion of implementing KPIs, we need to examine why you want performance measures in your organization. There can be many reasons and some will most certainly lead to failure. Thus, at this point, let us look at some of the myths about performance measurement.

Myth 1: Measuring Performance Is Relatively Simple and the Appropriate Measures Are Very Obvious

Performance measurement is failing around the world because management is not aware of the unintended consequence of the performance measures they have picked. As mentioned already, all measures have a dark side. There is a possibility that the actions the measures cause may send performance in the wrong direction.

One of the characteristics of a key performance indicator (KPI) is that this "dark side," this unintended consequence, is very minor, and thus, KPIs have the holistic property of sending performance in the right direction.

Every measure that is to be used needs to be:

- Discussed with the relevant staff: "If we measure this, what will you do?"
- Piloted before it is rolled out.
- Abandoned if its dark side creates too much adverse action.

Myth 2: You Can Delegate a Performance Management Project to a Consulting Firm

For the past 15 years or so, many organizations have entered performance measure initiatives, and these have frequently been led by consultants. Commonly, a balanced-scorecard approach has been adopted based on the work of Kaplan and Norton. The approach, as I will argue, is too complex and leads to a consultant focused approach full of very clever consultants, undertaking this exercise with inadequate involvement of the client's staff. Although this approach has worked well in some cases, there have been many failures. I firmly believe in an in-house approach to this initiative, supported, when necessary, with an external facilitator.

The balanced scorecard has generated a billion-dollar industry of consultants taking organizations on a journey going nowhere quickly. Before you make this mistake ascertain:

- How many of the consultants have worked on a balanced-scorecard project that has worked well?
- Why are the consultants not questioning a methodology that is profoundly flawed in a few key areas?
- How many of the consultants have worked as a manager in your industry? In other words, have they had experience in "firing live rounds?"
- Are you wiser or quietly confused after the consultant's presentations?

Myth 3: Your In-House Project Team Can Achieve Success while Continuing with Their Other Duties

The winning KPIs methodology clearly states, "you can do this in-house." If you cannot, no one else can. KPI projects are in-house projects run by skilled individuals who know the organization, its success factors, and who have been unburdened from the daily grind to concentrate on this important project. In other words, these staff members have moved their family photographs, the picture of the 17-hand stallion, or their petite Bichon Frise dog and put them on their desks in the project office. Leaving the daily grind of firefighting, in their sphere of operations, to their second-in-commands who have now moved into their offices, on a temporary basis of course!

Myth 4: By Tying KPIs to Pay You Will Increase Performance

In all types of organizations, there is a tendency to believe that the way to make KPIs work is to tie KPIs to an individual's pay. KPIs are so important to an organization that performance in this area is a given, or as Jack Welch says, "a ticket to the game."[1] When KPIs are linked to pay, they become

EXHIBIT 2.1   Performance-Related Pay Systems That Will Never Work

Category	Perspective Weighting	Measure	Measure Weighting
Financial	60%	EVA	25%
		Unit profit	20%
		Market growth	15%
Customer	20%	Customer satisfaction survey	10%
		Dealer satisfaction survey	10%
Internal	10%	Above-average rank on process industry quality survey	5%
		Decrease in dealer delivery cycle time	5%
Innovation and		Suggestions/employee	5%
learning	10%	Satisfaction survey	5%

Source: International Institute of Management.

key political indicators (not key performance indicators), which will be manipulated to enhance the probability of a larger bonus.

Because KPIs are special performance tools, it is imperative that these are not included in any performance-related pay discussions. KPIs are too important to be manipulated by individuals and teams to maximize bonuses. Although KPIs will show 24/7, daily, or weekly how teams are performing, it is essential to leave the KPIs uncorrupted by performance-related pay. I have attached an article on the 10 rules of performance-related pay in Appendix A.

Performance bonus schemes using a balanced scorecard are often flawed on a number of counts:

- The balanced scorecard is often based on only four perspectives, ignoring the important environment, community, and staff satisfaction perspectives.
- The measures chosen are open to debate and manipulation.
- There is seldom a linkage to progress in the organization's critical success factors.
- Weighting of measures leads to crazy performance agreements such as Exhibit 2.1.

Myth 5: Most Measures Lead to Better Performance

Although it may appear logical that most measures lead to better performance, in fact, it is quite often the reverse. In order to get measures to work in the right direction requires you to be a bit of an amateur psychologist. You have to second-guess the behavior of the staff being measured. In his book *Transforming Performance Measurement*,[2] Dean Spitzer fires a broadside across the boughs of many of us who, one quiet afternoon, proceeded to dream up a new measure or two (see the section "Unintended Behavior: The Dark Side of Measures" in Chapter 1).

Myth 6: Performance Measures Are Mainly Used to Help Manage Implementation of Strategic Initiatives

The traditional balanced-scorecard approach uses performance measures to monitor the implementation of the strategic initiatives, and measures are typically cascaded down from organization measures such as "return on capital employed."

While this may look logical, it leads to mayhem. The cascading of measures has led many of the balanced-scorecard applications to have hundreds of measures in some form of matrix helping the organization to go, I believe, nowhere quickly.

Performance measures are not on this planet to monitor the implementation of strategies. The main purpose of performance measures is to ensure that staff members spend their working hours focused primarily on the organization's critical success factors.

The winning KPI process states:

- Measures are derived from the critical success factors first and then the success factors.
- There is no cascading down of measures.
- Monthly measures will never be important to management as they report progress too late.
- It is the critical success factors, not the strategic initiatives, that influence the day-to-day running of the business.

Exhibit 2.2 shows the difference in the two approaches. Winning KPI methodology states that you derive the measures from the critical success factors. Deriving your measures from your strategic initiatives will create a

EXHIBIT 2.2   How Strategy and the Critical Success Factors Work Together

large number of unimportant measures, largely ignoring the important daily "business as usual" issues.

Many strategic initiatives are controlled by special project teams undertaking secretive work, such as acquiring new operations or technologies. They will monitor their progress through project reporting. These new initiatives will become business as usual only when the new business or product is part of daily activities.

Although some strategic initiatives will impact directly on business as usual the impact of these initiatives can be managed better through monitoring measures in the critical success factors.

Myth 7: The Balanced Scorecard Was First Off the Blocks

Hoshin Kanri business methodology, a balanced approach to performance management and measurement, was around well before the balanced scorecard. It has been argued that the balanced scorecard originated from the adaptation from *Hoshin Kanri*.

As I understand it, translated, *Hoshin Kanri* means a business methodology for direction and alignment. This approach was developed in a complex Japanese multinational where it is necessary to achieve an organization-wide collaborative effort in key areas.

One tenet of *Hoshin Kanri* is that all employees should incorporate into their daily routines a contribution to the key corporate objectives. In other words, staff members need to be made aware of the critical success factors and then prioritize their daily activities to maximize their positive contribution in these areas.

In the traditional form of *Hoshin Kanri,* there is a grouping of four perspectives. It is no surprise that the balanced-scorecard perspectives are mirror images (see Exhibit 2.3). An informative paper on the comparison

EXHIBIT 2.3   Similarities between *Hoshin Kanri* and Balanced-Scorecard Perspectives

Hoshin Kanri	Balanced Scorecard
Quality objectives and measures	Customer focus
Cost objectives and measures	Financial
Delivery objectives and measures	Internal process
Education objectives and measures	Innovation and learning
Both of these approaches should be augmented by:	
Staff satisfaction	Staff satisfaction
Environment and community	Environment and community

Source: David Parmenter, *Key Performance Indicators: Developing, Implementing, and Using Winning KPIs,* 2nd ed. Copyright © 2010 by David Parmenter. Reprinted with permission of John Wiley & Sons, Inc.

EXHIBIT 2.4   How Late Planes Impacts Most, If Not All Six, Perspectives

				Perspectives		
	Financial	Customer Satisfaction	Staff Satisfaction	Innovation and Learning	Internal Process	Environment and Community
Late planes in the sky over 2 hours late	√	√	√	√	√	possible

of *Hoshin Kanri* and the balanced scorecard has been written by Witcher and Chau.[3]

Myth 8: Measures Fit Neatly into One Balanced-Scorecard Perspective

One dilemma for many users of the balanced scorecard is where to report the measure. Taking one KPI, called "late planes in the sky," as an example, should the performance measure be reported as a customer, financial, or an internal process measure? In fact, in this example, late planes in the sky affects all six perspectives, as shown in Exhibit 2.4.

Myth 9: The Balanced Scorecard Can Report Progress to Both Management and the Board

One certainly needs to show the government or board the state of progress. However, it is important that governance information is shown rather than management information. The measures that should be reported to the board are key result indicators.

We need to ensure that the management-focused performance measures (KPIs, result indicators, and performance indicators) are only reported to management and staff. Examples of the differences between reporting to management and the board are shown in Chapter 14, Reporting Performance Measures.

Myth 10: There Are Only Four Balanced-Scorecard Perspectives

For almost 20 years, the four perspectives listed in Kaplan and Norton's original work[4] (financial, customer, internal process, and learning and growth) have been consistently reiterated by Kaplan and Norton through to the

FINANCIAL	CUSTOMER	ENVIRONMENT AND
Assets utilization, sales growth, risk management, optimization of working capital, cost reduction	Increase customer satisfaction, targeting customers who generate the most profit, getting close, noncustomers	**COMMUNITY** Employer of first choice, linking with future employees, community leadership, collaboration
INTERNAL Delivery in full on time, optimizing technology, effective relationships with key stakeholders	**STAFF SATISFACTION** Right people on the bus, empowerment, retention of key staff, candor, leadership, recognition	**INNOVATION AND LEARNING** Innovation, abandonment, increasing expertise and adaptabilty, learning environment

EXHIBIT 2.5   Balanced Scorecard with Six Perspectives

present time. For example, they have argued successfully that a supplier perspective is often not wanted because it is not a point of difference. Your competitors have access to them as well.

I recommend that these four perspectives be increased by the inclusion of two more perspectives, and that the learning and growth perspective be reworded as innovation and learning (see Exhibit 2.5). This last change is a very important and recent change in my work because it lifts the profile of innovation, which has been emphasized by all the great business writers like Peter Drucker, Jim Collins, Thomas Peters, and Robert Waterman.

I have added *staff satisfaction* and *environment and community* to the traditional four perspectives. These two perspectives were underestimated in the original work of Robert Kaplan and David Norton.

Having a separate *staff satisfaction perspective* emphasizes the importance of measuring the key drivers of employee satisfaction such as the amount and regularity of recognition (e.g., how many recognition events are planned for the next week or two, how much recognition has been made this week, the past two weeks, and this month). It will also support the need for more regular staff satisfaction surveys performed on a rolling-sample basis.

The environment and community perspective has been managed brilliantly by some leading CEOs, helping to create a major asset for the human-resources team, assisting the organization in becoming an employer of choice. Other benefits include staff learning new skills through doing voluntary work in the community, reducing costs through minimizing waste, creating positive press, and increasing higher staff morale by implementing green initiatives. Leading CEOs intuitively work in this area. They realize that the community is the source of your current and future employees and customers. They see the linkage of initiatives in this area to positive customer perceptions.

Example: Scoring Goals with the Community—Your Future Customers

On a flight I had the pleasure of sitting next to a person who once worked for Virgin Atlantic. She told me that whenever a new route was opened, Virgin Atlantic founder Richard Branson would fly in, achieve a prominent photo in the local press, and hold a party. All staff members were told to bring their partners and their best friends.

Throughout the evening, Branson would pose for photographs with groups of guests. Every person had a signed photo at the end of the evening. Where do you think these photos ended up? In a box under the bed? I do not think so. They were put in a place of pride, center of the mantelpiece, wedding photo moved to the right! Every time your friends look at the photograph, what would they think? What a great night, and how much they value your friendship.

In a single evening, Branson enhanced staff morale and satisfaction, created free press exposure, and linked the Virgin Group to new customers. What airline would you fly if you had a photo, on your mantelpiece, of you meeting Richard Branson?

Kaplan and Norton's later work on strategic mapping[5] also alludes to the importance of staff satisfaction and the environment and community perspectives. This modification is important because it means the balanced scorecard now incorporates all triple-bottom-line issues.

Myth 11: Strategy Mapping Is a Vital Requirement

If strategy maps help management make some sense out of their strategy, then, as a working document, they must be useful. However, I am concerned with the "simplified" use of cause-and-effect relationships, a major component of strategy mapping (see Exhibit 2.6). It has led to the demise of many performance-measurement initiatives. From these oversimplified relationships come the strategic initiatives and the cascading performance measures. Strategy mapping, in the wrong hands, can give birth to a monster.

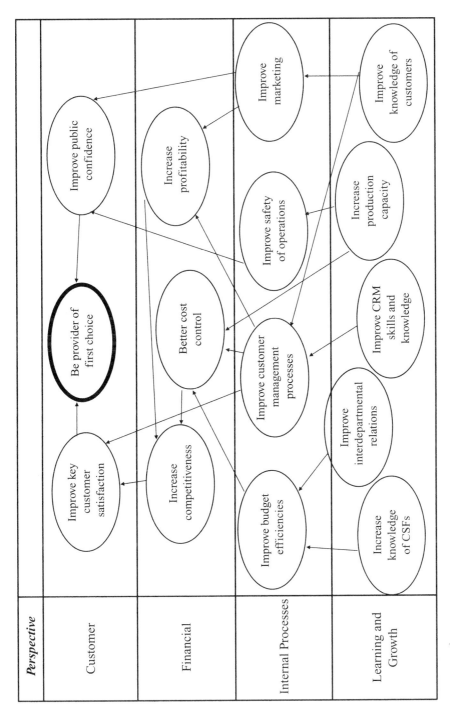

EXHIBIT 2.6   Strategy Mapping

21

The cause-and-effect diagrams of strategic mapping, where initiatives/ success factors neatly fit into a balanced-scorecard perspective and create one or possibly two cause-and-effect relationships, are full of intellectual thought signifying nothing in many cases. I am sure there are many consultants who can use strategy mapping effectively to help businesses have a better understanding of its likely impact. However, it is a dangerous tool in the wrong hands, particularly if it is the source of all performance measures in the organization.

These strategy map diagrams are flawed on a number of accounts:

- Success factors do not fit neatly within a balanced-scorecard perspective; the more important they are, the more perspectives they impact, and hence, some success factors would need to be drawn across the whole page of a strategy map. This is clearly too untidy for the strategy-map designers.
- If you are bright enough, you can argue a totally different causal route for your arrows in your strategic mapping. Every action an organization takes has a number of different impacts. To restrict oneself to one or two relationships in strategy mapping is at best too simplistic, at worst totally naive.
- When I ask workshop attendees to map the impact of late planes on the success factors of an airline, they come up with at least 20 impacts. Strategy mapping cannot cope with multi-relationships and, thus, cannot cope with the reality of day-to-day business.
- Actions that employees take, on a daily basis, are influenced by many factors, they cannot be simplified to one or two causal impacts. The secret is to understand those employee actions that lead either to success or failure and thus direct the staff to move in the right direction (i.e., one consistent with interests of the organization's long-term strategy).

Myth 12: All Performance Measures Are KPIs

One important difference between the winning KPI approach and the traditional balanced-scorecard approach is that in winning KPIs there is a definition of what a KPI is. This has a very profound impact on non profit and government agencies. My definition of a KPI, in Chapter 6, includes that a KPI is 24/7, daily, or weekly, and it is nonfinancial. Many agencies state that they can only realistically measure performance monthly. To this I say read on and I will show you a number of daily measures that your organization should have.

The winning KPIs methodology clearly indicates that KPIs are rare. These KPIs are reported immediately, and thus, should never find their way into a balanced scorecard that is reported two or three weeks after the month end to the senior management team.

Myth 13: Monitoring Monthly Performance Measures Will Improve Performance

Show me a monthly performance measure and I will show you a result indicator, a key result indicator, or a performance indicator. It will never be a KPI! How can it be key to your business when you are looking at the measure well after the damage has been done? It is as useful as telling a trainer that his prize racehorse escaped the stables, sometime last month.

If you want something to happen, something to change, then measurement has to be timely. Imagine saying to your teenage son, once a month, "You had an untidy room 28 out of the 30 days this month." All you would achieve is an argument. Instead, a clever parent says, "Pat, an untidy room equals no allowance." When the room is tidy on Saturday, you can get the pocket money. A constant weekly behavioral change program will win through. Soon they will say, "Dad, Mom, come and look at my room."

Staff members are no different than wayward teenagers. Sometimes they could be worse. To get a change, a chief executive officer needs to focus on the critical success factors and act on the KPIs that will align the appropriate behavior.

Myth 14: KPIs Are Financial and Nonfinancial Indicators

Financial measures are a quantification of an activity; we have assigned a value to the activity. Thus, behind every financial measure is an activity. I call financial measures "result indicators"; a summary measure. It is the activity that you will want more or less of. It is the activity that drives the dollars, pounds, yen. Thus, as I argue in Chapter 6, financial measures cannot possibly be KPIs.

In our organizations, we need to find the activities that support the critical success factors and find appropriate measures that we can focus on, such as "late planes in the sky two hours late."

Myth 15: The More Measures the Better

The traditional balanced-scorecard approach is to cascade measures down from an organizational measure such as return on capital employed. This process, along with balanced-scorecard applications, leads to myriad ill-defined measures that, at best, will do no harm, at worse take the organization on an expensive journey to oblivion.

British Airways was reportedly turned around by Lord King in the 1980s by focusing on one KPI, late planes in the sky. The story is one that certainly changed my life as I realized its significance to the development of performance measures that drove change. I have analyzed this measure in Chapter 6, The Great KPI Misunderstanding.

Myth 16: Indicators Are Either Lead (Performance Driver) or Lag (Outcome) Indicators

I have lost count of the number of times I read Kaplan and Norton's[6] original masterpiece to try and understand the lead-lag-indicators argument before I realized my difficulty in understanding lead-lag indicators was a result of flawed logic.

The lead-lag indicator differentiation should be consigned to the rubbish bin, as 24/7 KPIs simultaneously are both a lead and a lag indicator. Late planes in the sky, a common KPI for airlines, has clearly arisen out of past events and will have a major impact on future events—the late arrival will make the plane late in leaving. Instead of lead-lag the winning KPIs methodology sees a measure as a past (last week last month), current (yesterday's or today's activities—the here and now), or future (monitoring now the planning and preparation for events/actions that should occur in the future).

Myth 17: We Know What Good Performance Will Look Like Before the Year Starts and, thus, Can Set Relevant Year-End Targets

Jeremy Hope, of *Beyond Budgeting* fame,[7] was the first writer to clearly articulate that a fixed annual performance contract, such as the annual budgeting process, was doomed to fail. Hope and Fraser, pioneers of the *Beyond Budgeting* methodology, have pointed out the trap of the annual budget process. If you set an annual target during the planning process, typically 15 or so months before the last month of that year, you will never know if it was appropriate, given that the particular conditions of that year will never be guessed correctly. You often end up paying incentives to management when, in fact, you have lost market share. In other words, your rising sales did not keep up with the growth rate in the marketplace.

When we compare performance among peers and against external benchmarks, such as the market share, we are looking at relative performance targets measures. Thus, the financial institutions that are making super profits out of this artificial lower-interest-rate environment would have a higher benchmark set retrospectively, when the actual impact is known.

As Jeremy Hope points out, not setting an annual target beforehand is not a problem as long as staff members are given regular updates about how they are progressing against the rest of the market. He argues that if you do not know how hard you have to work to get a maximum bonus, you will work as hard as you can.

Notes

1. Jack Welch and Suzy Welch, *Winning* (New York: HarperBusiness, 2005).

2. Dean R. Spitzer, *Transforming Performance Measurement: Rethinking the Way We Measure and Drive Organizational Success* (New York: AMACOM, 2007).

3. Barry J. Witcher and Vinh Sum Chau, "Balanced Scorecard and Hoshin Kanri: Dynamic Capabilities for Managing Strategic Fit," University of East Anglia UK, *Management Decision,* 45, no. 3 (2007): 518–538.

4. Robert S. Kaplan and David P. Norton, *The Balanced Scorecard: Translating Strategy into Action* (Cambridge, MA: Harvard Business Press, 1996).

5. Robert S. Kaplan and David P. Norton, *Strategy Maps: Converting Intangible Assets into Tangible Outcomes* (Cambridge, MA: Harvard Business Press, 2004).

6. Kaplan and Norton, *The Balanced Scorecard.*

7. Jeremy Hope and Robin Fraser, *Beyond Budgeting: How Managers Can Break Free from the Annual Performance Trap* (Cambridge, MA: Harvard Business Press, 2003).

CHAPTER 3

Revitalizing Performance Management

Performance management has been much misunderstood, misused, and abused, thereby preventing too many organizations from reaching their potential. Before we can get performance measures to work in government and non profit agencies, we need to understand considerably more about performance management.

To assist in this learning process, I have developed a model to help revitalize performance management (Exhibit 3.1). At first, this model may appear to go well beyond the brief of this book. Once understood though, it will identify why your organization is failing to meet its potential and why many performance-management initiatives, like the balanced scorecard, fail.

This model comprises five foundation stones that need to be put in place before you can handle the facets of performance that need to be managed in order to have a balanced performance.

The foundation stones and facets that need to be handled to revitalize performance management are discussed in detail next.

Foundation Stone 1: Understanding Human Behavior

As mentioned in Chapter 1, every measure can have a dark side, a negative consequence. In order to make measures work, you need to understand human behavior and minimize the dark side of performance measures.

The key is to find it first and then tweak how the measure is used so that the behaviors it will promote are appropriate. I suspect well over half the measures in an organization may well be encouraging unintended negative behavior.

EXHIBIT 3.1   Revitalizing Performance Management Model

Dean Spitzer's book[1] *Transforming Performance Measurement* has a vast array of examples of dysfunctional performance. Here are some of my favorite stories:

Public-Sector Examples

- Experienced caseworkers in a government agency will work on the easiest cases and leave the difficult ones to the inexperienced staff because they are measured on the number of cases closed.
- An Australian city rail service penalized train drivers for late trains, resulting in drivers skipping stations in order to get on-time schedules.
- A UK accident and emergency department was measuring timely treatment of patients. The nurses then delayed the ambulances from offloading until they could see them achieving a zero time difference. Within hours of implementation of this measure, ambulances were circling the hospital as the ambulance bay was full. The follow-on result was obvious: ambulances arriving late at an incident.

Private-Sector Examples

- A fast-food restaurant manager was striving to achieve an award for zero wastage of chicken. The manager won the chicken efficiency award by waiting until the chicken was ordered before cooking; the long wait time that resulted meant a huge loss of customers.
- A company that was measuring product that left the factory on time had a 100 percent record, yet 50 percent of customers complained about late delivery. The reason was that nobody cared about what happened next after the product left the factory.
- Sales staff met their targets at the expense of the company, offering discounts and extended payment terms, selling to customers who would never pay . . . you name it, they will do it to get the bonus!
- Purchasing departments awarded for receiving large discounts started to buy in too large a quantity, creating an inventory overload.
- Stores maintained low inventory to get a bonus and had production shut down because of stock outs.

Spitzer's statement that "People will do what management inspects, not necessarily what management expects" is worth repeating again here.

One of the most primitive beliefs is that the primary driver of staff is money, and thus, one needs incentives in order to get great performance. Although this is the case with employees who are situated within the first two tiers of Maslow's hierarchy of needs, it does not apply to many managers or staff. Recognition, self-worth, and self-actualization are more important drivers. This factor has a big impact on how we treat KPIs.

Thus, the greatest danger of performance management is dysfunctional behavior. As Spitzer says, "the ultimate goal is not the customer—it's often the scorecard." Spitzer has heard executives, when being candid, say "We don't worry about strategy; we just move our numbers and get rewarded."

To help assess the potential damage in your organization, I have developed a checklist (Exhibit 3.2).

Foundation Stone 2: Knowledge of the Paradigm Shifters (Drucker, Collins, Welch, Hamel, Peters, Waterman, and Others)

Many performance management initiatives will fail simply because the organization is still wedded to antiquated and broken management systems. There have been many paradigm shifters who have for years laid out a new pathway for management. Unfortunately, for many reasons, much of middle and senior management are either unaware of the new approaches,

EXHIBIT 3.2   Dysfunctional Performance Measures Checklist

	Does it happen?	
1. Is the reward structure tied to the key performance indicators?	☐ Yes	☐ No
2. Are measures constructed by teams or individuals based on what they think will work?	☐ Yes	☐ No
3. Are annual targets set that will trigger bonuses if met?	☐ Yes	☐ No
4. Does the organization believe that performance can only be achieved if there is a financial reward attached to that performance?	☐ Yes	☐ No
5. Are measures typically adopted by whoever dreams them up, without the necessity to trial them to assess their potential negative behavioral impact?	☐ Yes	☐ No
6. Are there instances where staff are asked "to force" compliance to a measure just to achieve a target even though the action may damage the organization's reputation?	☐ Yes	☐ No
7. Have you got some measures that are leading to dysfunctional behavior?	☐ Yes	☐ No
8. Have you had to remove measures due to the damage they have created?	☐ Yes	☐ No
9. Do you have measures that are solely used to make departments look good rather than the benefit they might give to the organization?	☐ Yes	☐ No
10. Do you have instances in your organization where the messenger has been shot when they report the "bad news"?	☐ Yes	☐ No
11. Do you have a history of "gaming" performance measures in the organization?	☐ Yes	☐ No
12. Do you have over 100 measures in your organization?	☐ Yes	☐ No
13. Are measures implemented without a full cost-benefit analysis performed?	☐ Yes	☐ No
14. Is there a high degree of cynicism about the effectiveness of performance measures in your organization?	☐ Yes	☐ No
15. Is the CEO and senior management team naïve when it comes to performance management?	☐ Yes	☐ No

Your score: Every yes indicates a problem.
With over 5 affirmatives, it may be best to put a stop to all new performance measures and start again with how you build performance measures.

unable to gather enough momentum to change, or simply too busy to make a change process work.

Peter Drucker is considered the father of management. His work contains many gems that have been overlooked. Alongside Drucker there are some brilliant writers like Jim Collins, Jack Welch, Gary Hamel, Thomas Peters, and Robert Waterman who have now taken the baton. The only problem is that many of us are too busy to read and absorb their work.

It should never be underestimated the impact these great thinkers and writers can have if one spends enough time understanding their wisdom. To assist you on your journey of discovery below you will find some major lessons and how they apply in performance measurement and your KPIs.

Peter Drucker's Lessons for Performance Management

The more I read Peter Drucker's work, the more I realize that his wisdom will transcend time. We will look at his writing the way we look at Shakespeare's work, and will say, shaking our heads, "How did he do it?"

Table 3.1 provides a quick overview of some of his Drucker's statements that have an impact on performance management. Some of his books make specific reference to the issues that face government and non profit agencies.[2]

For management to undertake their role without an in-depth understanding of Drucker is like deciding to sail around the world with your family without having completed a harbor-master's course. Yes you can do it, yes you may arrive safely, but you have put everybody at risk.

Jim Collins's Lessons for Performance Management

I am a fan of Jim Collins's work. His analysis, understanding, and communication of his concepts are without peer. His books are must-haves on the thoughtful person's bookshelf. (See Table 3.2.)

Jack Welch's Lessons for Performance Management

Straight talking Jack Welch and his book *Winning*,[3] co-written with Suzy Welch, is a must-read. Welch was profoundly influenced by Peter Drucker, therefore, you are getting another slice of Drucker's wisdom. Welch has not held back any punches, and gets to the point effectively. (See Table 3.3.)

TABLE 3.1   Peter Drucker's Lessons for Performance Management

Peter Drucker's Wisdom	Impact on Performance Management
Know your customers. Explicitly defining customer groups is the foundation stone of an outside-in perspective. One charity Drucker noted had 46 customer segments.	This will impact measurement because we can now measure the key segments more frequently for revenue, satisfaction, growth, and so on.
Have an outside-in focus to your business. See the operation from your customers' perspective, especially the perspectives of your important customers.	Outside-in initiatives will be measured, particularly as a future orientated measure. For example, date of next customer feedback survey. Implementation of survey recommendations being monitored weekly after the survey report is issued.
Focus on your noncustomers. Which of your noncustomers should you be doing business with?	We will need to measure the success we have in doing business with new targeted customers.
Look for opportunities as if your life depended on it. Drucker emphasized the importance of innovation	Measurement of innovation will be very important.
Management versus Leadership. Management is ensuring that staff are doing *things right* and leadership is ensuring that staff are *doing the right thing.*	Measurement of the progress with leadership training and development will be very important.
Recruitment is a life and death decision. Drucker was adamant about the significance of recruiting the right staff.	The recruiting of the KPI team should be done very carefully, ensuring they have the right mix of knowledge, experience, and credibility within the organization to be successful. Many government and non profit agencies focus on "recruiting the right people all the time" as a critical success factor, and they will need to develop specific measures to track recruitment processes.
Do not give new staff new assignments. He referred to these jobs as widow makers, jobs where the incumbent did not have a chance to succeed.	In this KPI project, it is important to ensure that the project team is made up of experienced staff who know the critical success factors and the members of the senior management team. Bringing in consultants to lead the KPI project will doom it to failure. Drucker told you so.

TABLE 3.1   *(Continued)*

Peter Drucker's Wisdom	Impact on Performance Management
The scarce resource in an organization is performing people. Drucker highlighted that these scarce resources need to be specifically monitored and not taken for granted. Their goals should be hard enough to stretch them and keep them interested.	Performance measures will be designed to monitor high performing staff.
Outstanding performance is inconsistent with a fear for failure. Without the will to take risks, to venture into the unknown and let go of the familiar past, an organization cannot thrive in the 21st century.	Measuring the go-forward nature of the organization and the measurement of the mistakes will flag whether we are moving quickly enough. Mistakes are seen as necessary learning experiences.
Today's advanced knowledge is tomorrow's ignorance. Drucker saw it as very important to harness knowledge in every aspect of the organization.	It is necessary to measure the extent the organization is gathering, sharing, and using knowledge.
Abandonment. Drucker said: "The first step in a growth policy is not to decide where and how to grow. It is to decide what to abandon. In order to grow, a business must have a systematic policy to get rid of the outgrown, the obsolete, the unproductive." He also said: "Don't tell me what you're doing, tell me what you've stopped doing." Measuring the extent of innovation and abandonment will help focus management's attention on these two important areas. Abandonment is a sign that management are recognizing that some initiatives will never work as intended and it is better to face this reality sooner than later.	Promote Peter Drucker's concept of abandonment. Many existing measures should be abandoned along with processes and reports. The KPI project needs space to work. Other systems need to be abandoned to allow enough time for the KPIs to function properly. The amount of abandonment will need to be measured.

(continued)

TABLE 3.1   *(Continued)*

Peter Drucker's Wisdom	Impact on Performance Management
Collaborate with other organizations, even your competitors. Jack Welch turned GE into a powerhouse by striving to focus on what GE was good at. This led Welch to follow Drucker's advice on collaboration, and he pointed out that "Your back room is someone's front room." In other words, if others can do a job better than you can, subcontract to them rather than diverting energy to be good at everything, a task that is impossible to achieve.	We will need to measure the extent to which collaboration is happening. The date of the next collaboration meeting, the date of the next shared collaboration, the date of the next agreement to contract out a service can all be measured.
Know what information you need to do your job and from whom you need it. When and how? By answering these basic questions, we can streamline much of the reporting formats, dispsensing with those reports that add no value.	We can measure the reports that have been removed from circulation.
Understand the importance of self-renewal. Drucker emphasized the importance for leaders to have balance, to have interests outside the work environment that help them maintain a balanced perspective.	The chief executive officer (CEO) should monitor the extent to which the senior management team and their direct reports are investing in self-renewal.
Have three test sites. Drucker pointed out that to do one pilot was never enough.	On a KPI project, we should follow the sage's advice and pilot the KPI project in three entities.
Place people according to their strengths. Drucker was adamant that you focus on what people can do rather than focus on what they cannot do well.	The selection of the KPI team should focus on the candidates' strengths. Organizations can highlight those staff members that are not in the right place (e.g., not performing) and take action to reposition them or assist them to find the right job elsewhere.
Generate three protégés for each senior position.	Status of succession planning for all key positions should be monitored on a quarterly basis. Following Drucker, any shortage from the three protégés for each senior position should be reported as an exception once a month.

TABLE 3.2   Jim Collins's Lessons for Performance Management

Jim Collins's Wisdom	Impact on Performance Management
Importance of level-five leadership. Collins points out that level-five leaders have a blend of personal humility and ambition. Their ambition is first and foremost for the organization and not for themselves.	By measuring the next occurrence of balanced feedback on key managers (360-degree feedback) we will ensure managers get appropriate feedback on their leadership.
Getting the right people on the bus. Collins emphasized the need for organizations to place more emphasis on recruiting.	The recruiting for the KPI team should be conducted carefully. Organizations can measure a manager's rate of success at recruiting. Managers who have a record of failure should be retrained or relieved of recruiting duties.
Getting the wrong people off the bus. Collins is very consistent with Drucker. Move staff on if they are a poor fit with the organization's values.	Organizations can highlight those staff members who are not in the right place (e.g., not performing) and take action to reposition them or assist them in finding the right job elsewhere.
The "hedgehog" concept. Collins points out that organizations need to know what they can be the best in the world at, what they are deeply passionate about, and what drives their economic engine. Organizations need to translate that understanding into a simple, crystal clear concept that guides all their efforts.	By understanding an organization's critical success factors and deriving performance measures from them, you will create an alignment that is consistent with Collins's thinking.
The flywheel effect. This refers to forward steps consistent with the hedgehog concept. The resultant accumulation of visible results will lead to a lineup of people energized by the results.	By measuring within the critical success factors, we will be consistent with Collins's thinking.
Big Hairy Audacious Goals (BHAGs).[4] Jim Collins and Jack Welch are at one here. They say incremental improvement will never stretch your thinking. We are asking what would we need to do to achieve this BHAG. It is not implying that falling short of the BHAG is a failure or that bonuses will not be paid.	The KPI team needs to set some BHAGs for the project that will stretch the KPI team's thinking.

(continued)

TABLE 3.2 *(Continued)*

Jim Collins's Wisdom	Impact on Performance Management
The silent creep of impending doom. Collins warns us about the first stage of decline "Hubris born of success," excessive pride leading the management team down the slippery slope. An organization always needs to focus on its economic engine, make sure its flywheel is turning and maintain a profound understanding of the fundamental reasons for success.	The highlighting of the critical success factors coupled with the KPIs will ensure the senior management team focus on what matters to their flywheel.
Try a lot of stuff and keep what works. Collins points out that visionary companies often made their best moves not by detailed strategic planning, but rather by experimentation, trial and error, opportunism, and in some cases, by accident. Collins compared innovation to branching and pruning. Clever gardeners let a tree add enough branches (variation) and then prune the dead wood (selection).	The CEO and senior management team need to encourage innovation. The number of innovations by team should be measured. The benchmark is Toyota, which has an average of ten implemented innovations per employee per year.
Risks above or below the waterline. Collins specifies that, when making decisions, you need to know if they will they affect you above or below the waterline if they go wrong. Those below the waterline will obviously sink the organization. Government and non profit agencies are protected by their surety of annual income from the public purse and, hence, are so easily blind to these risks.	The focus on the right measures will give clarity and purpose.
Grasping for salvation. Collins points out the propensity for organizations in this stage to bring in an outside CEO to be the savior. These initiatives fail more often than they succeed. As Welch observes, to bring in a CEO from outside is a sure sign that your organization failed to nurture protégés. In the public sector, it is even worse where excellent protégés are deliberately overlooked to bring in an external person.	It is important for government and non profit agencies to revisit their values and to include a bold statement that indicates they should develop their own leaders. The progress in this development of in-house leaders should be measured.
In the private sector this stage of decline is categorized, as Collins points out, by the silver bullet, a massive merger that will turn the organization around. Naturally enough, less than one in six of these mergers ever breaks even.	We can also measure the number of protégés for all senior positions.

TABLE 3.3   Jack Welch's Lessons for Performance Management

Jack Welch's Wisdom	Impact on Performance Management
Candor. Welch has reinvigorated this word and placed it in front of management. He said "It is a leader's obligation to tell their staff how they are doing and how they can improve performance in a candid way." As Welch points out, candor allows more people to participate in the conversation, generates speed, cuts costs, and encourages underperformers to reflect on their achievements and move forward or move on.	The KPI team needs to ensure that it is open and honest about performance measurement in the organization.
Jack Welch's 20/70/10 "differentiation" rule. Tied to candor is Welch's 20/70/10 "differentiation" rule. The top 20 percent of performers should be promoted into jobs that are a good fit for their strengths, assist the next 70 percent to better meet their potential, and make it clear to the bottom 10 percent that their future lies elsewhere. Good communication will see these staff members moving on to better pastures for themselves; failing that, these staff members need to be assisted in moving on.	It is important for government and non profit agencies to measure the handling of poor performers. Staff in the wrong positions may be a significant issue for the organization. Organizations can measure managers' success rate at recruiting.
A cluster of mentors. As Welch says "There is no right mentor for you; there are many right mentors." He sees mentoring more holistically. A mentor can come from a staff member many levels below who passes their knowledge on to you. In *Winning*, Welch was forever grateful for the young human resources (HR) advisor who patiently helped him master e-mail.	Ensure that all KPI team members have appropriate mentor support. Measures need to be developed to monitor take-up of mentors by management and staff. First, target senior managers who do not have a mentor.

(continued)

TABLE 3.3   *(Continued)*

Jack Welch's Wisdom	Impact on Performance Management
Read, read, read. Great leaders have a thirst for knowledge and are constantly looking at ways to move their learning on; they are constantly reinventing themselves. Welch was an avid reader of the financial and management press and journals. He makes it very clear that it is a leader's role to be up to date.	The KPI team will need to read the books indicated in the Epilogue. Organizations can measure the extent to which the senior executives are maintaining their learning, especially the CEO.
Raise the profile of human resources in your organization. Great leaders like Jack Welch have always recognized that the human resources team are vital to the organization. At GE, the head of HR was a member of the senior management team and the team was involved in all recruiting, promoting, training, and disciplining processes.	The KPI team should work closely with the HR team. The HR team will be able to help sell the required change and get more senior managers on board. In some organizations, the balanced scorecard has been implemented by the HR team. Performance measurement initiatives will work much better with skilled HR input. Leaving human resources to a young graduate to write meaningless policy inserts for a never-read manual is a surefire way to run down an organization.
Make innovation work. Welch was a champion of innovation. He wanted innovation to be part of the culture. Workshops were held called "work-out process" where groups discussed better practices and at least 75 percent of all recommendations from the brainstorming sessions had to be given. A yes or no by the manager at the close of the workshop and the remaining recommendations had a maximum 30-day gestation period before a decision had to be made. This technique forced the decision makers to apply innovation practices, which allowed for some failure but ensured much success at the same time.	Innovation needs to be measured both in the past ("How many innovations did each team do last month?") and in the future ("How many innovations will be up and running in the next two weeks, four weeks?").

TABLE 3.3 *(Continued)*

Jack Welch's Wisdom	Impact on Performance Management
Recognition and celebration. Welch says great leaders celebrate more. As he points out "Work is too much a part of life not to recognize moments of achievement." You can sense from listening to his webcasts that his celebrations would have been fun to attend. Welch was all about making business fun. Realize that it is not life or death, but a game you want to win.	The KPI project team will need to be active with recognition and celebration to assist with buy-in and maintain interest and momentum. Recognition and celebration needs to be measured both in the past ("How much recognition and celebration occurred last month") and in the future ("recognitions and celebrations planned for next week, next fortnight"). Government or non profit agencies also need to measure the number of positive press releases printed in the papers for, as sure as night follows day, the press will have a field day on the negative events that are press worthy and happen because of the very nature of the work a government or non profit agency performs.
Crisis management. All exceptional leaders are great in a crisis and Welch is no exception. He had a large realism streak in his body. He would take the necessary action, face the necessary music, and move on. Welch handled each crisis on the following assumptions: ▪ The crisis will be worse than it first appears. ▪ The bad news will come out sometime, so may as well face the music now. ▪ The situation will be portrayed in the worst possible light by the press. ▪ There will be carnage. ▪ His organization will survive.	It would be worth measuring the integrity gap within the organization, that is, the time between when an event is known about and when it is conveyed to the senior management team.

(continued)

TABLE 3.3   *(Continued)*

Jack Welch's Wisdom	Impact on Performance Management
Setting goals that stretch (Big hairy audacious goals, as Jim Collins would say). Welch liked to see goals that were a mix of possible and the impossible. He went on to say "Effective leaders are not afraid to envision big results." By raising the bar so high that staff and management were forced to totally rethink the route plan , new ways had to be found to succeed and so often this was achieved.	In performance measurement, it is a sure way to limit performance by linking KPIs to bonuses. The key driver here will be politics and questionable measurement practices. (See Appendix A.)
Be number one or two in the game. Welch was aware that many of GE's investments did not make sense. The answer would have been no to the Drucker question, "If you were not in the business would you enter it now?" Consequently Welch was known as ruthless for his directive of "Fix it, sell it, or close it" when a business did not meet the strict criterion of being either number one or two in that particular sector.	For government and non profit agencies it means do not provide services that other government and non profit agencies can do much better than you. Focus on what you can do well. We need to measure our success at service delivery and the amount of abandonment we are doing in those services that can be better done by other government and non profit agencies.

Thomas Peters and Robert Waterman's Lessons for Performance Management

Every now and again, there arises a masterpiece in thought, word, and deed. *In Search of Excellence*[5] is one such masterpiece that is a must-read because it is so timeless and encompassing. (See Table 3.4.)

Gary Hamel's Lessons for Performance Management

Gary Hamel for some time has been making management think about the future. His book, *The Future of Management*,[6] has many lessons to consider. (See Table 3.5.)

TABLE 3.4   Thomas Peters and Robert Waterman's Lessons for Performance Management

Peters and Waterman's Wisdom	Impact on Performance Management
Understand human motivations. In Chapter 3 of *In Search of Excellence,* Peters and Waterman go into much detail about behaviorist studies.	This book has as its foundation an emphasis on understanding human nature in order to minimize the carnage associated with performance measurement.
Importance of chaos rather than unnecessary order. Throughout the first three chapters of *In Search of Excellence* the importance of allowing overlap, internal competition, impromptu contact, while minimizing head office command and control was highlighted through the case studies quoted.	The project team needs to be wary of adopting the easier command and control approach. The KPI team must allow a fair degree of autonomy in the pilots and rollout stages so long as the foundation stones are intact.
A bias for action. The emphasis is on action, getting something into prototype, test, test, test rather than trying to second guess. The disbanding of committees that meet and do not convert anything to action is a very strong message.	The CEO should have a weekly record of the last meaningful action from every standing committee. If the last action was over six weeks ago, maybe it is time to abandon it.
Close to the customer. Being close to the customer does not only help with customer retention, it is the major source of innovation. Peters and Waterman found compelling evidence that customers are the main source of innovative ideas.	We need to measure the frequency of our interaction with customers: ■ Date of next contact with key customers. ■ Date of next customers' focus group. ■ Date of next research project into customer needs and ideas. ■ Follow-up on ideas from customers.
Autonomy and entrepreneurship. Peters and Waterman observed that radical decentralization and autonomy, with their attendant overlap, messiness, lack of coordination, and internal competition, were necessary in	We need to measure the speed of decentralization and empowerment until it is well and truly embedded.

(continued)

TABLE 3.4   *(Continued)*

Peters and Waterman's Wisdom	Impact on Performance Management
order to breed the entrepreneurial spirit and champions who were required to take risks in developing new ideas.	
■ Intense communication. ■ Tolerating failure. ■ Internal competition. ■ Promote legends. ■ Absence of overplanning and paperwork.	
Productivity through people. Peters and Waterman noted that the following were evident in the best-run organizations:	The KPI team will need to apply these techniques to be successful.
■ Unabashed hoopla. ■ Internal competition. ■ Family atmosphere. ■ Available information. ■ Trust. ■ Keeping units small and fast and flexible.	
Stick to the knitting. Peters and Waterman coined this famous phrase, and it is consistent with Jim Collins's, "hedgehog" concept. *Simple form, lean staff.* Peters and Waterman offered the following advice:	We can measure the degree to which resources and time are directed away from the core activities, indicating a loss of focus. We can report the levels of command, the headcount of head office, and the numbers of staff reporting to managers.
■ Avoid the trap of economies of scale—they seldom eventuate. ■ Avoid constantly hiving off into new divisions. ■ Maintain a small corporate office. ■ Keep a flatter organizational structure.	

TABLE 3.5   Gary Hamel's Lessons for Performance Management

Gary Hamel's Wisdom	Impact on Performance Management
Continuous management innovation. You need to have a process for continuous management innovation. To be an organization that is capable of trauma-free renewal rather than one that is moved to change through a crisis.	The KPI team needs to be very open to new management thinking and processes. It is very important that new management concepts are embraced by the project team.
Creative apartheid. Hamel points out that most human beings are creative in some sphere of their lives. The point he makes is that this creativity needs to be embraced at the workplace. He believes that creativity can be strengthened through instruction and practice, e.g., Whirlpool has trained more than 35,000 employees in the principles of business innovation.	The KPI team must be open to new ideas during the project. Be flexible with how workshops are run, ensuring that creativity is given time to flourish.
Too much hierarchy, too little community. Hamel points out hierarchies are good at aggregating effort (coordinating activities) but not good at mobilizing effort (inspiring people to go above and beyond). The more you consolidate power in the hands of a few leaders, the less resilient the system will be.	The KPI team must promote a community feel to the project, selling the benefits through the emotional drivers and gaining credibility by abandoning process, measures, and reporting that is not delivering.
Aggregate collective wisdom. Hamel points out the compelling evidence that "large groups of people are often smarter than the smartest people in them."	The KPI team should consult widely and hold sessions during each workshop to ensure an adequate chance for all to have their say. This is best done by limiting each workgroup in the workshop to no more than seven. The Internet and intranet should be used widely by the KPI team to tap into the collective wisdom within the organization.
Embrace differences. Hamel is very consistent about the need to: ■ Embrace irregular people; their irregular ideas can be very valuable. ■ Look for positive deviants.	The KPI team should be selected from all experienced employees. It is important to consider those employees who have always shaken the cart. They may have the X factor to make this project work.

(continued)

TABLE 3.5   *(Continued)*

Gary Hamel's Wisdom	Impact on Performance Management
Mission matters. The mission must be compelling enough to overcome the gravitational pull of the past and spur individual renewal.	The KPI team should ensure its mission statement is worded carefully so it will energize and assist with the selling of the winning KPI methodology.
Opt-in commitment. Hamel believes organizations should have an opt-in and self-chosen commitment.	The KPI team should have an open selection process so that a wide net is cast for the best team members. Passion for performance management will be a very important attribute to look for.
New management order. Hamel wants to see a new management order and the signs are there in how the Internet works. He points out that the reason the Internet is so successful is:	The KPI team members should become familiar with Gary Hamel's book *The Future of Management.*

- Everyone has a voice.
- The tools of creativity are widely distributed.
- It is easy and cheap to experiment with.
- Capability counts more than credentials and titles.
- Commitment is voluntary.
- Authority is fluid and contingent on value added.
- The only hierarchies are "natural" hierarchies.
- Just about everyone is decentralized.
- Ideas compete on an equal footing.
- It's easy for buyers and sellers to find each other.
- Resources are free to follow opportunities.
- Decisions are peer based.

Foundation Stone 3: Using an Appropriate Strategy

As the Mad Hatter said in *Alice in Wonderland*: "If you don't know where you are going, any road will take you there." Peter Drucker reinforced the importance of having the right strategy for the organization—a strategy that was relevant for this Lego world we live in, a world in which independent service providers can be put together in a seamless way to the customer. He stated that there was not competition, just better solutions. Drucker saw collaboration as the key, collaboration even with an organization that was previously seen as a competitor. Jack Welch pointed out "Your back room is somebody's else front room."

In government and non profit agencies, collaboration has the same barriers as in the private sector: egos and past institutional memories that seem to prohibit staff from striking effective alliances with other organizations that can perform the service better and cheaper. Drucker went on to say that an organization could achieve almost all functions from collaboration. Drucker saw only marketing and innovation as being sacrosanct in-house activities.

Setting out one's strategy is covered in Chapter 5, Strategy and Its Relevance to Performance Measures.

Foundation Stone 4: Critical Success Factors Known by All Staff

It is interesting that such a basic premise that all staff in the organization should know what is important and thus be able to prioritize their activities is not universal.

I argue that, unless this foundation stone is in place, each manager, in their own empire, will have what is important to them embedded in the way things are done. Many counterproductive activities will occur based on this false premise, that is, what is important to me is important to the organization.

For a CEO to steer the ship, everybody needs to know the journey, what makes the ship sail well, and what needs to be done in difficult weather.

(For a more detailed explanation of how an organization can find its critical success factors, see Chapter 7, Finding Your Organization's Critical Success Factors.)

Foundation Stone 5: Abandon Processes That Do Not Work

In the next few centuries, Peter Drucker will be revered in the way Leonardo da Vinci is today. He created many management and leadership principles that we forget at our peril. His concept of abandonment is the most profound of those principles. He saw abandonment as the source—the fountain of innovation. His argument was so simple: We undertake tasks, we embed processes, we attend meetings, we monitor measures, we write reports that are broken and that exist only because they were done last week, last month, last quarter.

In many government and non profit agencies, we could well abandon:

- All measures and restart the exercise, basing them on the critical success factors. Some measures will no doubt be reinstated but many will remain discarded.
- Performance reports that have no relevance to the critical success factors and strategy. They are completed the same way they were done last month, and the month before with nobody reading them. Every report should have a small box on the front page explaining how it is relevant to the critical success factors and strategy of the organization.
- The balanced-scorecard application, if it is based on the cascading of measures down from an organizational measure resulting in hundreds of meaningless measures.
- A scorecard that has been proved to be dysfunctional, with many measures encouraging staff to act in a direction that is not beneficial to the organization. The scorecard can be rebuilt.
- Meetings that have become a ritual, held because they were held last week, last month, and yet the action points are never cleared. They just fall off the to-do list over time. Every meeting should have a clear statement of its purpose, a record of what it has actioned, and the cost per hour to the organization. In one organization, the CEO would randomly interrupt meetings and ask each attendee why they were present, and what they could add. Attendees who were there to fill out the numbers were requested to get back to work. Although an extreme management practice, it had the desired impact.
- Performance-related pay where it is linked to annual targets, which will either be too easy or too hard. (See Appendix A.)
- The annual planning process as it is currently set up. It is really only an annual political event serving no purpose. (See Appendix C.)
- A dysfunctional scorecard where there are hundreds of measures. We can recycle the application but the scorecard needs to be a casualty.
- Annual performance reviews. Nobody likes receiving them, managers hate preparing them, they do not help with remuneration, and in any case, managers should be giving feedback on a regular basis—at least monthly to their staff.

Rejuvenating Human Resources

One of the most disconcerting departures from better practice has been the demise of the human resources (HR) team's influence in organizations. When recruitment is left to managers, chaos ensues. Jack Welch's view is that the senior HR manager should sit alongside the chief information officer and chief financial officer, with equal standing and remuneration.

Most readers can look back to a recruitment process, which, on reflection, did not work out as well as intended. In most cases, this would have been based on interviews and references. HR practitioners have found there is a far more effective way to recruit, by starting with an in-depth focus on the job requirements and following with behavioral event interviews, simulated exercises, and assessment centers. All this takes experienced in-house resources to manage and consequently deliver. As we all know, the cost of appointing the wrong person can be much greater than just the salary costs.

Without an active and informed HR department, an organization cannot possibly function. This situation can be no more clearly illustrated than with the process of performance management. Read Jack Welch's book, *Winning*,[7] to understand the issues.

At the center of all organizations are people practices; these are integral to all the elements of best practice. Examples of people practices that leading organization's adopt include:

- Effective, integrated top-down and bottom-up communications.
- Focus on and measurement of employee satisfaction.
- Training and development processes that promote career paths (including mentorship programs, empowerment programs, leadership training, running in-house development centers, etc.).
- Excellent occupational health and safety practices.
- Focus on internal (and external) customers.
- Innovative staff recognition systems (including CEO success express weekly newsletters, CEO awards).
- Focus on daily innovation at the workface (e.g., doing what we do better every day).
- Performance-based remuneration that relies on relative measures rather than performance against an annual fixed target.
- Migration away from the classic annual or half-yearly staff performance review cycle, which is cumbersome, expensive, and too late to be of any use.

Performance-Related Pay: Correcting the Errors

Never in the history of management has so little rigor been applied in such an important area. Performance bonuses give away billions of dollars each year based on methodologies to which little thought has been applied. Who are the performance bonus experts? What qualifications do they possess to work in this important area other than prior experience in creating the mayhem we currently have?

When one looks at the skill base of compensation experts, one wonders why they get listened to in the first place. Which bright spark advised the hedge funds to pay a $1 billion bonus to one fund manager who created a paper gain that never eventuated into cash? These schemes were flawed from the start; "super" profits were being paid out, there was no allowance made for the cost of capital, and the bonus scheme was only "high side" focused.

There are a number of foundation stones that need to be laid down and never undermined when building a performance bonus scheme. These foundation stones have been addressed in Appendix A.

Reviewing an Individual's Performance

This is a more informal weekly or monthly activity, and not an overly structured and time consuming once-a-year or half-yearly process. Many writers have pointed out that the performance review monster needs to be put down humanely. In its place, we need to put a better or more robust system.[8]

Getting the Right People on the Bus

Why do we accept jobs we never should have or appoint staff who started to fail from week one?

Drucker saw recruiting as a life and death decision, which should be taken with great care. When discussing recruiting issues with managers, I like to reinforce the importance of recruitment and promotion. Get it right, and you have laid a "clutch of golden eggs," get it wrong, and you have a disaster affecting the whole team for months.

You simply either spend 40 hours at the top of the cliff or 400 hours at the bottom with the casualty and its impact on the rest of the team.

In Jim Collins's *Good to Great,*[9] an important factor was that great organizations "get the right people on the bus."

Jack Welch embedded a culture of careful selection, and GE became expert at selecting quality candidates from the army and less-well-known colleges and universities. Welch did not subscribe to the theory that the best candidates were in the Ivy League business schools. He looked at the attributes the individual would bring to the organization rather than the circumstances that attributed to giving the applicant the Ivy League business school opportunity.

Welch saw recruiting or promotion activity as among the most important things you ever do. He said that it was important to get "into the candidate's skin" to find out what they were really made of, to find out if they had a passion for the business, and what their values really are. It was deemed imperative that the applicant's values be consistent with the GE values.

This is so fundamental to performance measurement that I would argue that, if you have the wrong staff on board, you will never get your measures to work.

To assist you with recruiting, I have set out in Appendix B the necessary questions you need to ask to ascertain whether there is an appropriate fit.

Jack Welch's 20/70/10 Differentiation Rule

Jack Welch's 20/70/10 differentiation rule caused a huge furor when he first talked about it. It was thought to be very politically incorrect. As mentioned earlier, he believes that in every team you have 20 percent of high performers, 70 percent of good solid people, and 10 percent who never should have been employed. The 10 percent employees do not have the skills or the passion to succeed in the organization.

To reiterate Welch's point: Promote your top 20 percent of performers into jobs that are a good fit for their strengths, assist the next 70 percent to better meet their potential, and make it clear to the bottom 10 percent that their futures lie elsewhere. Welch points out, why make these staff members redundant, as this act costs the organization and rewards poor performance. Instead tell the person "we made a mistake recruiting you, and you made a mistake joining us. You deserve to work in an environment where you are passionate about what you do and where you can succeed." With this candor and open communication, it is likely that these staff members will want to move on to better pastures for themselves.

I place this 20/70/10 differentiation rule so highly because, in every organization, mistakes are made in recruitment. The issue now is how you deal with it. Performance management can never work if you have staff members who are not passionate about their work, are not respected by their managers, and who would leave if a better position was available. Applying this rule will help focus staff recruitment within the organization.

I recommend that you listen to Jack Welch describe his differentiation rule on YouTube.

Secrets from High-Performing Teams

We can all learn so much from replicating the secrets of those gifted managers who have transformed performance. Many better practices are discussed in the books by Welch, Collins, Peters, Waterman, and Hamel. These books have been analyzed in this chapter.

Many of the leadership traits featured in these books can be implemented in a short timeframe, as long as you are consistent with the implementation and lock in the changes, once a week over a 13-week period.[10]

Toyota's 14 Principles

Where does one start? We start with what I believe to be the greatest company in the world. Toyota has understood the basics of running a multinational business and it is able to embed its culture in all countries it operates within. Its Kentucky plant exceeded all Toyota expectations with its acceptance of the Toyota way.

I believe that Toyota's 14 principles should be embedded in all government and non profit agencies. They would make a profound impact on the organizations benefiting the staff, management, board/government agencies and, of course, the public they serve. These 14 principles have been well-analyzed in Jeffrey Liker's book *The Toyota Way*[11] and include:

Principle 1: Base your management decisions on a long-term philosophy, even at the expense of short-term financial goals.

Principle 2: Create continuous process flow to bring problems to the surface.

Principle 3: Use pull systems to avoid overproduction.

Principle 4: Level out the workload (*Heijunka*).

Principle 5: Build a culture of stopping to fix problems, to get quality right the first time.

Principle 6: Standardized tasks are the foundation for continuous improvement and employee empowerment.

Principle 7: Use visual control so no problems are hidden.

Principle 8: Use only reliable, thoroughly tested technology that serves your people and processes.

Principle 9: Grow leaders who thoroughly understand the work, live the philosophy, and teach it to others.

Principle 10: Develop exceptional people and teams who follow your company's philosophy.

Principle 11: Respect your extended network of partners and suppliers by challenging them and helping them improve.

Principle 12: Go and see for yourself to thoroughly understand the situation (*Genchi Genbutsu*).

Principle 13: Make decisions slowly by consensus, thoroughly considering all options and then implement the decisions rapidly.

Principle 14: Become a learning organization through relentless reflection (*Hansei*) and continuous improvement (*kaizen*).

Role of Performance Measures: Implementing Winning KPIs

The great power of performance measures can only be successfully unleashed if you understand what they are, where they come from, and ensure the senior management team lives and breathes them. The rest of the chapters of this book address why and how you implement winning KPIs.

Quarterly Rolling Planning: The Setting of Targets

As mentioned in Chapter 2 on the myths of performance measurement, setting an annual performance agreement is doomed to failure. One of the most significant breakthroughs in performance management has been the realization that planning should be done on a quarterly rolling basis rather than on the traditional annual cycle as set out in Exhibit 3.3. In this process, each quarter in the second week of the third month (June, September, December, and March in this example) management is asked:

- What are your goals for the next quarter?
- What resources do you really need to achieve these goals?
- What resources might you need for quarters 2, 3, 4, 5, 6?

Each quarter, before approving the next quarter's targets and funding, the senior management team and board forecast the bigger picture six quarters out. While firming up the short-term numbers for the next three months, each forecast will also update the annual forecast. Budget holders are encouraged to spend half the time on getting the details of the next three

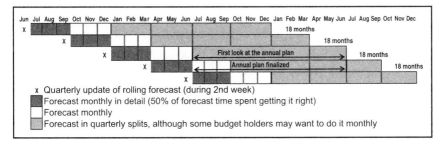

EXHIBIT 3.3   The Quarterly Rolling Planning Process

Source: David Parmenter, *Winning CFOs: Implementing and Applying Better Practices,* Copyright © 2011 by David Parmenter. Reprinted with permission of John Wiley & Sons, Inc.

months right, because these will become targets, on agreement, and the rest of the time on the next five quarters. Each quarter forecast is never a cold start because budget holders have reviewed the forthcoming quarter a number of times. Provided appropriate forecasting software is available, management can do its quarterly forecasts very quickly; it takes one airline three days! The overall time spent in the four quarterly forecast updates should be no more than five weeks.

Most organizations can use the cycle set out in Exhibit 3.3 if their year-end falls on a calendar quarter-end. Some organizations may wish to stagger the cycle, say May, August, November, and February.

This quarterly rolling planning is so important I have dedicated Appendix C to further explain this major development to you.

Reporting Performance

Many management reports are not management tools; they are merely memorandums of information. As a management tool, management reports should encourage timely action in the right direction. Organizations need to measure and report on those activities on which the board, management, and staff need to focus. The old adage, "What gets measured gets done," is still true.

For management reporting to become a management tool, monthly reporting must be combined with daily and weekly reporting. It is of little help to tell the senior management team that the horse has bolted halfway through the next month. If management is told immediately that the stable door has been left open, most management will take action to close it.

Decision-based reporting has a profound impact on the KPI reporting, which needs to be timely, brief, and informative.

Reporting performance requires that we have an understanding of the rules surrounding data visualization—the method by which we make information useable for the reader.

Data visualization is an area that is growing in importance. No longer is it appropriate for well-meaning accountants and managers to dream up report formats based on what looks good to them. There is a science behind what makes data displays work. The world expert on this is Stephen Few who has written the top three bestselling books on Amazon in this field.[12]

A must visit for all people involved in report design is Stephen Few's company web site where he has lodged many high quality white papers on the topic of graphical displays (www.perceptualedge.com/articles).

Outside-In View

We cannot hope to get performance right if we do not have the Peter Drucker outside-in view of your business.

Drucker made it clear that leaders need to look at their organization from outside-in. His work in this area is beautifully summarized in a book called *The Definitive Drucker*.[13] He said that chief executive officers needed to define their business from the customer perspective. They have to be aware of all the noncustomers out there, asking how could we tap that potential.

Drucker commented that great organizations would ensure that the senior management team spent some time each year directly interfacing with the customer (e.g., having a week where they serve customers as frontline workers). One great CEO I have met, George Hickton, has used this technique in every organization he has led. After the hands-on week, the senior management are refreshed, more aware of the silly bureaucracy that is getting in the way, and are a much tighter-knit team. Drucker singled out Jack Welch as an example of a great outside-in leader.

Drucker was adamant that leaders must constantly look into the future from the customers' perspective, thus ensuring that CEOs would be quicker to realize when cash-cow businesses were in decline.

Organizations all face times when change is catastrophic; change suddenly comes with a factor-10 force. During these times, great leaders have seen the warning signs, made the painful decisions to ditch once successful businesses, and refocused into new business areas where they can once again be a market leader. One great book on the topic is Jim Collins's *How the Mighty Fall*.[14]

Adopting *Kaizen*

Although *Kaizen* was covered in the 14 Toyota principles, discussed earlier, it is so important to government and non profit agencies that it is separated out in this model. *Kaizen* should be a way of life for staff in every organization. It is the acceptance that everything we do each day can be improved if you put your mind to it.

In government and non profit agencies, far too often innovation is stifled. Young bright graduates are trained to stop challenging the system and follow what we have done for the last decade.

The cost of this lost opportunity to change is immense. The lack of *Kaizen* is costing the public purse billions. Management would be mortified if they knew their reluctance to embrace innovation means fewer roads, fewer hospitals, fewer operations, and so on.

Working Smarter Not Harder

There is no point in having all the foundation stones in place and then having an office environment in which bad practices absorb too much time. These bad practices were featured in my management book[15] and include:

- Not adopting action meetings—a new revolution in how to handle meetings.
- Scheduling meetings in the mornings, the most productive time in the day, when many could be held in the afternoon.
- Trying to sell change by logic instead of the emotional drivers of the audience.
- Not putting enough weight behind a mentorship program—frequently they are present in government and non profit agencies but they are failing through lack of nourishment.
- Limiting performance feedback for the staff to the formal process that occurs once or twice a year. Management is a process that is 24/7, so staff recognitions should be given when good performance is noted and reprimands handled swiftly, ending on a positive note as prescribed by the *One Minute Manager*.[16]
- Making work a burden instead of fun. Typically, the main culprit is not celebrating achievements enough. As Jack Welch says, "Work is too important a part of life not to celebrate achievements when you have them."
- Lack of collaboration both internally and externally. This has been covered in Drucker's wisdom earlier in this chapter.

Getting Technology to Deliver

There is a major issue with technology and applications. The issue is that applications are being delivered by very clever young staff who have never operated in business. I call them freshly minted MBAs.

Jeremy Hope, coauthor of *Beyond Budgeting*,[17] points out that of the millions spent on systems, where is the paperless office?

Toyota, the cautious and thinking company, interestingly enough has avoided the major technology mistakes of other large organizations. They have a principle:

Toyota Principle 8: Use only reliable, thoroughly tested technology that serves your people and processes.

This has meant they are naturally skeptical about new systems and their claims until they have seen them working elsewhere and then they improve the system to fit the Toyota way. This principle of caution has enabled them to ensure technology when implementation will deliver what is required.

Moving from Management to Leadership

As Peter Drucker said "Management is about doing things right and leadership is about doing the right things." To revitalize performance management in an organization, there has to be a massive switch in thinking. We need the organization to invest in their leaders, ensuring that they have the training and opportunity to grow, that they work in an environment in which mistakes are seen as a learning experience rather than as a reason for a court martial, and that they have created a place where they breed the chief executive officers of the business.

Organizations, and particularly government and non profit agencies, that consistently recruit their CEOs externally, are saying we have failed. In my view any board that presides over this catastrophe should step down. They have failed the very basic 101 test: How to grow leaders.

Notes

1. Dean Spitzer, *Transforming Performance Measurement: Rethinking the Way We Measure and Drive Organizational Success* (New York: AMACOM, 2007).
2. Peter F. Drucker, *Managing the Non-Profit Organization* (New York: HarperBusiness, 2006).
3. Jack Welch and Suzy Welch, *Winning* (New York: HarperBusiness, 2005).
4. Jim Collins and Jerry Porras, *Built to Last: Successful Habits of Visionary Companies* (New York: HarperBusiness, 1994).
5. Thomas J. Peters and Robert H. Waterman, *In Search of Excellence: Lessons from America's Best Run Companies* (New York: Harper & Row, 1982).
6. Gary Hamel, *The Future of Management* (Cambridge, MA: Harvard Business School Press, 2007).
7. Welch and Welch, *Winning*.
8. For more information, see David Parmenter, *The Leading-Edge Manager's Guide to Success: Strategies and Better Practices* (Hoboken, NJ: John Wiley & Sons, 2011).
9. Jim Collins, *Good to Great: Why Some Companies Make the Leap and Others Don't* (New York: HarperBusiness, 2001).

10. For examples of high performing teams, see David Parmenter, *The Leading-Edge Manager's Guide to Success: Strategies and Better Practices* (Hoboken, NJ: John Wiley & Sons, 2011).

11. Jeffrey K. Liker, *The Toyota Way: 14 Management Principles from the World's Greatet Manufacturer* (New York: McGraw-Hill, 2003).

12. Stephen Few, *Show Me the Numbers: Designing Tables and Graphs to Enlighten* (Burlington, CA: Analytics Press, 2004); *Information Dashboard Design: The Effective Visual Communication of Data* (Sebastopol, CA: O'Reilly Media, 2006); *Now You See It: Simple Visualization Techniques for Quantitative Analysis* (Burlington, CA: Analytics Press, 2009).

13. Elizabeth Haas Edersheim, *The Definitive Drucker: Challenges for Tomorrow's Executives—Final Advice from the Father of Modern Management* (New York: McGraw-Hill, 2006).

14. Jim Collins, *How the Mighty Fall: And Why Some Companies Never Give In* (New York: HarperCollins, 2009).

15. See also Parmenter, *The Leading-Edge Manager's Guide to Success.*

16. Ken Blanchard and Spencer Johnson, *One Minute Manager* (New York: Morrow, 1982).

17. Jeremy Hope and Robin Fraser, *Beyond Budgeting: How Managers Can Break Free from the Annual Performance Trap* (Cambridge, MA: Harvard Business School Press, 2003).

CHAPTER 4

Measurement Leadership Has to Come from the Chief Executive Officer

As Dean Spitzer[1] argues, one of the fundamental issues of the implementation of performance measurement is *measurement leadership*. Only when the chief executive officer (CEO) is passionate and knowledgeable about measurement will you have the opportunity to get twenty-first-century measurement to work effectively and efficiently.

Barriers to Measurement Leadership

The CEO and senior management team need to minimize the barriers to measurement leadership which include the following:

- CEOs who lack the knowledge to have the requisite expertise to run the organization. As Dr. Scott Gardner, Associate Professor at Murdoch University (Perth, Western Australia), said to me one day

    "Experience plus knowledge equals expertise."

- Far too often, CEOs are completely unaware of management thinking or literature because their pursuit for learning ceased soon after graduation.
- CEOs who are motivated to retain the existing measurement system because they benefit from the flaws with a large year-end bonus.
- CEOs who are addicted to action and quick fixes rather than a well-thought-out, slow but effective implementations of change.
- CEOs who are happy to run the business on intuition rather than on facts.

- CEOs who have become immune to waste, who have worked with so many dysfunctional systems that they consider them part of the surroundings.
- CEOs who have very narrow understanding of the work of leading leadership and management writers, such as Peter Drucker, Jim Collins, Peters and Waterman, Gary Hamel, and Jack Welch.

The Way Forward for the Chief Executive Officer

To really get started, CEOs need to go through a crash course in twenty-first-century management practices. Naturally, this would at first appear insulting to many CEOs who, have not only an undergraduate degree but also a master's or PhD.

There are a number of major steps CEOs need to create to get performance measurement to work in their organization. Let us call them the top 10:

1. Disband any form of primitive performance-based pay mechanism that ties pay to either annual performance targets or performance measures and rebuild when a better understanding has been gained on foundation stones of performance-related pay.
2. Realize that you have reached the highest echelon of achievement a CEO can reach without the requisite knowledge. Although your *experience* will obviously be sound, you need to avail yourself of the *knowledge* from the greatest thinkers of our time. There is plenty of time to rectify this. You can start by the referring to the reading list (see Exhibit 4.1).
3. Apply the practices of winning leadership featured in my management book.[2]
4. Abandon processes that are not working.
5. Find your organization's critical success factors by following the steps in Chapter 7 and embed them in every team in the organization, for without them, everything will drift from one crisis to another.
6. Become a Toyota convert, embedding as many of its 14 principles as possible. See Toyota's 14 Principles in Chapter 3 for more details.
7. Commence the KPI project using handpicked in-house resources giving them time, resources, and support so they will have a chance to succeed. It is important that you champion the KPI project 24/7 by having a direct reporting link from the KPI team to you.
8. Appoint someone as the chief measurement officer, as outlined later in this chapter.

EXHIBIT 4.1   Minimum Reading List Required to Move Forward

- Jack Welch with Suzy Welch, *Winning* (HarperBusiness, 2005). Take a crash course in Peter Drucker's wisdom by reading *The Definitive Drucker: Challenges for Tomorrow's Executives–Final Advice from the Father of Modern Management* (Elizabeth Haas Edersheim), McGraw-Hill, 2006
- Jeffrey K. Liker, *The Toyota Way: 14 Management Principles from the World's Greatest Manufacturer*, McGraw-Hill, 2003
- Jeremy Hope and Robin Fraser, *Beyond Budgeting: How Managers Can Break Free from the Annual Performance Trap*, Harvard Business Press, 2003
- Jim Collins, *Good to Great: Why Some Companies Make the Leap . . . and Others Don't*, HarperBusiness, 2001 and *How the Mighty Fall: And Why Some Companies Never Give In*, HarperCollins, 2009
- Thomas J. Peters and Robert H. Waterman, *In Search of Excellence: Lessons from America's Best Run Companies*, Harper and Row, 1982
- Chapters 1 to 8 in this book

9. Create a new vision, mission, and values statement that ensures only like minded management and staff will join the organization in the future.
10. Make entire staff aware that all KPIs are all non financial and are monitored 24/7, daily, or weekly (see "Seven Characteristics of KPIs," in Chapter 6).

Armed with this knowledge it will be logical for you to challenge the myths and establish a simple yet effective measurement system in your organization. You will need to champion this process, in the same way the famous CEOs listed in Exhibit 4.2 did. You need to be the figure head of this change process like Jack Welch was in implementing Six Sigma and e-commerce within GE. You will need to select your most talented staff to lead this change to making measurement an activity that will lead to greater staff satisfaction.

EXHIBIT 4.2   CEOs Who Have Championed Measurement Successfully

- Jack Welch, former CEO, GEC
- Bob Gavin, former CEO, Motorola
- Larry Bossidy, CEO, Honeywell
- Carlos Ghosn, CEO, Nissan and Renault
- Frederick Smith, President, FedEx Corporation

Appoint a Chief Measurement Officer

To improve the likelihood of success with performance measurement, Dean Spitzer suggests appointing a chief measurement officer. This person would:

- Be knowledgeable in all the facets of performance management.
- Understand the psychology working behind performance measures.
- Have excellent communication skills, including the vital trait of management by walkabout.
- Be able to run workshops to train staff in finding performance measures.
- Exude passion for performance measurement.

Notes

1. Dean R. Spitzer, *Transforming Performance Measurement: Rethinking the Way We Measure and Drive Organizational Success* (New York: Amacom, 2007).
2. See David Parmenter, *The Leading-Edge Manager's Guide to Success: Strategies and Better Practices* (Hoboken, NJ: John Wiley & Sons, 2011).

CHAPTER 5

Strategy and Its Relevance to Performance Measures

S trategy is the way an organization intends to achieve its vision. In a competitive environment, your strategy will distinguish you from your competition. In the public sector, your strategy determines the way you can best marshal your resources to achieve desired outcomes.

An organization's strategy is related to performance measures through a series of linkages as shown in Exhibit 5.1.

I have seen far too many strategic plans go nowhere quickly. I often mention that, if you suffer from insomnia, read the first page of your organization's strategic plan and you will be asleep by the second page. Many organizations could inflict damage onto their major competitor if they planted an original copy of their organization's strategy into the competitor's possession. Because, as night follows day, the organization will be miles away from the intended route set out in the strategy and thus the competitor's reactive initiations will be in the wrong direction.

Peter Drucker was adamant that government and non profit agencies need, like their private sector counterparts, to get their strategy right. Although government and non profit agencies suffer less when strategy is not appropriate, it is the public at large that bears the cost. Here are some of my thoughts on this important matter.

Define Your Organization's Mission, Vision, Values

Too many government and non profit agencies have not spent enough time defining their mission, vision, and values statements in a way that communicates the direction to staff. Understanding the difference between a mission, vision, values, and strategy is vital. To aid clarity in this area, I offer you the simple definition that I first saw in Paul Niven's book on the balanced scorecard.[1]

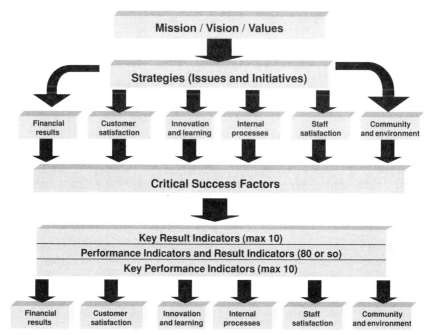

KPIs, RIs, and PIs in a balanced scorecard for Management and KRIs for the Board dashboard

EXHIBIT 5.1   Linkages between Strategy and KPIs

The *mission* is like a timeless beacon that may never be reached (e.g., a multinational in the entertainment business has a mission "to make people happy," and 3M's mission is "to solve unsolved problems innovatively"). A mission statement can remain the same for decades if crafted well.

The *vision* outlines what the organization wants to be by a certain time frame. A vision statement is more specific in terms of both the future state and the time frame. A vision describes what will be achieved if the organization is successful. The vision can galvanize your organization if it is stated with enough clarity, is time bound, and is supported continually by the senior management team. There are some very famous visions, most notably John F. Kennedy's when he said, "I believe that this nation should commit itself to achieving the goal, before this decade is out, of landing a man on the moon and returning him safely to the earth." This simple statement galvanized the U.S. scientific community and the management and staff of organizations in a herculean effort to achieve this vision. From the moment it was spoken, NASA experts began to plan how the millions of essential building blocks required to achieve this vision needed to combine together.

The *values* are what your organization stands for: "We believe..." (e.g., a public sector entity has the values "seek innovation and excellence, engage constructively, ask questions, support and help each other, bring solutions, see the bigger picture"). With the passing years, I realized that the organization's values are paramount. They should create a template that will help recruitment. Eminent organizations are very effective at recruiting staff who have the same values as the organization.

Create a Strategy That Is Understood by Staff

Organizations are waking up to the fact that strategic planning processes must be much more inclusive if your organization is to reap benefits. Staff members need to understand the organization's mission, vision, values, and strategy if they are to be "fast, focused, and flexible," says Bruce Holland,[2] a respected New Zealand strategic planner and communicator.

Holland strongly advocates that, "If you have done your job properly, you should be able to rip up the final document, as staff and management have the linkage imprinted in their memory." Achieving this level of understanding is much quicker and easier than most managers and CEOs believe. Getting people throughout the organization involved can generate high levels of understanding, energy, goodwill, and commitment.

The great management writers such as Jim Collins, Tom Peters, Robert Waterman, Gary Hamel, and Jack Welch have pointed out that prominent organizations are not great because they have the largest strategic plan. In fact, it is quite the reverse; the poorly performing organizations are the ones that spend the most time in strategy and the dreaded annual-planning process.

The people involved in strategic planning would normally make any task complicated. Their role is, of course, the reverse—to make strategy understandable by all. I call it passing the "14-year-old" test.

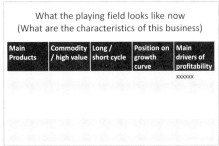

EXHIBIT 5.2   Extract from the Strategy Slides in Appendix D

Jack Welch says that strategy should be able to go on five slides. Although this may not be achievable, the points he says that should be covered could certainly fit within 10 slides. See Exhibit 5.2 for an extract of two of the slides, and see Appendix D for an interpretation of Welch's advice on strategy from his must read book *Winning*.[3]

As an observer of strategy implementation, I make the following observations: There are two types of strategic initiatives: those that improve "business as usual" and those initiatives that will create "new business." We monitor and report them differently because they are implemented differently.

New business initiatives are frequently run by small teams reporting directly to the CEO, and there is limited knowledge of the activities because some are highly confidential.

The business-as-usual strategies need to be communicated to staff so they understand and implement them.

Ensure That Your Strategy Is Balanced

In their ground breaking book *The Balanced Scorecard*,[4] Kaplan and Norton pointed out that strategy has to be balanced and the strategic initiatives reflect this balance. They observed that many strategies were not "balanced" because they do not map to all the balanced-scorecard perspectives. As mentioned in Chapter 2, it is a myth to believe that there are only four balanced-scorecard perspectives, as six balanced-scorecard perspectives provides a much better balance.

In Exhibit 5.3, the organization's strategies only map to five of these six perspectives; therefore staff do not need to link to the Environment and Community perspective in order to be compliant with the organization's strategy. This is clearly an unsatisfactory result.

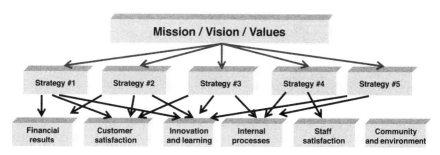

EXHIBIT 5.3   Mapping Strategies to the Six Balanced-Scorecard Perspectives

Progress Against Strategy

Status as 30 June xx

● Warning: little progress made
◐ Some progress but behind schedule
○ On track or finished

		Comments (required action if yellow or red)
Strategy one xxxxxxxxxxxxxxxxxxxxxxx		
A1	Initiative xxxx xxxx xxxxxx xxx xxx	○ Completed in third week of May
A2	Initiative xxxx xxxx xxxxxx xxx xxx	● xxxxxxxxx xxxxxxx xxxx xxxx xxxx xxxx xxxxx xxxxx xxxxxxx xxxx xxxx x xxxxxx x xxxxxx xxxxxxxx xxxx xxxx
A3	Initiative xxxx xxxx xxxxxx xxx xxx	◐
Strategy two xxxxxxxxxxxxxxxxxxxxxxx		
B1	Initiative xxxx xxxx xxxxxx xxx xxx	◐ xxxxxxxxxx xxxxxxx xxxx xxx xxxx xxxxx xxxx xxxxxx xxxxxxxx xxxx xxxx x xxxxxx x xxxxxx xxxxxxxx xxxx xxxx
B2	Initiative xxxx xxxx xxxxxx xxx xxx	○ Completed in March
B3	Initiative xxxx xxxx xxxxxx xxx xxx	○ On track, completion date mid Sept
Strategy three xxxxxxxxxxxxxxxxxxxxxxx		
C1	Initiative xxxx xxxx xxxxxx xxx xxx	○ Completed in third week of May
C2	Initiative xxxx xxxx xxxxxx xxx xxx	◐ Completed in third week of May
C3	Initiative xxxx xxxx xxxxxx xxx xxx	○ On track, completion date end Dec
Strategy four xxxxxxxxxxxxxxxxxxxxxxx		
D1	Initiative xxxx xxxx xxxxxx xxx xxx	● xxxxxxxxxx xxxxxxx xxxx xxx xxxx xxxxx xxxx xxxxxx xxxxxxxx xxxx xxxx x xxxxxx x xxxxxx xxxxxxxx xxxx xxx xxxxxxxxxx xxxxxxx xxxx xxxx xxxx xxxxx xxxx xxxxxx xxxxxxxx xxxx xxxx x xxxxxx x xxxxxx xxxxxxxx xxxx xxx
D2	Initiative xxxx xxxx xxxxxx xxx xxx	◐
D3	Initiative xxxx xxxx xxxxxx xxx xxx	○ Completed in third week of May

EXHIBIT 5.4 Report Format to Help You Report Progress, on a Monthly Basis, against the Strategic Objectives

Source: David Parmenter, *Winning CFOs: Implementing and Applying Better Practices*, Copyright © 2011 by David Parmenter. Reprinted with permission of John Wiley & Sons, Inc.

Monitor Implementation of Your Strategy

One of the greatest gifts given by Kaplan and Norton has been highlighting the lack of implementation of organizational strategy—strategic initiatives left to die in the bulky strategic plan that has been beautifully written by the senior managers who have come fresh out of their MBA program.

If an organization does not regularly report its progress against strategy, you may as well have played golf at the strategic-planning retreat.

In Exhibit 5.4, I set out a report format to help you report progress, on a monthly basis, against the strategic objectives/themes and the initiatives within them. The example uses a simple traffic light display.

Creating the Future

Executives need to be fully conversant with the thoughts of Peter Drucker, Jim Collins, Gary Hamel, and Jack Welch about how they should go about creating their organization's future. (Some of their relevant thinking has been addressed in Chapter 3.)

Exhibit 5.5 will help you spend more time creating your organization's future.

EXHIBIT 5.5   Steps to Help Implement Strategy

	Actioned	
1. Find your organization's critical success factors in a two-day in-house workshop.	☐ Yes	☐ No
2. Hold a strategic think tank facilitated by a strategy expert.	☐ Yes	☐ No
3. Hold a training session to cover the thinking of Drucker, Collins, Welch, Peters and Waterman, and Hamel.	☐ Yes	☐ No
4. Read Chapter 11 on Strategy in Jack Welch's book *Winning*.	☐ Yes	☐ No
5. Read Chapters 4 and 5 in Jim Collins *Good to Great*.	☐ Yes	☐ No
6. Have a road show to explain the critical success factors, and the "business as usual" strategy to staff.	☐ Yes	☐ No
7. Create a weekly and monthly monitoring regime to ensure strategic initiatives are implemented.	☐ Yes	☐ No
8. Find your KPIs to lock in a 24/7 daily adherence to the critical success factors.	☐ Yes	☐ No
9. Schedule a "blue sky" morning, once a week, once every two weeks, of 4 to 5 hours in a quiet space free from phones, emails and meetings where all you dwell on is the future.	☐ Yes	☐ No
10. Meet with your mentor once a month to dwell on the future.	☐ Yes	☐ No

Replace the Annual Planning Process with Rolling Planning

Annual planning will only ensure there is a total disconnect between action and strategy. Organizations in the government and non profit sectors need to implement quarterly rolling planning. This is discussed in more detail in Appendix C.

Notes

1. Paul R. Niven, *Balanced Scorecard: Step-by-Step for Government and Nonprofit Agencies* (Hoboken, NJ: John Wiley & Sons, 2008).
2. Bruce Holland has a very insightful newsletter accessible from www .virtual.co.nz/index.php/StrategicSnippets/StrategicSnippets.
3. Jack Welch with Suzy Welch, *Winning* (New York: HarperBusiness, 2005).
4. Robert S. Kaplan and David P. Norton, *The Balanced Scorecard: Translating Strategy into Action* (Cambridge, MA: Harvard Business Press, 1996).

PART II

Winning KPIs Methodology

CHAPTER 6

The Great KPI Misunderstanding

Many companies are working with the wrong measures, many of which are incorrectly termed key performance indicators (KPIs). As mentioned in Chapter 2, it is a myth to consider all performance measures to be KPIs. There are four types of performance measures (see Exhibit 6.1):

1. Key result indicators (KRIs) tell you how you have done in a balanced-scorecard perspective or critical success factor.
2. Result indicators (RIs) tell you what you have done.
3. Performance indicators (PIs) tell you what to do.
4. KPIs tell you what to do to increase performance dramatically.

Many performance measures used by organizations are, therefore, a mix of these four types.

An onion analogy can be used to describe the relationship of these four measures. The outside skin describes the overall condition of the onion, the amount of sun, water, and nutrients it has received, as well as how it has been handled from harvest to the supermarket shelf. The outside skin is a key result indicator. However, as we peel the layers off the onion, we find more information. The layers represent the various performance and result indicators and the core of the onion represents the key performance indicator.

Key Result Indicators

What are KRIs? KRIs are measures that often have been mistaken for KPIs. For government and non profit agencies, *Key Result Indicators* would include:

- Availability of the major services we offer—average waiting time for service.

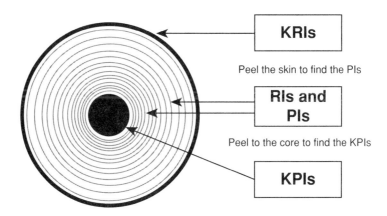

EXHIBIT 6.1   Four Types of Performance Measures

Source: David Parmenter, *Key Performance Indicators: Developing, Implementing, and Using Winning KPIs*, 2nd ed. Copyright © 2010 by David Parmenter. Reprinted with permission of John Wiley & Sons, Inc.

- Customer satisfaction (by customer group, showing the trend over an 18-month period).
- On-time implementation of infrastructure projects.
- Membership numbers (for professional organizations).
- Employee suggestions implemented (by groups showing the trend over an 18-month period).
- Employee satisfaction (by groups showing the trend over an 18-month period).

For the private sector, these measures would also include:

- Net profit before tax.
- Profitability of key customer groups.
- Return on capital employed.

The common characteristic of these measures is that they are the result of many actions. They give a clear picture of whether your organization is traveling in the right direction. They do not, however, tell you what you need to do to improve these results. Consequently, KRIs provide information that is ideal for the board or government official (i.e., those people who are not involved in day-to-day management).

KRIs typically cover a longer period of time than KPIs; they are reviewed on monthly/quarterly cycles, not on a daily/weekly basis as KPIs are. Separating KRIs from other measures has a profound impact on reporting, resulting in a separation of performance measures into those impacting governance and those impacting management. Accordingly, an organization should have a governance report (ideally in a dashboard format), consisting of up to 10 measures providing high-level KRIs for the board, and a balanced scorecard comprising up to 20 measures (a mix of RIs, and PIs) for management reports at month-end or a couple of times during the month. The KPIs are reported immediately outside the scorecard.

In between KRIs and true KPIs are numerous performance and result indicators. These complement the KPIs and are shown on the monthly scorecard for the organization, as well as on the relevant division, department, and team scorecards.

Performance and Result Indicators

The 80 or so performance measures that lie between the KRIs and the KPIs are the performance and result indicators (PIs and RIs). The performance indicators, although important, are not crucial to the business. The PIs help teams to align themselves with their organization's strategy. PIs are nonfinancial and complement the KPIs; they are shown on the organization, division, department, and team scorecards.

For government and non profit agencies, *Performance Indicators* that lie beneath KRIs could include:

- Abandon rate at call center—caller gives up.
- Number of media coverage events planned for next month, months 2 to 3, and months 4 to 6.
- Number of initiatives implemented from the staff survey.
- Date of next customer focus group.
- Number of staff innovations implemented, by team.
- Number of training hours booked for next month, months 2 and 3, and months 4 to 6—in both external/internal courses.

For the private sector, these measures would also include:

- Number of visits to key customers last month.
- Customer complaints from key customers.
- Sales calls organized for the next week, two weeks, and so forth.
- Late deliveries to key customers.

The RIs summarize activity and all financial performance measures are RIs (e.g., daily or weekly sales analysis is a very useful summary, but it is a result of the effort of many teams). To fully understand what to increase or decrease, we need to look at the activities that created the result.

For government and non profit agencies, *Result indicators* that lie beneath KRIs could include:

- Number of initiatives completed from the recent customer satisfaction survey.
- Number of employees' suggestions implemented in past 30 days.
- In-house courses scheduled to be held within three weeks where attendee numbers are below breakeven.
- List of abandonments by team in past month (reported monthly).
- Number of managers who have attended leadership training (reported quarterly, by manager level).
- Staff trained to use specified systems.
- Number of initiatives implemented to improve customer satisfaction.

For the private sector, these measures could also include:

- Net profit on key product lines.
- Sales made yesterday.
- Customer complaints from key customers.
- Weekly hospital bed utilization.

Key Performance Indicators

What are *KPIs*? KPIs represent a set of measures focusing on those aspects of organizational performance that are the most critical for the current and future success of the organization.

KPIs are rarely new to the organization. Either they have not been recognized or they were gathering dust somewhere unknown to the current management team. KPIs can be illustrated by two examples.

Example: An Airline KPI

This example concerns a senior British Airways (BA) official in the 1980s, who reportedly set about turning the airline around by concentrating on one KPI. He was notified, wherever he was in the world, if a BA plane was delayed. The BA manager at the relevant airport knew that if a plane was delayed beyond a certain threshold, he would receive a personal call from the BA official. It was not long before BA planes had a reputation for leaving on time. This KPI affected all six of the balanced-scorecard perspectives. Late planes:

1. Increased cost in many ways, including additional airport surcharges and the cost of accommodating passengers overnight as a result of planes being curfewed due to noise restrictions late at night.
2. Increased customer dissatisfaction and alienation of people meeting passengers at their destination (possible future customers).
3. Increased contribution to ozone depletion (environmental impact) because additional fuel was used in order to make up time during the flight.
4. Had a negative impact on staff development as they learned to replicate the bad habits that created late planes.
5. Adversely affected supplier relationships and servicing schedules, resulting in poor service quality.
6. Increased employee dissatisfaction, as they were constantly fire-fighting and dealing with frustrated customers.

Example: A Distribution Company

A distribution company's chief executive officer (CEO) realized that a critical success factor for the business was for trucks to leave as close to capacity as possible. A large truck, capable of carrying more than 40 tons, was being sent out with small loads because dispatch managers were focusing on delivering every item on time to customers.

Each day by 9 A.M., the CEO received a report of those trucks that had been sent out with an inadequate load the previous day. The CEO called the dispatch manager and asked whether any action had taken place to see if the customer could have accepted the delivery on a different date that would have enabled better utilization of the trucks. In most cases, the customer could have received it earlier or later, fitting in with a past or future truck going in that direction. The impact on profitability was significant.

In a scenario similar to the airline example, staff members did their utmost to avoid a career-limiting phone call from the CEO.

(Both these examples are provided in greater detail in my webcast, "Introduction to Winning KPIs," which can be accessed via www.davidparmenter.com.)

Seven Characteristics of KPIs

From extensive analysis and from discussions with over 3,000 participants in my KPI workshops, covering most organization types in the public and private sectors, I have been able to define what are the seven characteristics of KPIs:

1. Are nonfinancial measures (e.g., not expressed in dollars, yen, pounds, euros, etc.).
2. Are measured frequently (e.g., 24/7, daily, or weekly).
3. Are acted on by the CEO and senior management team (e.g., CEO calls relevant staff to enquire what is going on).
4. Clearly indicate what action is required by staff (e.g., staff can understand the measures and know what to fix).
5. Are measures that tie responsibility down to a team (e.g., CEO can call a team leader who can take the necessary action).
6. Have a significant impact (e.g., affect one or more of the critical success factors and more than one balanced-scorecard perspective).
7. They encourage appropriate action in the right direction (e.g., have been tested to ensure any potential dark side is minimal and that they have a significant positive impact on performance).

When you put a dollar sign on a measure, you have already converted it into a result indicator (e.g., daily sales are a result of activities that have taken place to create the sales). The KPI lies deeper down. It may be the number of visits to contacts with the key customers who make up most of the profitable business. As discussed in Chapter 2, it is a myth of performance measurement that KPIs can be financial and non financial indicators. I am adamant that all KPIs are non financial measures.

KPIs should be monitored 24/7, daily, or perhaps weekly for some. As stated in Chapter 2, it is a myth that monitoring monthly performance measures will improve performance. A monthly, quarterly, or annual measure cannot be a KPI, as it cannot be key to your business if you are monitoring it well after the horse has bolted. KPIs are current- or future-oriented measures as opposed to past measures (e.g., number of key customer visits planned in the next month or a list by key customer of the dates of the next planned visits). Most organizational measures are very much past indicators measuring events of the last month or quarter. These indicators cannot be and never were KPIs.

All KPIs make a difference; they have the CEO's constant attention due to daily calls to the relevant staff. Having a career-limiting discussion with the CEO is not something staff members want to repeat, and in the airline example, innovative and productive processes were put in place to prevent a recurrence.

A KPI should tell you what action needs to be taken. The British Airways late-plane KPI communicated immediately to everyone that there needed to be a focus on recovering the lost time. Cleaners, caterers, ground crew, flight attendants, liaison officers, and air traffic controllers would all work some magic to save a minute here and a minute there while maintaining or improving service standards.

A KPI is deep enough in the organization that it can be tied to a team. In other words, the CEO can call someone and ask, "Why?" Return on capital employed has never been a KPI, because it cannot be tied to a manager—it is a result of many activities under different managers.

A KPI will affect one or more of the critical success factors and more than one balanced-scorecard perspective. In other words, when the CEO, management, and staff focus on the KPI, the organization scores goals in all directions. In the airline example, the late-plane KPI affected all six balanced- scorecard perspectives. As mentioned in Chapter 2, it is a myth to believe that that a measure fits neatly into one balanced-scorecard perspective.

Before becoming a KPI, a performance measure needs to be tested to ensure, it creates the desired behavioral outcome (e.g., helping teams to align their behavior in a coherent way to the benefit of the organization). There are many examples where performance measures have led to dysfunctional behavior. There are two examples discussed in the section, "Unintended Behavior: The Dark Side of Measures," in Chapter 1.

For government and non profit agencies, *KPIs* could include:

- Number of CEO recognitions planned for next week or two weeks.
- Staff in vital positions who have handed in their notice on a given day. (The CEO has the opportunity to try to persuade the staff member to stay.)
- Key position job offers issued to candidates that are more than 48 hours outstanding. (The CEO has the opportunity to try to persuade acceptance of offer.)
- List of late projects, by manager, reported weekly to the senior management team.
- Number of vacant leadership positions at an in-house training course (reported daily to the CEO in the last three weeks before the course is due to run).
- Emergency response time over a given duration (reported immediately to the CEO).
- Number of initiatives implemented after the staff satisfaction survey (monitored weekly for up to three months after survey).
- Number of confirmed volunteers to be street collectors for the annual street appeal (monitored daily in the four to six weeks before the appeal day).

Difference between Key Results Indicators and KPIs

During workshops, one question emerges time and time again: "What are the differences between KRIs and KPIs, and RIs and PIs?" Exhibits 6.2 and 6.3 clarify the differences.

A car's speedometer provides a useful analogy to show the difference between a result indicator and a performance indicator. The speed the car is traveling is a result indicator, because the car's speed is a combination of what gear the car is in and how many revolutions per minute the engine is doing. Performance indicators might be how economically the car is being driven (e.g., a gauge showing how many miles per gallon), or how hot the engine is running (e.g., a temperature gauge).

EXHIBIT 6.2   Difference between KRIs and KPIs

KRIs	KPIs
Can be financial and nonfinancial (e.g., Return on capital employed, and customer satisfaction percentage)	Nonfinancial measures (not expressed in dollars, yen, pounds, euros, etc.)
Measures are performed mainly monthly and sometimes in a quarterly time period	Measured frequently (e.g., 24/7, daily or weekly)
As a summary of progress in an organization's critical success factor, it is ideal for reporting progress to a board	Acted on by the CEO and senior management team
It does not help staff or management because nowhere does it tell what you need to fix	All staff understand the measure and what corrective action is required
Commonly, the only person responsible for a KRI is the CEO	Responsibility can be tied down to a team leader
A KRI is designed to summarize activity within one critical success factor	A KPI impacts more than one of the critical success factors and more than one balanced-scorecard perspective
A KRI is a result of many activities managed through a variety of performance measures	A KPI is a unique measure that encourages appropriate action in the right direction
Normally reported by a monthly trend graph covering at least the last 15 months of activity	Normally reported by way of an intranet screen indicating activity, person responsible, past history, so a meaningful phone call can be made

EXHIBIT 6.3   Difference between RIs and PIs

RIs	PIs
Can be financial and nonfinancial	Nonfinancial measures (not expressed in dollars, yen, pounds, euros, etc.)
Measured daily, weekly, every two weeks, monthly, or sometimes quarterly	Measured daily, weekly, every two weeks, monthly, or sometimes quarterly
Cannot be tied to a discrete activity	Tied to a discrete activity and thus to a team
Does not tell you what you need to do more or less of	All staff understand what action is required to improve performance
Designed to summarize *some activity* within a critical success factor/success factor	Specific activity impacts on one of the critical success factors/success factors
Result of more than one activity	Focuses on a specific activity
Normally reported in a team scorecard	Normally reported in a team scorecard

Lead and Lag Confusion

Many management books that cover KPIs talk about lead and lag indicators; this merely clouds the KPI debate. Using the new way of looking at *performance* measures, we dispense with the terms *lag* (outcome) and *lead* (performance driver) indicators. At my seminars, when the audience is asked "Is the late-planes-in-the-air KPI a lead indicator or a lag indicator?" the vote count is always evenly split. The late plane in the sky is certainly both a lead and lag indicator. It talks about the past and it is about to create a future problem when it lands. Surely this is enough proof that *lead* and *lag* labels are not a useful way of defining KPIs and should be counted among the myths of performance measurement.

KRIs and RIs replace outcome measures. KRIs typically look at activity over months or quarters, whereas RIs can have a shorter time frame (e.g., sales made yesterday). PIs and KPIs are now characterized as past-, current-, or future-focused measures. *Current measures* refers to those monitored 24/7 or daily (e.g., late/incomplete deliveries to key customers made yesterday). *Future measures* are the record of a future commitment when an action is to take place (e.g., date of next meeting with key customer, date of next product launch, date of next social interaction with key customers). In your organization, you will find that your KPIs are either current- or future-oriented measures.

In workshops, I ask participants to write a couple of their major *past* measures in the worksheet shown in Exhibit 6.4 and then restate the

EXHIBIT 6.4   Past/Current/Future Performance Measures Analysis Worksheet

Past Measures (last week/2 weeks/ month/quarter)	Current Measures (real-time/ today/yesterday)	Future Measures (next week/ month/quarter)
E.g., number of late planes last week/ last month	E.g., planes over 2 hours late (updated continuously)	E.g., number of initiatives to be commenced in the next month/2 months to target areas that are causing late planes

Source: David Parmenter, *Key Performance Indicators: Developing, Implementing, and Using Winning KPIs,* 2nd ed. Copyright © 2010 by David Parmenter. Reprinted with permission of John Wiley & Sons, Inc.

measures as *current* and *future* measures. Take time out now and restate three measures.

The lead/lag division did not focus adequately enough on current or future-oriented measures. Most organizations that want to create alignment and change behavior need to be monitoring what corrective action is to take place in the future. Examples of future measures include the following:

- To be an innovative organization, we need to measure the number of initiatives that are about to come online in the next week, in two weeks, and in a month.
- To increase staff satisfaction, we need to monitor the number of planned celebrations in the next week/next two weeks. This measure will be maintained weekly by each manager.
- To develop leadership skills, we need to ensure in-house courses are being planned and staff are registering to attend. We should record the date of the next leadership program and the list of attendees registered to date (reported weekly to CEO).
- To maintain the profile of our CEO, we need to monitor the public relation events that have been organized in the next one month to three months, four months to six months, and seven months to nine months.
- To maintain staff recognition, the CEO needs to monitor the formal recognitions planned next week/two weeks by the CEO and senior management team.

All these future measures would be reported in a weekly update given to the CEO. Although CEOs may let a couple of weeks pass with gaps appearing on these updates, they will soon start asking questions. Management would take action, prior to the next meeting, to start filling in the gaps to ensure they avoided further uncomfortable questioning.

10/80/10 Rule

Kaplan and Norton recommend no more than 20 KPIs. Hope and Fraser[1] suggest fewer than 10 KPIs. The 10/80/10 rule is a good guide. That is, there are about 10 KRIs, up to 80 RIs and PIs, and 10 KPIs in an organization (see Exhibit 6.5). Very seldom are more measures needed, and in many cases, fewer measures will suffice. As explained in Chapter 2, it is a myth that the more measures there are, the better performance measurement will be. In fact, as has no doubt been witnessed by many readers, the reverse is true.

For many organizations, 80 RIs and PIs will at first appear totally inadequate. Yet, on investigation, you will find that separate teams are actually

EXHIBIT 6.5   10/80/10 Rule

Types of Performance Measures (PMs)	Number of PMs	Frequency of Measurement
1. Key result indicators (KRIs) give an overview on the organization's past performance and are ideal for the board as they communicate how management have done in a critical success factor or balanced-scorecard perspective.	Up to 10	Monthly, quarterly
2. Result indicators (RIs) give a summary on a specific area and they tell staff what they have done (e.g., yesterday's sales).	80 or so. If it gets over 150, you will begin to have serious problems	24/7, daily, weekly, every two weeks, monthly, quarterly
3. Performance indicators (PIs) are targeted measures that tell staff and management what to do (e.g., number of sales visits organized with key customers next week/biweekly).		
4. Key performance indicators (KPIs) tell staff and management what to do to increase performance dramatically (e.g., planes that are currently over two hours late).	Up to 10 (you may have considerably less)	24/7, daily, weekly

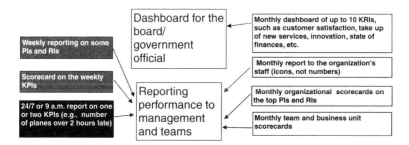

EXHIBIT 6.6   Suggested Reporting Framework

working with variations of the same indicator, so it is better to standardize them (e.g., a "number of training days attended in the past month" performance measure should have the same definition and the same graph).

Many KPI project teams will also, at first, feel that having only 10 KPIs is too restrictive and may wish to increase KPIs to 30. With careful analysis, that number will soon be reduced to the 10 suggested, unless the organization is composed of many businesses from very different sectors. If that is the case, the 10/80/10 rule can apply to each diverse business, providing it is large enough to warrant its own KPI rollout.

Importance of Timely Measurement

Before proceeding further, we will look at the importance of timely measurement. It is essential that measurement is timely. Today, a KPI provided to management that is more than a few days old is useless. KPIs are prepared in real time, with even weekly ones available by the next working day. The suggested reporting framework of performance indicators is set out in Exhibit 6.6. Frequently, staff working for government and non profit agencies tell me that we do not have any measures that we need to monitor frequently. I beg to differ. Review Appendix F for examples of common measures that will be useful for government and non profit agencies.

Some of the KPIs will be updated daily or even 24/7 (as in the British Airways case), whereas the rest of the KPIs will be reported weekly. Performance measures that focus on completion should be included. In organizations where finishing is a problem, a common weekly KPI is the reporting of projects and reports that are running late to the senior management team. Such reporting will revolutionize project and task completion in your organization.

The RIs and PIs will be reported in various time frames from daily, weekly, and fortnightly to monthly. The KRIs, which are best used to report performance to the board, will, therefore, be based around the timing of the board meeting.

Note

1. Jeremy Hope and Robin Fraser, *Beyond Budgeting: How Managers Can Break Free from the Annual Performance Trap* (Cambridge, MA: Harvard Business Press, 2003).

CHAPTER 7

Finding Your Organization's Critical Success Factors

I was first introduced to critical success factors by the talented people who wrote the KPI manual for AusIndustry (an Australian government department). They defined critical success factors as the "list of issues or aspects of organizational performance that determine ongoing health, vitality, and well-being."[1]

The Missing Link

In Chapter 2, the common myth that performance measures are mainly used to help manage implementation of strategic initiatives was highlighted. Instead, the main purpose of performance measures is to ensure that staff members spend their working hours focused primarily on the organization's critical success factors.

You could be in your tenth year with a balanced scorecard and still not know your organization's critical success factors. I believe it is like going to soccer's World Cup without a goalkeeper, or at best, an incompetent one.

The term *critical success factors* does not appear to be addressed by some of the leading writers of the past 30 years. Peter Drucker, Jim Collins, Gary Hemel, Tom Peters, Robert Kaplan, and David Norton all appear to ignore the existence of critical success factors.

In Chapter 3, I pointed out that having critical success factors known by all staff is one of the five foundation stones to revitalizing performance management. I went on to say:

> *I argue that, unless this foundation is in place, each manager, in their own empire, will have what is important to them embedded in the way things are done. Many counterproductive activities will occur based*

on this false premise, that is, what is important to me is important to the organization.

For a chief executive officer to steer the ship, everybody needs to know the journey, what makes the ship sail well, and what needs to be done in difficult weather.

It can come as no surprise when I say that the term critical success factors could be a major missing link in balanced-scorecard and other methodologies.

Importance of Knowing Your Organization's Critical Success Factors

The relationship between critical success factors and KPIs is vital, as illustrated in Exhibit 5.1 which is repeated here as Exhibit 7.1. If you get the

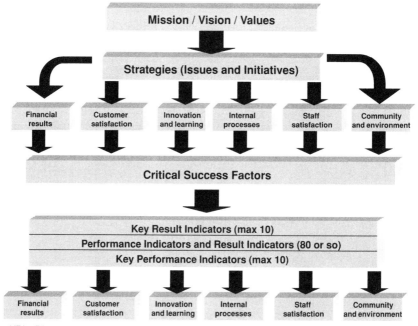

KPIs, RIs, and PIs in a balanced scorecard for Management and KRIs for the Board dashboard

EXHIBIT 7.1   How Critical Success Factors Drive the Performance Measures

critical success factors right, it is very easy to find your winning KPIs (e.g., once the "timely arrival and departure of planes" was identified as being the top critical success factors, it was relatively easy to find the KPI: planes late over a certain time).

As Exhibit 7.1 indicates, critical success factors cut across a number of balanced-scorecard perspectives (e.g., the timely arrival and departure of planes impacts nearly all the balanced-scorecard perspectives of an airline).

Limit to Five to Eight Critical Success Factors

Better practice suggests that organizational critical success factors should be limited to between five and eight, regardless of the organization's size. Some government or non profit agencies may have operations that are significantly different from each other, such as an ambulance service being run alongside a service offering overnight accommodation for the homeless. Accordingly, there would be a collection of critical success factors in this organization greater than the suggested five to eight.

Critical Success Factors Based Around the Organization

In order to create alignment between teams in an organization, it is important that there be only one set of between five and eight critical success factors (CSFs) for the organization. If you allow teams, departments, or divisions to create their own CSFs, you will have chaos. Teams will follow their own agendas.

Many head office teams will note that quite a few of their daily activities are not very aligned with the CSFs. Their alignment comes from focusing more on assisting the departments and teams who are working directly on the CSFs. In other words, support teams' alignment with the CSFs is achieved through other teams' efforts.

Critical Success Factors Are Not Key Result Areas

Since the beginning of my employment, I have seen the words "key result areas" (KRAs) plastered all over my job descriptions, and it was very helpful. However, KRAs are not critical success factors.

In fact, I would argue that everyone's job description should have a new section pointing out the organization's CSFs and how the incumbent should maximize alignment of his or her duties with them.

This would help to clarify the difference between KRAs and CSFs. The KRAs are those duties and tasks that the incumbent must be able to perform, and the organizational CSFs are the guiding force ensuring that everyday staff treat activities that align well with the CSFs as a priority.

Relationship between Critical Success Factors and Strategy

It is important to understand the relationship between CSFs and strategy. An organization's CSFs are impacted by a number of features. Most government and non profit agencies will have one or two generic critical success factors (e.g., "Stay, say, strive engagement with staff", "Recruit the right people all the time"), but each organization will also have some unique temporary conditions (e.g., a sudden drop in government tax intake will mean some CSFs will be introduced until the funding crisis is over). Some CSFs will be determined by strategy and others will be related to normal business conditions (see Exhibit 7.2).

Critical Success Factors Are the Origin of Performance Measures

The traditional balanced-scorecard (BSC) approach uses performance measures to monitor the implementation of the strategic initiatives, and measures are typically cascaded down from a top-level organizational measure such as return on capital employed. This cascading of measures from one another will often lead to chaos, with hundreds of measures being monitored by staff in some form of BSC reporting application.

The organization's five to eight CSFs should be the source of all performance measures that really matter, the KPIs. Getting staff to focus every day on the organization's CSFs is the El Dorado of management. Thus instead of using the strategies as the source of your measures, clarify what your

EXHIBIT 7.2   What Impacts the Critical Success Factors

Source: David Parmenter, *Winning CFOs: Implementing and Applying Better Practices,* Copyright © 2011 by David Parmenter. Reprinted with permission of John Wiley & Sons, Inc.

organization's CSFs are and then determine what measures would enforce alignment to these CSFs. You will find that your CSFs will create the vital linkage between daily activities and the organization's strategies.

Critical success factors are the origin of the performance measures that really matter, the KPIs. It is the CSFs, and the performance measures within them, that link daily activities to the organization's strategies. The CSFs impact the business all the time, 24/7, and it is therefore important to measure how the staff in the organization are aligning their daily activities to these CSFs.

Exhibit 7.3 shows that strategic initiatives, although their progress will be monitored, are not as fundamental to the business as monitoring the day-to-day alignment with the organization's CSFs.

Most organizations know their success factors; however, few organizations have:

- Worded their success factors appropriately.
- Segregated success factors from their strategic objectives.
- Sifted through the success factors to find their critical ones—their CSFs.
- Communicated the CSFs to staff.

If your organization has not completed a thorough exercise to know its CSFs, performance management cannot possibly function. Performance measurement, monitoring, and reporting will be a series of random processes, creating an army of measurers producing numerous numbing reports, full of measures that monitor progress in a direction very remote from the strategic direction of the organization. Very few, if any, of the measures in these reports could be defined as "winning KPIs" as they have been derived independently from the CSFs.

EXHIBIT 7.3 How Strategy and the Critical Success Factors Work Together

The Characteristics of Critical Success Factors

There are a number of characteristics of CSFs that are worth dwelling on. Critical success factors:

- Are worded so a 14-year-old could understand them and realize what is important to the organization.
- Will be no surprise to management and the board/government official, as they will have talked about them as success factors.
- Apply to more than one balanced-scorecard perspective (e.g., "Innovation is a daily activity" impacts nearly all the balanced-scorecard perspectives of a government and non profit agency).
- Are focused on the organization and thus should not be broken down into department CSFs.
- Are few in number; five to eight is sufficient.
- Have a great influence on other success factors.
- Are focused in a precise area, rather than being the bland statements that strategic objectives often are.

Selection of the Critical Success Factors Is a Very Subjective Exercise

The selection of the CSFs is a very subjective exercise, and the effectiveness and usefulness of those CSFs chosen is highly dependent on the degree of analytical skill of those involved. Active leadership by senior management in this step is, thus, mandatory.

Linkage to the Paradigm Shifters

In Chapter 3, Revitalizing Performance Management, the second foundation stone was the knowledge of the paradigm shifters (Drucker, Collins, Welch, Hamel, Peters, Waterman, and others). We need to apply this knowledge, as set out in Exhibit 7.4.

EXHIBIT 7.4   Lessons from the Paradigm Shifters (featured in Chapter 3)

Lesson	Implication
Focus on the "hedgehog" concept that differentiates the organization, gives it world leadership, fits with the organization's passion, and has an economic engine behind it. (Jim Collins)	By measuring within the critical success factors, we will be consistent with Jim Collins's thinking.
Staying focused on the flywheel. (Jim Collins)	

Four Tasks For Identifying Organization-Wide Critical Success Factors

To help organizations around the world find their five to eight critical success factors, I have developed a four-task process.

Task 1: Documenting the Already Identified Success Factors

Set up a small team who are to undertake the KPI project, let us call them the KPI team. The members of this team need to be assisted by a workshop facilitator who will run the workshop in task 2.

The KPI team needs to review the strategic documents in your organization covering the last 10 years. Then, extract and develop success factors from these documents. You may find an old strategic document written by an executive, long since moved on, which could prove very helpful because the success factors are still relevant.

The KPI team should interview as many of the organization's "oracles" as possible, along with the entire senior management team. From this information, you will be able to come up with a list of success factors.

I have prepared a generic list of success factors by major government and non profit agency type in Appendix E. Exhibit 7.5 provides an example of such a list.

Success factors should be:

- Worded so a 14-year-old could understand them and realize their importance to the organization.
- Focused in a precise area, rather than being the bland statements so often characterized by strategic objectives. Examples of unhelpful and bland statements are "increased profitability," "retention of key customers," "maximizing the use of our most important resource—our people."

Success factor for **Schools/Universities** by balanced-scorecard perspective	Environment and Community	Internal process	Finance	Customer	Innovation and learning	Staff satisfaction
Common critical success factors						
• "Stay, say, strive engagement with staff"	Y	Y	Y	Y	Y	Y
• Recruiting the right people all the time	Y	Y	Y	Y	Y	Y
• Develop exceptional people and teams who follow our company's philosophy		Y	Y	Y	Y	Y
• Grow leaders who thoroughly understand the work, live the philosophy, and teach it to others	Y		Y		Y	Y
• Innovation is a daily activity (finding better ways to do the things we do every day)		Y	Y	Y	Y	Y
• Willingness to **abandon** initiatives, opportunities that are not working or unlikely to succeed		Y	Y	Y	Y	Y
• Abandonment is necessary and right		Y	Y	Y	Y	Y
• Make decisions slowly by consensus, thoroughly considering all options; implement decisions rapidly (Toyota)		Y	Y	Y	Y	Y
• Delivery in full on time, all the time to our students (and their parents, for schools)		Y		Y		Y

EXHIBIT 7.5   Extract of the Success Factor Matrix in Appendix E

Once you have ascertained what you consider to be a good first cut, ask one or two members of the senior management team to review the list of success factors, provided they understand the rules on the wording. You have now created a list of success factors mapped against the six balanced-scorecard perspectives ready for the workshop attendees to review in task two.

Task 2: Determining the Critical Success Factors in a Workshop

From my experience in this area, most organizations will need to run a two-day workshop attended by experienced staff from around the organization, as much of the senior management team as possible, and the chief executive officer (CEO). The CEO needs to attend the first half day and the last session after the afternoon break on the second day. However, in CSF workshops I have delivered for organizations, many CEOs have said they regretted not being available for the whole two days. The staff who are likely to be on the KPI team should also attend.

It is important to have experienced staff (the oracles) attend this workshop, as you are trying to ascertain the organization's success factors and then determine which ones are critical. It is not a workshop for staff new to the organization. The organization's oracles are the individuals everyone refers you to when you need something answered (e.g., "You need to talk to Pat").

To assist organizations in finding their CSFs, I have provided the templates I personally use when facilitating the workshop. The draft letter invitation, workshop agenda, and workshop exercises are set out in the Critical Success Factors Kit, Chapter 7 in my companion book.[2] These CSF templates were not provided again in this book as they cover over 20 pages, but are available electronically free to all readers of this book via my web site, www.davidparmenter.com For an example of one of these templates, see Exhibit 7.6

The two-day workshop needs to cover the following:

- The new thinking on key performance measures, as outlined in Chapter 6.
- The agreement of the organization's success factors, which have been gathered in Task 1: Documenting the Already Identified Success Factors.
- How to perform relationship mapping to ascertain CSFs from the success factors.
- The identification of the organization's CSFs through the application of the relationship-mapping process on the organization's success factors, as outlined later in this chapter.
- The 12-step winning KPI process, set out in Chapter 9 (8-step process if less than 200 full-time employees in the organization).

EXHIBIT 7.6   Extract of the Agenda for the Two Day CSF Workshop

Day 1	
From 8:30 A.M.	Registration and breakfast
9:00	Opening remarks by CEO—Setting the context of the workshop
9:10	The new thinking on Key Performance Indicators.
	▪ The difference between the four types of performance measures
	▪ The characteristics of a winning KPI—two stories
	▪ The 10/80/10 rule for performance measures
	▪ The importance of knowing your organization's critical success factors
	▪ A case study on success factors
10:00	Presentation on success factors
10:20	Commence Workshop #1: Revisiting your organization's success factors (SFs). All work that has been already done in this area will be tabled to attendees (e.g., from a review of the last few years' strategic plans)
10:40	Morning break
	Note: template continues for the remaining two days at this level of detail

- How to brainstorm performance measures from the organization's CSFs.
- How to report performance measures to staff, management, and the board. The designing of report formats that begins during this workshop is to be finished afterwards.
- The commencement of brainstorming organizational and team performance measures from the CSFs.
- Presentations by each work group covering their next steps to complete their scorecard, new measures they wish to use, and existing measures they wish to discard.

FINDING THE CSFs THROUGH A RELATIONSHIP MAPPING PROCESS   To find your five to eight CSFs, a good technique is to type all your success factors into numbered boxes on a large sheet of paper (A3/U.S. fanfold). Each team of five to seven people is then asked to map the relationships, drawing an arrow to reflect the direction of influence.

The mapping process is performed by the team members, starting with one success factor and then looking at each other success factor and asking "does it impact this success factor?" It is understandable that some relationships are two-way. In these cases we draw two arrows.

In most organizations, you will be handling over 40 success factors. As such, each arrow is shown leaving one box, with the number of the box it is going to, and then another arrow entering that box with the number of the box it has come from (see Exhibit 7.7). This exercise is slow to start with and then becomes quicker as teams remember where the success factors are positioned.

As mentioned, this process is very subjective and it is now necessary to put attendees' knowledge of the organization to full use. I always give the following instructions:

- If one member of the team sees a linkage, other members of the team should draw the relationship without debate. This speeds up the process.
- Although the magnitude of the relationships will clearly be different, teams should pretend they are all equal for the time being.
- Each team should mentally jump into one success factor box at a time and look out at the other success factors, drawing the relationships they find.
- After a couple of success boxes have been mapped and there is a common understanding of the exercise, each group should split into smaller teams of two or three people, each looking into a designated number of success factors.

There is an alternative method of mapping relationships, shown to me by a clever attendee at an in-house workshop I was running, which involves mapping the relationships on a spreadsheet matrix (see Exhibit 7.8). This method is preferred by some and also creates easy to review documentation of the process.

HANDLING THE DIVERSITY OF RELATIONSHIP MAPPING BY THE TEAMS   The beauty of this exercise is that it does not matter if one team has 10 arrows out of a success factor and another team has 16 arrows out of the same success factor. Each team will have a different materiality level when establishing the arrows; that is, one team may find 20 relationships from "timely arrivals and departures of planes," while other groups may find 10, 12, or 15.

I ask each team to give me their top five success factors, the ones with the most arrows out. Some of the top five success factors may have the same score, in which case I give them a position of joint second or joint third place. Thus, the scores from one team may be (1st, 2nd, =3rd, =3rd, 4th), and another team may have (=1st, =1st, =2nd, =2nd, 3rd) for its top five success factors. I list their rankings on a summary chart; see Exhibit 7.9, to see which success factors selected are the most significant.

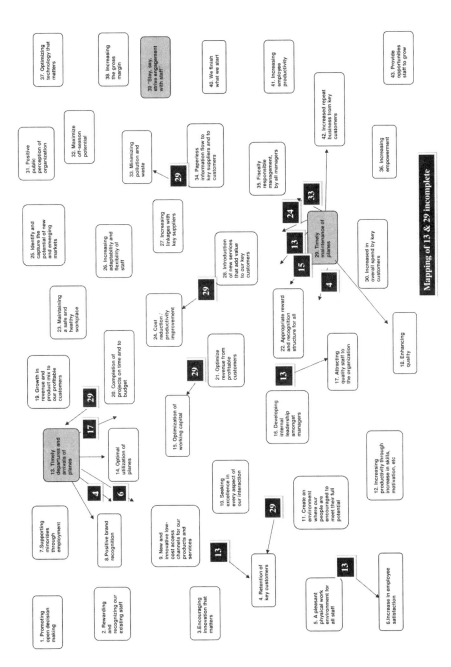

EXHIBIT 7.7 Example of Critical Success Factor Relationship-Mapping Exercise

95

Success Factor Number

#	Success Factor	Count	1	2	3	4	5	6	7	8	9	10	11	12	13	14	15	16	17	18	19	20	21	etc.	etc.
1	Positive public perception of XXX	5		X								X		X	X		X	X		X					
2	Be seen in the community as an employer of first choice	1	X																	X	X		X		
3	Minimizing pollution and waste	3	X																						
4	Encouraging voluntary assistance by staff to the local community	2	X																						
5	Supporting local businesses (% of purchases to have local content)	3	X												X							X			
6	Delivery in full on time, all the time to our key customers	5	X											X	X		X			X					
7	Finding better ways to do the things we do everyday	4								X						X	X				X				
8	Maintaining a safe and healthy workplace	3	X	X													X								
9	Enhancing operational/communication efficiency, e.g., reducing cost per transaction	2								X															
10	Increasing linkages with key suppliers	9	X									X	X		X	X	X	X	X	X		X	X		
11	XXXX	3	X	X																X		X	X		
12	XXXX	8																					X		
13	XXXX	3																X	X						
14	XXXX	1																X				X			
15	XXXX	0																							
16	XXXX	0																							
etc.	XXXX	3	X																		X				
etc.	XXXX	2	X																						
	Count (# of relationships between success factors)		10	3	0	0	1	1	1	3	2	2	2	3	6	5	4	0	5	3	1	3	2		0

This X represents an arrow from success factor #1, "Positive pubic perception of XXX," to "Be seen in the community as an employer of first choice."

This X represents an arrow from success factor #8, "Maintaining a safe and healthy workplace," to "Be seen in the community as an employer of first choice."

These are all the mind-mapped success factors

This shows the total amount of relationships formed between Success Factors. The higher number, the greater the likelihood of being a Critical Success Factor

EXHIBIT 7.8 A Spreadsheet Matrix of Success Factor Relationships

96

EXHIBIT 7.9   Summarizing the Teams' Top Five Success Factors from the Mapping Process

	Team 1	Team 2	Team 3	Team 4	Team 5	Team 6	# of Times Selected
Be seen in the community as an employer of first choice	=5		=4			=1	3
Supporting minorities through employment							
Delivery in full on time, all the time to our key customers	1	=3	1	1	1	=2	6
Finding better ways to do the things we do every day	=5						1
Optimizing technology that matters			2		4		2
Completion of projects on time and to budget							
Encouraging innovation that matters		1		4			2
Enhancing quality		=3					1
Timely, accurate, decision-based information							
We finish what we start	4	2	=4	2	3	=2	6
Reducing supply chain costs		=3	=5		2	=1	4
"Stay, say, strive engagement with staff"	2		3	3	5	3	5
Increase in employee satisfaction	3						1
Appropriate reward and recognition structure for all				5			1
Increasing recognition throughout the organization							
A pleasant physical work environment for all staff							

Source: David Parmenter, *Key Performance Indicators: Developing, Implementing, and Using Winning KPIs,* 2nd ed. Copyright © by David Parmenter. Reprinted with permission of John Wiley & Sons, Inc.

I avoid the temptation to use a weighting, as we are trying to add certainty to a subjective process. It is my belief that success factors that are rated in the top five by most or all of the teams are the most likely to be the organization's critical success factors.

FINE TUNING THE FIRST CUT OF THE CRITICAL SUCCESS FACTORS During this exercise, you will note that some attendees have a gift for this mapping process. Identify four to six of these attendees and extract them for a special exercise: remapping the 12 or so success factors that have been identified as possible CSFs.

As before, the mapping process is performed by starting with one success factor and then looking at whether it is impacted by each other success factor.

The purpose of this exercise is to test the robustness of the short cut list and then to shortlist the five to eight success factors with the highest scoring relationships. Again we do not use the exact count of outward arrows to prioritize, as not all of the arrows are equal. We simply assume, for example, that success factors with 20 outward arrows will be more important than success factors with 8 outward arrows.

TESTING THE CSFs When the first cut of the CSFs has been ascertained the KPI project team test the list of the top five to eight critical success factors against the six balanced-scorecard (BSC) perspectives and the organizations strategic objectives (see Exhibits 7.10 and 7.11).

EXHIBIT 7.10 How Do Your Top Five to Eight CSFs Cover the Six Balanced-Scorecard Perspectives?

Critical Success Factor	Perspectives					
	Financial	Customer Satisfaction	Staff Satisfaction	Innovation and Learning	Internal Process	Environment and Community
E.g., timely arrival and departure of planes	√	√	√	√	√	possible
xxxxxx		√			√	√
xxxxx	√					
xxxxx	√			√		
Xxxx			√		√	
xxx	√	√		√		√

EXHIBIT 7.11   Testing That Your Top Five to Eight CSFs Link to Your
Strategic Objectives

Critical Success Factor	Strategic Objectives (SO)					
	SO #1	SO #2	SO #3	SO #4	SO #5	SO #6
E.g., timely arrival and departure of planes	√		√			possible
1. xxxxx		√			√	√
2. xxx	√					
3. xxxxx			√			
4. xxx	√	√			√	
5. xxxxx			√			√
6. xxxx			√			
7. xxxx	√		√		√	

Source: David Parmenter, *Key Performance Indicators: Developing, Implementing, and
Using Winning KPIs*, 2nd ed. Copyright © 2010 by David Parmenter. Reprinted with
permission of John Wiley & Sons, Inc.

RUNNING THE WORKSHOP   This workshop needs to be facilitated by a skilled
presenter familiar with the content in my companion KPI book.[3] Accredited
coaches in this methodology are being trained. For registration details see
www.davidparmenter.com.

While every facilitator has a unique style, one universal teaching technique is to always demonstrate to the whole group what is intended before
commencing an exercise. Hand out the written instructions and then read
the instructions twice.

I ensure that each workshop group is between five and seven people
and consists of employees from different functions within the organization.

I always ask for a volunteer chairperson, telling the workshop group,
"If you do not want to give feedback to the whole group, volunteer
to be the chairperson, and then you can delegate the feedback task to
someone else."

If you have set up the workshop properly, you will find that the work
groups start this exercise quickly. A sign of success is that you can leave
the room for a period of fifteen minutes or so, leaving the workgroups to
make their own way.

To ensure that each work group documents all progress, it is necessary
that one attendee in each group brings a laptop and that the electronic
templates they are to use are loaded on the laptop. Work groups will then
be able to update the success factor template, record their measures, and
start drafting new report formats during the workshop.

As mentioned, to help organizations find their CSFs, I have provided free to all readers of this book via my web site www.davidparmenter.com the templates I personally use when facilitating the CSF workshop.

Task 3: Presenting the Critical Success Factors

The KPI team prepares and delivers a presentation on the organization's CSFs to facilitate discussion and agreement with the senior management team and then the Board. See Appendix G for the suggested content for this presentation.

The presentation will cover:

- The history of performance measurement within the organization.
- The top five to eight CSFs and their impact on the organization (see Exhibit 7.12).
- The process used to discuss these CSFs with employee representatives and staff.
- Permission to proceed to next stage finding the winning KPIs (selection of the team, steps to do, time frame, costs, etc.).

Task 4: Explaining the Critical Success Factors to Employees

Once final CSFs have been agreed upon, communicate them to all management and staff. If CSFs are not going to be discussed with employee representatives and conveyed to staff, the benefits of knowing them will be limited. If staff are told what is important, they can align their daily activities to maximize their contribution. I came across a brilliant example of how to communicate to staff what is important. In Exhibit 7.13, the company in question prepared a cartoon representation of what it wanted to achieve in the year and staff pinned it on their office walls. It was printed on U.S. fanfold (A3) paper in full-color. I believe this concept is an ideal way to present the CSFs to staff.

Strategy Mapping

The reader who is conversant with Kaplan and Norton's work will note that I have not supported the concept of strategy mapping. In Chapter 2, I point out that it is a myth that strategy mapping is a vital requirement for ascertaining performance measures. In Chapter 2, I explained:

> *If strategy maps help management make some sense out of their strategy, then, as a working document, they must be useful. However, I am concerned with the "simplified" use of cause-and-effect relationships,*

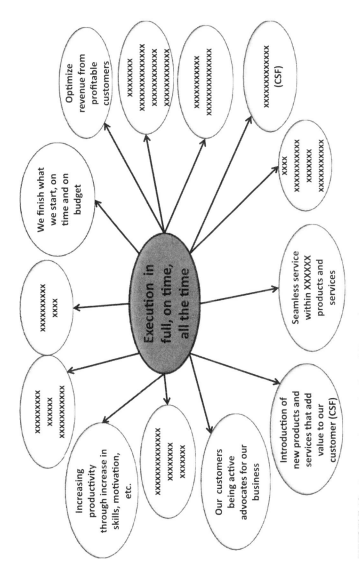

EXHIBIT 7.12   Presentation to the Board Example

EXHIBIT 7.13   Communicating Critical Success Factors to Staff Example

Source: Energy Efficiency and Conservation Authority 2009/2010 Plan.

a major component of strategy mapping. It has led to the demise of many performance-measurement initiatives. From these oversimplified relationships come the strategic initiatives and the cascading performance measures. Strategy mapping, in the wrong hands, can give birth to a monster.

Should you wish to use strategy mapping, please ensure you have read and understood my critique in Chapter 2.

Notes

1. "Key Performance Indicators Manual: A Practical Guide for the Best Practice Development, Implementation and Use of KPIs" (Aus-Industries 1996). Now out of print.
2. For examples of a draft letter invitation, agenda, workshop exercises,, see David Parmenter, *Key Performance Indicators: Developing, Implementing, and Using Winning KPIs,* 2nd ed. (Hoboken, NJ: John Wiley & Sons, 2010).
3. For more information on running a workshop, see David Parmenter, *Key Performance Indicators,* Chapter 7, Critical Success Factors Kit and Chapter 4, KPI Team Resource Kit. All the templates from these two chapters can be acquired electronically from www.davidparmenter .com.

CHAPTER 8

Foundation Stones for Implementing Key Performance Indicators

Successful development and utilization of key performance indicators (KPIs) in the workplace is determined by the presence, or absence, of seven foundation stones (see Exhibit 8.1). In my original work,[1] I came to the conclusion that there were four foundation stones. The seven foundations stones are:

1. Partnership with the staff, unions, and third parties.
2. Transfer of power to the front line.
3. Measure and report only what matters.
4. Source KPIs from the critical success factors.
5. Abandon processes that do not deliver.
6. Understand human behavior.
7. Organization-wide understanding of winning KPIs definition.

"Partnership with the Staff, Unions, and Third Parties" Foundation Stone

The successful pursuit of performance improvement requires the establishment of an effective partnership among management, local employee representatives, unions representing the organization's employees, employees, major customers, and major suppliers. Implications of the partnership foundation stone include:

■ Recognition by all stakeholders that significant organizational and cultural change requires a mutual understanding and acceptance of the need for change and how it is to be implemented.

KPIs - Key Performance Indicators
PIs - Performance Indicators
KRIs - Key Result Indicators
RIs - Result Indicators

10 Winning KPIs

10 KRIs

80 PIs & RIs

| Partnership with the staff, unions, and third parties | Transfer of power to the front line | Measure and report only what matters | Source KPIs from the critical success factors | Abandon processes that do not deliver | Understand human behavior | Organization-wide understanding of winning KPI definition |

EXHIBIT 8.1   Seven Foundation Stones for KPI Development

- Commitment to the establishment and maintenance of effective consultative arrangements with unions, employee representatives, and employees.
- Joint development of a strategy for the introduction of best practice and KPIs.
- Extension of the notion of partnership to include and involve the organization's key customers and key suppliers.

If you want to improve satisfaction with your major customers, would it not make sense to sit down with them and ask, "What should we measure to better manage the delivery of our products and services to you?" If you want your key suppliers' performance to improve, would you not visit them and discuss your expectations? What is important to you? What do you want to measure?

Example: An Airline Working with Its Suppliers

When team members were discussing how to improve performance with late planes that were about to land, they soon realized how important their key suppliers were. Instead of calling their cleaners and aviation fuel supplier numerous times each day, saying "Please treat these planes as a priority," they simply gave their key suppliers read-only access to their late-planes screen. They said, "Whenever a plane is over, say, one hour late, you have our pre-approved authority to speed the process up." The cleaners doubled the cleaning crew and thus halved the cleaning time, and the aviation fuel supplier had its staff awaiting the plane's arrival so refueling could commence as soon as it was safe to do so.

"Transfer of Power to the Front Line" Foundation Stone

Successful performance improvement requires empowerment of the organization's employees, particularly those in the operational "front line." To fully understand transfer of power, I recommend that the reader become familiar with the work of the paradigm shifters—Drucker, Collins, Welch, Hamel, Peters, and Waterman—discussed in Chapter 3.

Implications of the foundation stone "transfer of power to the front line" include:

- The operation of effective top-down and bottom-up communication, including a welcoming of candor, staff being able to challenge and pass up observations that may well be bad news (e.g., no longer is the messenger of bad news shot; now they are rewarded).

- The empowerment of employees to take immediate action to rectify situations that are negatively impacting KPIs (e.g., able to authorize the doubling of cleaning staff to speed turnaround time for an anticipated late plane).
- Devolving responsibility to the teams to develop and select their own performance measures and to make more decisions.
- Provision of training on empowerment, decision making, KPIs, the organization's critical success factors.
- Exposure to process improvement methods (e.g., total quality management, Six Sigma).
- Additional support for those employees with literacy, numeracy, or other learning-related difficulties.

Example: Empowerment at a Car Manufacturer

Leading car manufacturers have long realized the importance of empowerment. When staff members on the production line see a quality defect, they place a tag on it. If they have time, they will start to fix it. The next person on the line spots the tag and, after completing designated tasks, also carries on the rectification work. When the next operator realizes that the fault cannot be fixed before it will be covered over by the installment of the next panel, he or she simply pulls the "cord" to stop production.

Management then organizes the fixing of the fault and restarts the line. They investigate whether the decision to stop the line was correct. If not, they see it as a failure of the training, not the fault of the individual, and simply discuss the matter with the staff concerned.

The ability of staff to stop a production line without consultation is a high-level form of empowerment. The key to the success of this method is that staff members are not only empowered, but feel confident to make the decision to stop the production line.

"Measure and Report Only What Matters" Foundation Stone

It is critical that management develop an integrated framework so that performance is measured and reported in a way that results in action. Organizations should be reporting events on a daily/weekly/monthly basis, depending on their significance, and these reports should cover the critical success factors. The human resources team has an important role to ensure that the workforce perceives performance measurement in a positive way (e.g., a way to increase their long-term job satisfaction, rather than the old views of performance measurement portrayed so well in the Peter Sellers film, *I'm All Right Jack*—a must-see for all of the KPI team).

Implications of the foundation stone "measure and report only what matters" include:

- Every report should link to a success factor or critical success factor; no report should exist because it was done last month and the month before. We should adopt Peter Drucker's abandonment mantra.
- We should measure only what we need to. Each measure should have a reason for existing, a linkage to a success factor or critical success factor.
- What gets reported should be followed by action. The chief executive officer has to commit to making phone calls: "Pat, why did BA235 leave 2.5 hours late?"
- There needs to be a major revamp of reporting so that it is more concise, timely, efficient to produce, and focused on decision making.
- Reporting should be prepared in accordance with the work of Stephen Few, the leading light in data visualization.
- Organizational performance measures will be modified in response to the performance measures developed at team level.

A great exercise to perform in an organization is to ask the chief executive officer to write a memo, requesting all staff and management to provide one copy of every report they work on in a given month. A person is designated to gather the reports, to ensure all management and staff have sent in their reports, and to weed out the duplications. In some organizations, the pile will be over four feet high. Put all the papers in a see-through container, and then make a container a quarter of the size and announce that this is the total amount of reporting allowed.

Example: Unnecessary Reporting in a Government Department

I once saw a pile of reports on a finance manager's desk. When I asked what they were, he said they were the budget holder's month-end reports. "What do you use them for?" I asked. There was a silence and then he replied in a low tone, "I do not use them. I call the relevant budget holder if I need an explanation of a major variance."

Hundreds of hours of budget-holder time were wasted each month when they could have been better spent getting home at a reasonable hour.

"Source KPIs from the Critical Success Factors" Foundation Stone

Critical success factors should be the source of all performance measures that really matter, the KPIs. It is the critical success factors and the performance measures within them that link daily activities to the organization's strategies. The critical success factors impact all the time, 24/7 on the business, therefore, it is important to measure how the staff in the organization are aligning their daily activities to these critical success factors.

As mentioned in Chapter 2, I believe the main purpose of performance measures is to ensure that staff members spend their working hours focused primarily on the organization's critical success factors. The traditional balanced-scorecard approach, however, sees the purpose of performance measures as helping to monitor the implementation of the strategic initiatives.

Performance measures should be brainstormed from thinking about how to measure performance within the critical success factors. Each measure being carefully checked for a potential dark side before it is used. There is, thus, a significant difference in how measures are produced in "winning KPIs" methodology and that of the traditional balanced-scorecard approach.

Exhibit 8.2 shows the linkage between performance measures and critical success factors.

Implications of this foundation stone, "source KPIs from the critical success factors," include:

- Before KPIs can be found, the critical success factors have to be determined in the process outlined in Chapter 7.
- If a measure is not linked to a critical success factor, it will not be a KPI and is unlikely to be very important to the organization and, therefore, should be screened for potential abandonment.

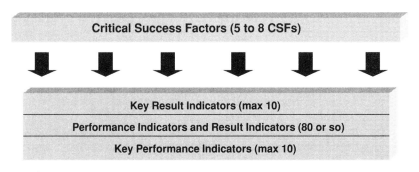

EXHIBIT 8.2   Linkage between Performance Measures and Critical Success Factors

- The KPIs, performance indicators, result indicators, and key result indicators that an organization is using should all be linked to either a critical success factor or a success factor. The database of measures that an organization utilizes should record this linkage.
- The current strategies, the critical success factors, and progress against them should be documented and reported to management and to staff.

"Abandon Processes That Do Not Deliver" Foundation Stone

This is a new addition to the four foundation stones of my earlier work.[2] The need for this foundation stone came about as a result of ferociously reading Peter Drucker's work. I knew if I absorbed his work, I would be able to improve my understanding of performance management.

Of all of his legendary insights, "abandonment" stands head and shoulders above them all. Drucker saw abandonment as the vital source, the fountain of innovation. Abandonment is a sign that management is recognizing that some initiatives will never work as intended and it is better to face this reality sooner than later. It is essential that the organization has freed up enough time to give the KPI project and the attendant balanced scorecard the time and commitment it deserves.

Implications of this foundation stone, that the organization needs to abandon processes that do not work, include the following:

- Create an abandonment day each month during which teams report back to the organization on what they have agreed to abandon.
- Measure the abandonment rate, which will be significant for the CEO.
- In some circumstances, it would be worth abandoning all performance measures in an organization and restarting the exercise basing performance measures on the critical success factors. Some measures will no doubt be reinstated, but many will remain discarded.
- Abandon reports that are completed the same way they were last month and the month before, with nobody reading them. Every report should have a small box on the front page explaining how it is relevant to the organization's critical success factors and strategy.
- Abandon meetings that have become a ritual, held because they were held last week and last month, and yet the action points are never cleared. They just fall off the "to-do" list over time. Every meeting should have a clear statement explaining why it is in existence, a record of what action it has taken, and the cost per hour to the organization.
- Abandon the existing balanced scorecard if it is not working. Then the KPI team can recycle the application if it is warranted, but the scorecard needs to be a casualty.

- Review the current projects schedule for projects that are no longer appropriate or needed.
- Re-evaluate, for their contribution to the organization, processes that are incurring a lot of time. Starting points include the following:
  - **Performance-related pay** when it is linked to annual targets, which will either be too easy or too hard. See Appendix A for some guidelines about how it should be restructured.
  - **The annual planning process** as it is currently set up. It really is only an annual political event serving no purpose. See Appendix C for an explanation of quarterly rolling planning.
  - **Annual or twice-yearly performance reviews.** Nobody likes receiving them, the managers hate preparing them, they do not help with remuneration, and managers, in any case, should be giving feedback on a regular basis, at least monthly, to their staff.

Abandonment has also been discussed in Chapter 3.

"Understand Human Behavior" Foundation Stone

This is a new addition to the four foundation stones of my earlier work.[3] My realization of the need for this foundation stone came about while reading Dean Spitzer's book *Transforming Performance Measurement*.[4] I now understand that the behavioral side of performance measures is paramount and that I had not provided enough focus on this aspect in my earlier work.

There needs to be a new approach to measurement, one that acknowledges the presence of the dark side to performance measures. Staff and management need to be confident that a measure will achieve the intended behavioral alignment to the organization's critical success factors and strategic direction.

Implications of this foundation stone, that there needs to be an "understanding of the behavioral consequences of a measure," include the following:

- The KPI team should be trained in all aspects of performance management and measurement that is discussed in this book and in others such as Spitzer's *Transforming Performance Measurement*.[5]
- All performance measures should be vetted for their potentially significant dark side by the KPI team.
- Consult with staff so that you have some idea of the possible unintended consequences of the measure. You have to ask staff. "If we measure XXX, what action will you take?"
- Pilot the performance measure to enhance its chance of success. Putting measures in without this piloting is simply being naive.

The need to understand human behavior has been discussed in detail in Chapter 3.

"Organization-Wide Understanding of Winning KPIs Definition" Foundation Stone

This is a new addition to the four foundation stones of my earlier work.[6] After working over 20 years analyzing what makes KPIs work, I have realized that unless the organization embraces the new definition of what a KPI is and what it is not, the progress will be limited very quickly.

I have repeatedly found that, once the organization has held the two-day critical-success-factor workshop, staff who have gone back to their offices soon start to call all measures KPIs again.

It is vital that the senior management team, led by the CEO, communicate the new meaning of a KPI and that all breaches of the term "*KPI*" are quickly picked up and staff and managers corrected.

Implications of this foundation stone, that there needs to be an "organization-wide understanding of the definition of winning KPIs," include the following:

- Teams will only have KPIs in their area if a KPI is significant to the organization.
- Most team measures will be PIs and RIs.
- The segregation of measures into KRIs, RIs, PIs, and KPIs will give clarity.

Notes

1. David Parmenter, *Key Performance Indicators: Developing, Implementing, and Using Winning KPIs*, 2nd ed. (Hoboken, NJ: John Wiley & Sons, 2010).
2. Ibid.
3. Ibid.
4. Dean R. Spitzer, *"Transforming Performance Measurement: Rethinking the Way We Measure and Drive Organizational Success* (New York: Amacom, 2007).
5. Ibid.
6. Parmenter, *Key Performance Indicators*.

CHAPTER 9

Implementing the 12-Step Process

O rganizations often select KPIs without the preparation that is indicated in the 12-step implementation plan outlined in this chapter. Like painting the outside of a house, 70 percent of a good job is in the preparation. Establishing a sound environment in which KPIs can operate and develop is crucial. Once the organization understands the process involved and appreciates the purpose of introducing KPIs, the building phase can begin.

A 12-step process has been developed to incorporate better practice and facilitate a swift introduction—in a 16-week time frame (see Exhibit 9.1). This can be condensed into a six-week time frame for organizations with less than 200 full-time employees where there is a motivated chief executive officer (CEO) and senior management team (see Exhibit 9.2).

To assist organizations in implementing the 12 steps, I have provided checklists, worksheets, and workshop agendas in Chapters 3 and 4 of my companion book.[1] These templates were not provided again in this book, as they cover over 30 pages and can be accessed electronically at www.davidparmenter.com.

How the 12-Step Model and the Seven Foundation Stones Fit Together

The seven foundation stones discussed in Chapter 8 will need to be in place in order for the implementation of the 12 steps to have a chance of success. It is just like building a house: The foundation stones have to be firmly in place for the house to stand properly. Exhibit 9.3 shows the connection between the foundation stones and the 12 steps.

Step One: Senior Management Team Commitment

The senior management team must be committed to developing and driving through the organization KPIs and any balanced scorecard that includes

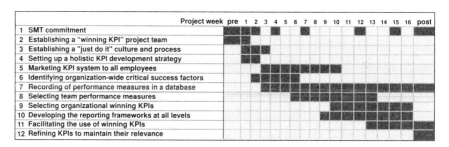

EXHIBIT 9.1   12-Step Implementation 16-Week Timeline

Source: David Parmenter, *Key Performance Indicators: Developing, Implementing, and Using Winning KPIs,* 2nd ed. Copyright © 2010 by David Parmenter. Reprinted with permission of John Wiley & Sons, Inc.

them. The senior management team's commitment creates a dynamic environment in which projects can thrive. Before the senior management team can do this, they need to be sold on the concept and fully understand why they should treat monitoring and follow up on the KPIs as a daily task.

By senior management team commitment, I mean that senior management will need to set aside time each week to perform exercises that include giving feedback on suggested measures, being available to the winning KPI team for interviews, visiting other government and non profit agencies, and approving investment proposals into new executive information systems that will be the main vehicle for reporting KPIs.

An attendee at one of my workshops made a profound observation that senior staff can simply view development of KPIs as an end in itself and go through with it "to keep the boss happy." They are not strategic in their perspective, so they don't see the KPIs and the associated balanced

Phase	Steps		Project week	pre	1	2	3	4	5	6	post
1	1, 4	Selling the change and agreeing on the appropriate timing									
2	1, 6, 7, 8	Workshop to find the organization's CSFs and start team scorecards									
3	2, 3	KPI project team trained and empowered									
4	7, 8	Teams complete their scorecards and record their measures									
5	9	Selecting organizational winning KPIs									
6	10	Developing the reporting frameworks at all levels									
7	11	Facilitating the use of winning KPIs									
8	12	Refining KPIs in 12 months to maintain their relevance									

EXHIBIT 9.2   A Six-Week Time Frame for Organizations with Less Than 200 Full-Time Employees

Source: David Parmenter, *Key Performance Indicators: Developing, Implementing, and Using Winning KPIs,* 2nd ed. Copyright © 2010 by David Parmenter. Reprinted with permission of John Wiley & Sons, Inc.

KPIs - Key Performance Indicators
CSFs - Critical Success Factors
SMT - Senior Management
PIs - Performance Indicators
KRIs - Key Result Indicators
RIs - Result Indicators

* 80 RIs and PIs collectively

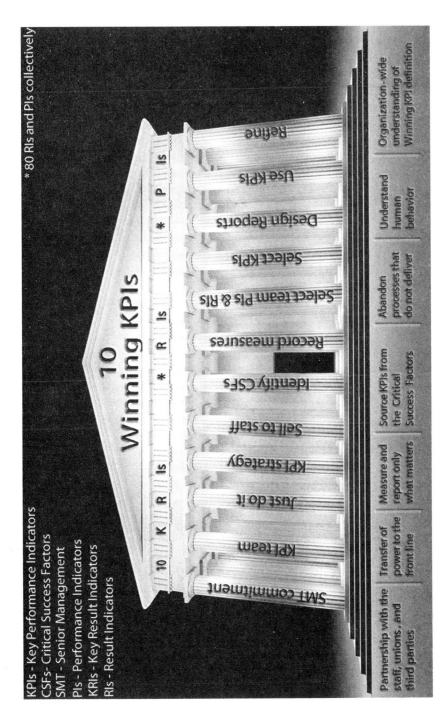

EXHIBIT 9.3   Connection between the Foundation Stones and the 12 Steps

117

scorecard (BSC) as tools to help them better understand and manage their organization. This can be reflected in a loss of interest when the process of development gets tough, such as deciding on KPIs to use and the tradeoffs to be made. Although the senior management team is important, I think the CEO is critical. The CEO must be the central driver, carrying around the embryonic KPIs all the time, talking about their importance frequently, and so on.

The CEO needs to locate an external facilitator, who will work with the senior management team to scope the project, facilitate senior management's commitment, help select the in-house KPI team, and support the KPI team in their journey of learning, discovery, and achievement. The facilitator needs to be experienced with performance measurement issues as well as how to develop and implement KPIs.

KEY STEPS FOR SENIOR MANAGEMENT TEAM COMMITMENT   The KPI team will need to incorporate the following five tasks in the work it performs in step 1:

Task 1. Project needs to be sold to the senior management team on emotional drivers, not logic. Nothing is ever sold by logic. You sell through emotional drivers (e.g., remember your last car purchase). Thus, we need to radically alter the way we pitch this sale to the senior management team and the board. We have to focus on the emotional drivers that matter to the senior management team and the governing body, as they will be different. Selling by emotional drivers is so important to this project that Chapter 12 is devoted to explaining it in more detail.

Task 2. Appointment of a facilitator. The CEO needs to locate an external facilitator who will work with the senior management team to scope the project, facilitate senior management commitment, help select the in-house KPI team, and support the KPI team in its journey of learning, discovery, and achievement. The facilitator needs to be experienced with performance measurement issues and given time to familiarize him- or herself with the development and implementation of KPIs.

Task 3. Facilitator delivers a half-day workshop to the senior management team to kick-start the project. This workshop will, among other things:
   - Explain the new thinking on performance measures.
   - Emphasize the importance of knowing the organization's critical success factors (CSFs).
   - Show that daily activities can be linked to the strategic objectives.
   - Convey the importance of monitoring and following up on the KPIs as a daily task.

- Explain the difference among key result indicators (KRIs), result indicators (RIs), performance indicators (PIs), and KPIs.

In the workshop, the facilitator needs to ensure that the senior management team understands the commitment they need to make each week. They will need to give feedback on suggested measures, be available to the project team for interviews, and possibly visit other organizations. Before running the workshop, the facilitator will send out the questionnaire in the resource kit.[2]

Task 4. Hold a one-day focus group workshop. A cross-section of 15 to 30 experienced staff members, encompassing the departments, teams, area offices, and head office, and covering the different positions, from administrators to senior management team members, come to a central location to help the formation of a KPI project that will work. The entire executive team should attend the morning session.

An outside facilitator, who delivers presentations and facilitates the workshops, runs the session.[3] It is essential that all potential candidates for the KPI project team be present. As a result of this workshop, the project implementation program will be tailored to cover the main institutional barriers, and the senior management team should be in a position to select the KPI team and commit to the project.

Example: Shortcut—Merge This Workshop with the Critical Success Factors Workshop in Step Six

By extending this focus-group session to two days and extending the audience, you can merge the focus-group outcomes with finding the CSFs. This is the approach I now adopt with most in-house workshops I perform. Benefits include the following:

- Because most attendees will be the same for both workshops, it saves a day and the extra costs associated with accommodation and travel.
- Finding the CSFs at an earlier stage gives a tangible benefit earlier on in the project.
- This method builds momentum for the project sooner, because after the workshop, advocates for the process will be preaching the gospel.

Task 5. Project team delivers two short workshops to the senior management team *during the project.* These workshops (about two to three hours long) help maintain the senior management team's interest, provide an opportunity for the senior management to give valuable input into the project, launch newly designed reports, and convey progress.

BENEFITS OF THIS STEP   The selling of this project to the senior management team, using emotional drivers, will ensure senior management's continued involvement. This KPI project will enhance their understanding of their operation, further develop their organization's strategies, and link day-to-day activities to the organization's strategic objectives.

Step Two: Establish a Winning KPI Team Working Full Time on the Project

A small well-trained team will have the best chance of success. Kaplan and Norton,[4] developers of the balanced-scorecard concept, have commented that KPIs have been successfully designed by an individual, without large consultations, but that this was an exception rather than the rule.

A project team of between two to four people is recommended, depending on the size of the organization. The chosen project team members need to be committed full time, and they need to report directly to the CEO (see Exhibit 9.4). Any layer in between the CEO and the team indicates that Step One has not been successfully achieved.

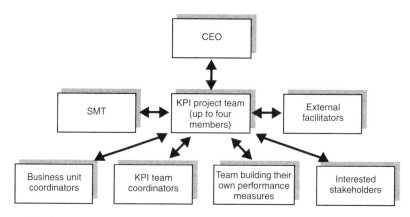

EXHIBIT 9.4   The KPI Team's Reporting Lines

Source: David Parmenter, *Key Performance Indicators: Developing, Implementing, and Using Winning KPIs,* 2nd ed. Copyright © 2010 by David Parmenter. Reprinted with permission of John Wiley & Sons, Inc.

This point is so important that the project should not proceed if the CEO does not wish to be involved in this way. The KPI project team members should have a proven track record of excellent presentation and communication skills, flair for innovation, ability to complete, knowledge of both the organization and sector, and have the ability to bring others on board.

The KPI project team members should be a balanced mix of oracles and young guns. Oracles are those gray-haired individuals whom you visit if you want to find out about what has happened in the past in the organization. Young guns are your young, fearless, and precocious leaders of the future, who are not afraid to venture into the unknown.

All departments and service teams should appoint a person who is sufficiently knowledgeable about their operation to provide information and feedback to liaise with the KPI team.

The interested stakeholders consist of those who can add a useful perspective to the project team, such as some members of the board, union representatives, representatives from some key suppliers, and key customers.

Do not include members of the senior management team on the KPI team, as they will be unable to meet the commitment required of being full time on this project.

In Chapter 3, Revitalizing Performance Management, the second foundation stone was knowledge of the paradigm shifters (Drucker, Collins, Welch, Hamel, Peters, Waterman, and others). We need to apply this knowledge in this step, as set out in Table 9.1.

KEY TASKS FOR ESTABLISHING A WINNING KPI PROJECT TEAM The KPI team will need to incorporate these four tasks among the work it performs in this step:

Task 1. External facilitator helps select the in-house KPI team. The external facilitator should help the senior management team pick a team. Research into personnel records is recommended, as many talented staff are found in obscure places, and some may already have some KPI experience. The facilitator is looking for staff members who have a proven track record of excellent presentation and communication skills, a flair for innovation, the ability to complete what they start, knowledge of both the organization and sector, the aptitude to bring others on board, and the ability to be cheerful under pressure.

The questionnaire in my companion book will help with the selection process. It is advisable to run some tests to assess the potential compatibility of prospect team members, such as personality and thinking preference, as it is likely they have never worked together on a large project before. The findings from these tests will

TABLE 9.1   Lessons from the Paradigm Shifters (featured in Chapter 3)

Lesson	Implication
Do not give new staff new assignments. Drucker[5] referred to these jobs as widow makers—jobs where the incumbent did not have a chance to succeed.	In this KPI project, it is important to ensure that the project team is made up of experienced staff who know the CSFs and the members of the senior management team. Bringing in consultants to lead the KPI project will doom it to failure.
Recruitment is a life and death decision. Drucker was adamant about the significance of recruiting the right staff.	The recruiting of the KPI team should be done very carefully ensuring they have the right mix of knowledge, experience, and credibility within the organization to be successful.
Embrace differences. Hamel[6] is very consistent with the need to: ■ Embrace irregular people, their irregular ideas can be very valuable. ■ Look for positive deviants.	The KPI team should be selected from all experienced employees. It is important to consider those employees who have always shaken the cart. They may have the X factor to make this project work.
A cluster of mentors. As Welch,[7] says, "There is no right mentor for you; there are many right mentors." He sees mentoring more holistically. A mentor can come from a staff person many levels below who passes on their knowledge to you. In *Winning* Welch was forever grateful for the young human-resources advisor who patiently helped him master e-mail.	Ensure all the KPI team members have appropriate mentor support.
Opt-in commitment. Hamel believes organization's should have an "opt-in" and "self-chosen" commitment.	The KPI team should have an open selection process so that a wide net is cast for the best team members. Passion for performance management will be a very important attribute to look for.

help the KPI team members understand how to work better with each other. The human resources manager will know about these tests.

Task 2. Facilitator negotiates for full-time commitment of KPI project team. The facilitator needs to convince management that these staff members are required to be committed *full time*.

A project office needs to be set up and the photos on the desk moved! The facilitator's second-in-command, who will now move into the vacated office, will fill the team's existing roles. Succession planning will be an additional benefit from this project. As stated in Chapter 2 it is a myth that this project can be handled while continuing on with other duties. If project staff members are still intending to start and finish the day at their desk, this project should be terminated.

Task 3. Team identifies coordinators. The team, with the help of the facilitator, needs to identify a liaison for each department or service team. This person needs to be knowledgeable about the operation, because his or her role is to provide the KPI team with detailed knowledge about their area of operation, to provide feedback, and so forth.

Task 4. Facilitator develops training schedule and holds training exercises for the KPI project team. The facilitator will need to establish the knowledge gaps and set up training and some team-building exercises for the team. The exercises might include:

- Preparing a presentation to sell an idea through the audiences' emotional drivers.
- Research exercises both through the company's files and the intranet; for example:
  - Find me the last five reports done internally on performance measurement issues.
  - Find me the articles and white papers written on the topic in major journals and respected web sites.
- Going away for a weekend on a team-building excursion.

The KPI team will need training and assistance. The type of training will include the following:

- A comprehensive understanding of this KPI book.
- How to pass on knowledge using better-practice teaching techniques.
- How to facilitate workshops, which they will be running.
- How to deliver informative presentations.
- How to design databases.
- Better-practice communication techniques.
- Maintaining a vibrant project team home page on the intranet.

For organizations with a staff of 3,000 or more, the facilitator will also be involved in training KPI teams in each department. A central team of trained in-house KPI consultants will support these teams. The facilitator will train the in-house consultants who then will train the KPI teams as the rollout occurs.

BENEFITS OF THIS STEP   The project will have a team with the capability to deliver, provided it is supported by a forward thinking senior management team. This team will have a good support network and a vibrant and informative intranet home page.

Step Three: Establish a Just-Do-It Culture and Process

Right the first time is a rare achievement; the balanced scorecard is no exception. The balanced scorecard is just like a piece of sculpture, you can be criticized on taste and content, but you can't be wrong. The senior management team and KPI project team need to ensure that the project has a just-do-it culture, not one in which every step and measure is debated as part of an intellectual exercise.

With this just-do-it culture comes a belief that we can do it, we do not have to rely on experts to run the project. As mentioned in Chapter 2, it is a myth that you can delegate a performance management project to a consulting firm. In any case, many CEOs are extremely cautious of those large projects that they perceive to be primarily run by external consultants. It is worth noting that experts, like artists, may not necessarily produce the sculpture that you want or need.

To give the team the confidence and knowledge they will need, the KPI team should set up a small reference library and all team members should read the following books:

- David Parmenter, *Key Performance Indicators: Developing Implementing, and Using Winning KPIs*, 2nd ed. (Hoboken, NJ: John Wiley & Sons, 2010).
- Robert S. Kaplan and David P. Norton, *The Balanced Scorecard: Translating Strategy into Action* (Cambridge, MA: Harvard Business Press, 1996).
- Dean R. Spitzer, *Transforming Performance Measurement: Rethinking the Way We Measure and Drive Organizational Success* (New York: Amacom, 2007).
- Paul R. Niven, *Balanced Scorecard: Step-by-Step for Government and Nonprofit Agencies* (Hoboken, NJ: John Wiley & Sons, 2008).
- Stephen Few, *Information Dashboard Design: The Effective Visual Communication of Data* (Sebastopol, CA: O'Reilly Media, 2006).

Establishing your winning KPIs is not complex, and the process should be carried out in-house, provided the team has the assistance of an experienced facilitator. The facilitator's role is principally that of a mentor to the project team and, thus, the facilitator should keep a low profile at balanced-scorecard presentations.

There is no need to heavily invest in balanced-scorecard applications during the first 12 months because the team should be utilizing existing spreadsheet, presentation, and database applications. This eliminates the delay caused by having to tender, select, and populate specialized software at this stage. This can be done more efficiently and effectively in the second year of the project when the organization has a better understanding of KPIs.

Applications such as SharePoint Team Services enable the KPI team to set up intranet pages that everyone with an interest in winning KPIs can access:

- Relevant memos and articles (programmed with expiration dates so only current and important pronouncements are available).
- Forums to discuss issues.
- KPI documentation that requires collaborative input.
- The master performance-measure database.

In Chapter 3, Revitalizing Performance Management, the second foundation stone was the knowledge of the paradigm shifters (Drucker, Collins, Welch, Hamel, Peters, Waterman, and others). We need to apply this knowledge in this step as set out in Table 9.2.

KEY TASKS TO ESTABLISH A JUST-DO-IT CULTURE AND PROCESS The KPI team will need to incorporate these five tasks within the work it performs in this step:

Task 1. Provide training and support to teams so they can develop their performance measures. Major breakthroughs in performance improvement will result from the application of KPIs in local teams or work groups. Recognize that significant educational resources and time are required to implement performance measures in teams.

Task 2. Introduce a moratorium on all existing KPIs. Every organization is likely to have a number of performance measures in place, even if they are not called KPIs. These existing measures need to be reviewed to fit them within the new four-tiered structure of performance measures (KRIs, RIs, PIs, KPIs). All new measures should be allowed to be developed only from the project; there must be a moratorium on measures developed elsewhere.

The organizational emphasis on the existing KPIs will be reduced as soon as senior management team members have been educated in what KPIs really are. All the existing measures will be included in the evaluation process with many being superseded.

TABLE 9.2   Lessons from the Paradigm Shifters (featured in Chapter 3)

Lesson	Implication
Abandonment. Drucker[8] said, "The first step in a growth policy is not to decide where and how to grow. It is to decide what to abandon. In order to grow, an organization must have a systematic policy to get rid of the outgrown, the obsolete, the unproductive."	Promote Drucker's concept of abandonment. Many existing measures should be abandoned along with processes and reports. The KPI project needs space to work. Other systems need to be abandoned to allow enough time for the KPIs to function properly.
Recruitment is a life and death decision. Drucker was adamant about the significance of recruiting the right staff.	Recruiting the KPI team should be done very carefully, ensuring they have the right mix of knowledge, experience, and credibility within the organization to be successful.
Have three test sites. Drucker pointed out that one pilot was never enough.	On a KPI project, we should follow the sage's advice and pilot the KPI project in three entities.
Recognition and celebration. Welch[9] says that great leaders celebrate more. As he points out, "Work is too much a part of life not to recognize moments of achievement." You can sense from listening to his webcasts that his celebrations would have been fun to attend. Welch was all about making work fun. Realizing that it is not life or death but a game you want to win.	The KPI project team will need to be active with recognition and celebration to assist with buy-in and maintain interest and momentum.

Task 3. Check back to the seven foundation stones. When a consensus has been reached on the agreed process for developing and using KPIs, a review must take place to ensure that all the steps are consistent with the seven foundation stones:

1. Partner with staff, unions, and third parties.
2. Transfer power to the front line.
3. Measure and report only what matters.
4. Source KPIs from the CSFs.
5. Abandon processes that do not deliver.
6. Understand human behavior.
7. Facilitate organization-wide understanding of Winning KPIs definition.

Task 4. Validate process and plan with stakeholders. An agreed process and plan for introducing KPIs should be developed in consultation with management, local employee representatives, unions representing the organization's employees, employees, major customers, major suppliers, and the board. Many of the concerns held about introducing measurement can be overcome at this stage if these stakeholders validate the process for developing KPIs.

Task 5. Determining the perspectives of the balanced scorecard. Take a practical approach and avoid getting involved with debates on perspectives and their names. For the first year, stick to the names already suggested and focus your energies elsewhere. You will need a name for each of these perspectives:

- Financial.
- Customer focus.
- Internal process.
- Innovation and learning.
- Staff satisfaction.
- Environment and community.

BENEFITS OF THIS STEP Establishing a just-do-it culture and process will enable the project team to cut through red tape and deliver a timely suite of performance measures, recognizing that it will require further tailoring and improvement at a review period six to eight months down the road.

Step Four: Set Up a Holistic KPI Development Strategy

This step involves ensuring that this is the right time for the project to be run in conjunction with concurrent projects within the organization. In addition, it is necessary to consider how best to run the implementation.

The most appropriate implementation is influenced by the size of the organization, the diversity of the departments, the organization's locations, and the in-house staff resources available for the project. Each implementation is like a fingerprint that is unique to the organization, and it should be designed in consultation with the stakeholders, the external facilitator, and with consideration of prior experiences that have worked and not worked in past implementation rollouts.

There are a number of questions to answer.

- What needs to be abandoned to make room for this project?
- Is this the right time to embark on this project?
- Do we have a window of opportunity to commit to this project?
- How should we best implement winning KPIs across our organization?
- Have we maximized the fit with the other changes our organization is pursuing to achieve world-class performance?

TABLE 9.3　Lessons from the Paradigm Shifters (featured in Chapter 3)

Lesson	Implication
Continuous management innovation. Gary Hamel[10] points out that you need to have a process for continuous management innovation; to be an organization that is capable of trauma-free renewal rather than one that is moved to change through a crisis.	The KPI team needs to be very open to new management thinking and processes. It is very important that the project team embraces new management concepts.
Creative apartheid. Hamel points out that most of us are creative in some areas of our lives. This creativity needs to be embraced at the workplace. He believes that creativity can be strengthened through instruction and practice.	The KPI team must be open to new ideas during the project. Be flexible with how workshops are run and ensure that creativity is given time to flourish.
Embrace differences. Hamel is very consistent about the need to: ■ Embrace irregular people, because their irregular ideas can be very valuable. ■ Look for positive deviants.	The KPI team should be selected from all experienced employees. It is important to consider those employees who have always shaken the cart. They may have the X factor to make this project work.
Mission matters. Hamel says that the mission matters—it must be compelling enough to overcome the gravitational pull of the past and spur individual renewal.	The KPI team should ensure that its mission statement is worded carefully so it will energize and assist with the selling of the winning KPI methodology.
Opt-in commitment. Hamel says organizations should have an opt-in and self-chosen commitment	The KPI team should have an open selection process so that a wide net is cast for the best team members. A passion for performance management will be a very important attribute to look for.

When you can answer these questions clearly, you will be able to locate winning KPIs in the total performance improvement game plan.

In Chapter 3, Revitalizing Performance Management, the second foundation stone was the knowledge of the paradigm shifters (Drucker, Collins, Welch, Hamel, Peters, Waterman, and others). We need to apply this knowledge in this step as, set out in Table 9.3.

KEY TASKS FOR SETTING UP A HOLISTIC KPI DEVELOPMENT STRATEGY   In this step, the KPI team will need to incorporate these five tasks within the work it performs:

Task 1. Ascertain what projects, performance measures, processes, and reports need to be abandoned to make room for the KPI project. Peter Drucker said, "Don't tell me what you're doing, tell me what you've stopped doing."[11] The KPI project needs space to work. Many projects fail because staff and management have to carry out all their existing workload as well as the new responsibilities of the new project. It does not take long before enthusiasm wanes and the project starts to come of its rails.

Task 2. Ascertain the existing measurement culture. Be aware of the current understanding of performance measurement and how it has been used in the organization. It takes time to adapt new approaches to performance measurement. It is, therefore, important to plan the introduction to KPIs with an appreciation of the organization's existing comfort (or discomfort) levels with performance measurement.

Task 3. KPI project phased approach. For organizations with fewer than 500 staff, a total rollout in 16 weeks is achievable. Organizations with over 500 full-time employees will require a phased approach. The larger the organization, the more focused the first phase must be. For an agency with 20,000 or more full-time employees, the first phase would be limited to three of the departments (as recommended by Drucker) where the benefits are the greatest, and it would be desirable to include one head office unit, because the head office units must be able to support this process early on. Exhibit 9.5 shows the indicative rollout duration for organizations of different sizes.

For organizations with more than 3,000 employees, there will be KPI teams in each main department. These teams will be supported by a central KPI team. This central KPI team, whose members will be trained by the facilitator, will effectively be in-house KPI consultants who travel in pairs to support the KPI teams in each main department. The size of the central KPI team varies according to the speed of rollout required.

The number of in-house consultants can be supplemented by external consultants, provided they have been trained in the methodology. The number of trained in-house KPI consultants required will vary depending on the complexity of the rollout and prior experience from other project rollouts in the organization.

EXHIBIT 9.5   Indicating Rollout Duration (use as a guide only)

Size of Organization (FTEs)	Less than 200	200 to 500	500 to 3,000	3,000 to 10,000	10,000+
First phase (2-person KPI project team)	6 weeks	18 weeks	16 to 20 weeks for first phase	Too small	Too small
First phase (4-person KPI project team)	6 weeks (no time saving but better product)	16 weeks	16 to 20 weeks for first phase	20 to 26 weeks for first phase	20 to 30 weeks for first phase
Rollout phases	Not required	Not required	10 weeks for each rollout phase	10 weeks for each rollout phase	10 weeks for each rollout phase

Source: David Parmenter, *Key Performance Indicators: Developing, Implementing, and Using Winning KPIs,* 2nd ed. Copyright © 2010 by David Parmenter. Reprinted with permission of John Wiley & Sons, Inc.

Each rollout can be performed by trained department-based project teams, which will be supported by a designated KPI project team member. It is unlikely that more than three departments can be rolled out simultaneously because there will be inadequate support from the central KPI team.

For those in the private sector who have operations in other countries, the rollout will meet different types of resistance and hurdles. Staff based in Asia may require more workshops than those in Europe, or vice versa. The rollout will also need to take into account the current significance of subsidiaries' operations and their long-term future (e.g., there may be no point embarking on a rollout to a foreign subsidiary if it is to be sold).

Task 4. Once started, ensure that every rollout phase is completed within a 16-week time frame. The rollout success will be dependent on maintaining momentum and energy. Once a department has been selected, there should be an intensive push to complete. Each rollout phase should not be allowed to take more than 16 weeks, because the groundwork already has been prepared. A department rollout could take as few as 10 weeks. It is unlikely to be shorter due to the level of consultation and the team-performance-measures-workshop rollout.

Task 5. Be flexible about the rate of progress required. KPIs do not have to be applied uniformly within the organization. Typically, the drive to introduce KPIs originates from senior or corporate levels of management, but it can also be pushed up from within the organization. Where flexibility is allowed, different parts of the organization can proceed with the introduction of KPIs at varying paces, according to their own requirements and readiness.

A flexible approach to the development of KPIs avoids at least two potential problems associated with centralized, universal implementation:

1. Too much top-down influence on KPI selection, resulting in a lack of ownership in the measures and resistance to their use.
2. Difficulties associated with coordinating and resourcing KPI development in several departments and work groups at the same time.

Example: Shortcut—Perform Part of This Step While You Are Performing Step One

It is important that KPI projects are not undertaken in an environment in which they are doomed to fail. The external facilitator should recommend deferral of the project if there are any doubts about conflicting priorities or adequacy of resources, because:

- It is far better to delay this project to a period in which management will assign adequate resources and have time to commit to it.
- Staff will not see performance measurement as a passing fad, or as yet another failed project initiated by management.

BENEFITS OF THIS STEP A coherent approach will be established that should encourage employee, senior management team, board, and union buy-in and commitment.

Step Five: Market the KPI System to All Employees

Employees need to be prepared for change. The project team and the senior management team need to:

- Convey what the organization's CSFs are and why employees need to focus their daily activities around them.

- Convince employees of the need for change by highlighting the performance gap between the organization and best practice.
- Outline what change is required.
- Show how KPIs contribute to the CSFs and the organization's strategy.
- Attract employees' interest so they want to participate by selling the change through their emotional drivers.
- Address employee's resistance to change and performance measurement.

A formal briefing program should be held to outline the changes associated with introducing KPIs into the organization. By its conclusion, all employees should at least believe that they need to do something differently, and a core group should be clear about implementation issues and how performance measures will be used. Those who have shown an aptitude for the new KPI model should become the team coordinators, who will support and help the KPI team to develop and implement KPIs.

In Chapter 3, Revitalizing Performance Management, the second foundation stone was the knowledge of the paradigm shifters (Drucker, Collins, Welch, Hamel, Peters, Waterman, and others). We need to apply this knowledge in this step, as set out in Table 9.4

TABLE 9.4   Lessons from the Paradigm Shifters (featured in Chapter 3)

Lesson	Implication
Aggregate collective wisdom. Hamel[12] provides compelling evidence that "large groups of people are often smarter than the experts in them."	The KPI team should consult widely and hold sessions during each workshop to ensure adequate chance for all to have their say. This is best done by limiting each workgroup in the workshop to no more than seven members.
Too much hierarchy, too little community. Gary Hamel points out that hierarchies are good at aggregating effort (coordinating activities), but not good at mobilizing effort (inspiring people to go above and beyond). The more you consolidate power in the hands of a few leaders, the less resilient the system will be.	The KPI team must promote a community feel to the project, selling the benefits through the emotional drivers and gaining credibility by abandoning process, measures, and reports that are not working.

KEY TASKS FOR MARKETING THE KPI SYSTEM TO ALL EMPLOYEES The KPI team will need to incorporate these five tasks within the work it performs in this step:

Task 1. Run a survey on a cross-section of staff. A survey is required to find out the current perceptions on existing performance monitoring in the organization, the current concerns about the new project, and what needs to be covered in the employee briefings. A survey template is set out in Chapter 4 of my earlier the KPI book.[13]

These worksheets should be completed by all teams involved in this process. With the help of the human resources team, make a selection of experienced staff covering all regions, levels of staff, and so forth. This cross-section sample should not be greater than 200, or 10 percent of total staff, and not less than 50 staff members. With these numbers, you can close off the survey with a 60 percent return rate and still have a valid survey. Too large a sample will make data mining more difficult and seldom raises any new issues.

Task 2. Build a case for change with public relations support. Demonstrate that KPIs are part of a senior management team-agreed package of initiatives to respond to the pressures on the organization. Spell out these pressures in terms that people can understand. Use comparative information from preliminary benchmarking to highlight the performance gap between your organization and best practice. It is important to utilize the services of an expert in public relations (PR).

As already stated, in selling the project to the senior management team in Step One, nothing was ever sold by logic! You sell through emotional drivers. Thus, you need to radically alter the way you pitch this sale to the staff. You have to focus on the emotional drivers that matter to them:

- The right mix of performance measures will make work more rewarding and enjoyable (e.g., greater staff recognition).
- The focus on the right measures would mean their work would be more effective (e.g., their day-to-day work would be better linked to the organization's strategic objectives).
- Over time, they would have more empowerment and autonomy (e.g., staff making more decisions).
- Winning KPIs will enhance profitability and thus offer greater job security and possibly increased remuneration (e.g., through profit-sharing arrangements).

Many initiatives fail at this hurdle because we attempt to change the culture through selling by logic, writing reports, and issuing commands via e-mail. It does not work. This project needs a PR machine behind it. No presentation, e-mail, memo, or paper should go out to staff unless it has been vetted by your PR expert. All your presentations should be road-tested in front of the PR expert. (See www.davidparmenter.com for webcasts where I discuss this in more detail and provide you with material to help the sales process.)

Task 3. Use the vision to attract the staff. Generate interest by painting a picture of how the workplace could look in two to three years once KPIs and other initiatives have taken hold. Over time, empowered staff will begin to generate their own versions of the vision for the workplace. However, in the beginning, it is critical that the KPI project team is passionate about the task. The PR expert is to ensure that all documentation sells this vision adequately (e.g., in memos, presentations, and the KPI team intranet pages).

Task 4. Roll out a road show to all staff. Structure road show briefings so that all employees get to hear the message, taking into account language skills, literacy, and shift work patterns. It is important to demonstrate the existence of a partnership in change. To this end, employee/union representatives should also address staff attending the road show, outlining their support for winning KPIs. The best workshops seem to be held in informal workplace settings, involving local management known to the audience, and to be structured to maximize attendee feedback. (In larger groups, the use of written questions submitted by the audience will encourage staff to raise issues.)

Task 5. Set up an intranet KPI home page. Set up an intranet KPI home page to describe the steps required to develop and implement KPIs, success stories as they arise within the organization, indicate duties of the KPI coordinators, and publish a time frame for project completion.

BENEFITS OF THIS STEP   Marketing the KPI system to all employees maximizes the commitment from a broad cross-section of employees.

Step Six: Identify Organization-Wide Critical Success Factors

This has been covered in Chapter 7.

Step Seven: Record Performance Measures in a Database

The KPI team will have gathered and recorded performance measures from information gained during discussions held with senior management,

Name of performance measure	Type of PM (KRI, RI, PI, KPI)	Person responsible	BSC perspectives	Time zone (past, current, future)	Frequency of measurement (24/7, daily, weekly, monthly)	Linkage to CSFs/SFs	Team xx	Team xx	Team xx	Team xx	Team xx	Team xx	Suggested target
Number of initiatives implemented from the quarterly rolling client survey	PI	JAK	CF	P	Weekly	Retain key customers Increased repeat business	✓	✓	✓				All by 3 months post survey
Late planes over 2 hours late	KPI	BT	CF IP F E & C	C	24/7	Timely arrival and departure of planes	✓	✓	✓			✓	< 3 per week
Number of initiatives to be implemented next month, months 2 to 3	KPI	CST	CF IP F E & C	F	Weekly	Timely arrival and departure of planes	✓	✓	✓	✓		✓	> 3 per month per team

EXHIBIT 9.6 Performance-Measure Database

Source: David Parmenter, *Key Performance Indicators: Developing, Implementing, and Using Winning KPIs,* 2nd ed. Copyright © 2010 by David Parmenter. Reprinted with permission of John Wiley & Sons, Inc.

revisiting company archives, reviewing monthly reports and external research from the beginning of the project. There will also be many performance measures generated from each team workshop.

Performance measures identified need to be collated in a database. This database needs to be up to date, complete, and made available to all employees to help support their understanding of performance measures and to assist with their selection of their team measures.

The database, as shown in Exhibit 9.6, should include the following fields:

- Description of the performance measure.
- The type of performance measure (KRI, RI, PI, KPI).
- Person responsible for reporting on the measure.
- Which balanced-scorecard perspective(s) the performance measure impacts.
- Frequency of measurement (24/7, daily, weekly, monthly).
- Suggested target.
- Time zone; whether it is a past, current, or future measure.

- Which critical success factor it is linked to (e.g., which critical success factor was being brainstormed when measure was discussed?).
- The teams who have chosen to measure it (this can act as a selection list). You may have a column for each team with a yes or √, indicating selection.

See Appendix F for a list of performance measures suitable for government and non profit agencies.

Key Tasks for Recording Performance Measures in a Database

The KPI team will need to incorporate these five tasks within the work it performs in this step:

Task 1. Select a database that has wide access within the organization and is user friendly. Most organizations operate database applications, which are underutilized. The KPI team must learn to use the in-house database application and design and build a performance-measure database that is easy to use. (Note: An Access performance-measure database is available from www.david parmenter.com for a small fee. Search in templates for the Performance Indicator Measures Ledger.)

Task 2. Build the performance-measure database. The database should include sections where teams:
- Select the CSFs/success factors that are relevant to them.
- Can interrogate the database using keywords to see if their measure is already included.
- Can add new performance measures. (Only the KPI team should have power to delete measures.)
- Record their selection of all the measures they are proposing to use.

Task 3. Populate the performance-measure database. On a daily basis, the measures that have been identified need to be input into the database to ensure that they are not lost in a mountain of paperwork. In order to maintain consistency of input, one person or a small team should be responsible for this action. An easy-to-use input form should be set up in the database to facilitate entering the measures in a timely manner.

Task 4. Train all teams to use the performance-measure database and to refine the performance measures constantly. The KPI team needs to train all the other teams, not only on how to use the database, but also the significance of each database field. This is best achieved through the rolling workshops they will be giving teams. Teams will be trained to review the database to see if any new measure has emerged that is very relevant for their team. This will be performed as part of a later step.

The team will need to refine the performance measures constantly by peeling more layers off the onion. In time, a clearer hierarchy of measures will develop, some will be discarded, and new measures will start emerging that will have a profound impact on the organization's future.

Task 5. Ensure that all database fields are complete for every performance measure. The project team needs to review the database constantly, cleanse it of duplication, and encourage teams to look at measures that have been selected by their peers.

BENEFITS OF THIS STEP   Recording measures in a performance-measure database creates a vital electronic working tool for the KPI project team and for teams selecting and recording their performance measures. This tool will ensure a high level of consistency throughout the organization.

Step Eight: Select Team-Level Performance Measures

This is a vital step in performance improvement. The appropriate performance measures will help teams to align their behavior in a coherent way for the benefit of the whole organization. This is achieved because teams are focusing on performance measures that are linked to the organization's CSFs.

Team performance measures will be comprised mainly of PIs and some of the organizations KPIs, where relevant (e.g., late planes measure would have been monitored by the front desk, engineering, catering, cleaning, etc. but not by the accounting team).

Although management often tends to become focused on achieving KPI introduction at the organization-wide level, in reality the critical issue is getting these KPIs embedded in the teams who need to take corrective action 24/7.

Thus, it is at the team level, Level 4 in Exhibit 9.7, that significant and sustainable performance improvement can be achieved through the use of performance measures.

Every CEO would wish that all employees' align day-to-day activities with the organization's strategic objectives. Yet this is seldom the case. Why does the marketing team measure all customer satisfaction infrequently when our CSF in that area might be "increased repeat donations from our main contributors"? Surely, a charity should be measuring the satisfaction of its main contributors regularly and surveying the other donors less

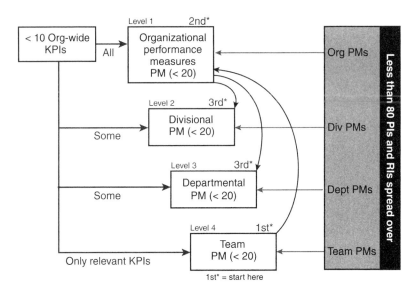

EXHIBIT 9.7   Interrelated Levels of Performance Measures in an Organization

Source: David Parmenter, *Key Performance Indicators: Developing, Implementing, and Using Winning KPIs,* 2nd ed. Copyright © 2010 by David Parmenter. Reprinted with permission of John Wiley & Sons, Inc.

frequently. Organizations should concentrate their efforts on their CSFs and reduce effort in less important areas; for example, staff in well-run hospitals will take infinitely more care in a patient's details prior to the patient going into an operating theater. Once staff members understand the CSFs and prioritize their daily activities around them, a magical alignment can occur between effort and effectiveness.

In Chapter 3, Revitalizing Performance Management, the second foundation stone was the knowledge of the paradigm shifters (Drucker, Collins, Welch, Hamel, Peters, Waterman, and others). We need to apply this knowledge in this step as set out in Table 9.5.

KEY TASKS FOR SELECTING TEAM-LEVEL PERFORMANCE MEASURES   The KPI team will need to incorporate these seven tasks within the work it performs in this step:

> **Task 1. Have teams complete preworkshop worksheets.** These worksheets are set out in Chapter 4 of my earlier KPI book.[14]

TABLE 9.5   Lessons from the Paradigm Shifters (featured in Chapter 3)

Lesson	Implication
Importance of chaos rather than unnecessary order. Gary Hamel[15] emphasizes the importance of chaos rather than unnecessary order. Peters and Waterman, throughout the first three chapters of *In Pursuit of Excellence*, stress the importance of allowing overlap, internal competition, impromptu contact, while minimizing head-office command and control.	The project team needs to be wary of adopting the easier command-and-control approach. The KPI team must allow a fair degree of autonomy in the pilots and rollout stages, so long as the foundation stones are intact.
Creative apartheid. Hamel points out that most of us are creative in some areas of our lives. This creativity needs to be embraced at the workplace. He believes that creativity can be strengthened through instruction and practice.	The KPI team must be open to new ideas during the project. Be flexible with how workshops are run, ensuring that creativity is given time to flourish.

These worksheets should be completed by all teams involved in this process.

Task 2. Roll out training workshops to all teams. The KPI project team must provide training and assistance to all teams so that they are equipped to select their own performance measures that are consistent with the organization's CSFs. It is a good idea to bring a number of teams together at the same time, as they will learn from each other's different views. Some workshop groups have up to 80 attendees doing the team performance measures exercise. Each team is broken into a discussion group of four to seven staff members. Encourage a balance in team performance measures. If the CSFs are clearly defined and related to the six BSC perspectives (customer focus, financial performance, innovation and learning, internal process, staff satisfaction, and environment/community), then team performance measures developed in this context generally will reflect the required balance.

Use the mind-mapping techniques set out in Chapter 10 during the brainstorming sessions (see Exhibit 9.8 for an example).

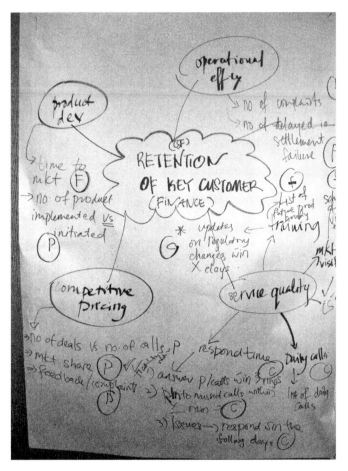

EXHIBIT 9.8   Example of Mind Mapping a Critical Success Factor

Example: Shortcut—Merge the Team Performance Workshops with the Road Show from Step Five

This is the approach I now adopt with most in-house workshops I perform.

Benefits include:

- Because most attendees at the two workshops will be the same, it saves having two disruptions to the same production, sales, and operations teams.

- Merging Steps Five and Eight helps staff understand more about the purpose behind having a team scorecard.
- This method builds momentum for the project earlier, because teams can start working with their scorecard sooner.

Task 3. Promote an appropriate mix of past-, current-, and future-looking measures. Current measures are measured 24/7 or daily, and future measures are the record of a future date when an action is to take place (e.g., date of next meeting with key customer, date of next product launch, date of next social interaction with key customers). (See Exhibit 9.9.)

Key result indicators and *result indicators* will all be past measures, whereas *performance indicators* and *key performance indicators* are now categorized as either past, current, or future measures. You will find that most of the KPIs in your organization will fit into the current or future categories.

The previous debate about lag (outcome) and lead (performance driver) indicators is now dispensed with. As pointed out in Chapter 2, the lag and lead classification of indicators does not work and serves to confuse.

Task 4. Permit team performance measures to evolve. Virtually no team will achieve a perfect set of performance measures at its

EXHIBIT 9.9   Taking a Past Measure and Restating as a Current and Future Measure

Past Measures (last week/2 weeks/month/quarter)	Current (real-time/today/yesterday) Measures	Future Measures (week/month/quarter)
Number of late planes this month	Late planes in the air over 2 hours late	Number of initiatives to be implemented this month to target areas that are causing late planes
Date of last visit by key customer	Cancellation of order by key customer (today)	Date of next visit to key customer
Sales last month in new products	Quality defects found today in new products	Number of improvements to new products to be implemented in next month, months 2 & 3

Source: David Parmenter, *Key Performance Indicators: Developing, Implementing, and Using Winning KPIs,* 2nd ed. Copyright © 2010 by David Parmenter. Reprinted with permission of John Wiley & Sons, Inc.

first or even its second attempt. Further, once a set of performance measures exists, individual indicators may need to vary as the team improves performance and then moves on to focus on other problem areas.

Task 5. Use Pareto's 80/20 rule when assessing how to calculate a measure. Encourage teams to be practical when assessing how to calculate their chosen performance measures. It is essential that the cost of gathering the measure is not greater than the benefit derived from the measure. For many measures, staff should be encouraged to either use sample techniques (e.g., measure late invoices one week a month) or assessment techniques (e.g., estimate the number of coaching hours received last month). Pareto's 80/20 rule encourages us to measure in detail only the KPIs (e.g., the late planes' tracking system would have warranted a multimillion-dollar investment).

Task 6. Never lose sight of team ownership. Remember that the primary purpose of team performance measures is to assist and help the team to improve their performance. It follows that their performance measures represent what they want to collect in order to contribute to improvement in the identified CSFs. The KPI team needs to steer them gently if they are off course.

Task 7. Set a maximum of 25 performance measures for a team. As a guide, 25 is probably the upper limit of performance measures that a team should select for regular use. Any more than this number may lead to resource problems and a lack of focus. These performance measures will include some of the organization's KPIs. Some teams may have up to three organizational KPIs in their team scorecard. Many head-office teams will not have KPIs in their scorecard, as they are not relevant to them (e.g., the British Airways accounting team would not have a late-planes measure). Remember that the KPIs affect the entire organization. Thus, there are no KPIs specific to one team.

BENEFITS OF THIS STEP   Selecting team-level performance measures puts measures in place that:

- Clarify the teams' objectives.
- Align daily team work to the organization's strategic objectives.
- Improve job satisfaction (e.g., measures that increase the level of staff recognition and celebration).
- Increase job security as teams contribute more to the bottom line.
- Provide a basis for recognizing and celebrating team achievements.
- Provide a better understanding and link to the organization's strategies.

Step Nine: Select Organizational Winning KPIs

It is recommended that the selection of organizational KPIs be started after progress has been made at the team level (Level 4 in Exhibit 9.7). The KPI team will have gained an insight into the organizational KPIs by working with teams. It is very much an iterative process, with findings being conveyed both up and down. Once Levels 1 and 4 (in Exhibit 9.7) are in a semifinalized state, the backfilling of the divisional or departmental measures (Levels 2 and 3) can take place. This process will ensure that there are appropriate measures for all levels.

This approach reflects the goal of empowerment and will ensure team ownership of their performance measures. It will also ensure that as performance measures are introduced at other levels in the organization, they will be influenced by:

- The organizational CSFs.
- The vital activities existing at the workplace that are creating success or failure.

No matter how complex your organization—whether a public body, a hospital, or a diverse manufacturer—team, department, and division performance measures should not be consolidated to become the organization's measures. This ends up in chaos; for example, some hospitals have over 200 measures at the organizational level! It is crucial that all staff members fully understand KPIs. Remember, finding appropriate KPIs is very much like peeling the layers off an onion to get to the core. Although it is relatively easy to produce a reasonable list of performance indicators, it is difficult to identify the key performance indicators, particularly when it needs to be recognized that there will be no more than ten in the entire organization.

In Chapter 3, Revitalizing Performance Management, the second foundation stone was the knowledge of the paradigm shifters (Drucker, Collins, Welch, Hamel, Peters, Waterman, and others). We need to apply this knowledge in this step as set out in Table 9.6.

TABLE 9.6   Lessons from the Paradigm Shifters (featured in Chapter 3)

Lesson	Implication
Have three test sites. Drucker pointed out that one pilot was never enough.	On a KPI project we should follow the sage's advice and pilot the KPI project in three entities.

KEY TASKS FOR SELECTING ORGANIZATIONAL WINNING KPIS   The KPI team will need to incorporate these five tasks within the work it performs in this step:

Task 1. Ensure that KRIs, RIs, PIs, and KPIs are balanced. The organization's KRIs, RIs, PIs, and KPIs should address all six BSC perspectives (customer focus, financial, innovation and learning, internal process, staff satisfaction, and environment/community). The worksheet in my companion book will assist with this process.

Task 2. Limit the organization-wide KPIs to no more than 10. There is no magic number, but few organizations will need more than 10 KPIs, and in fact many can operate successfully on fewer than 5 KPIs.

Task 3. Permit the KRIs, RIs, PIs, and KPIs to evolve. Virtually no KPI project team will achieve a perfect set of KRIs, RIs, PIs, and KPIs at its first or even its second attempt. Further, once a set of KPIs exists, information from the teams will shed light on enhancements to the KPIs.

Task 4. Ensure that all KPIs have most or all of the KPI characteristics. Ensure that all KPIs selected pass this checklist. The characteristics of a KPI include the following:

- Nonfinancial measures (e.g., not expressed in dollars, yen, euros, etc.).
- Measured frequently (e.g., 24/7, daily, or weekly).
- Acted on by CEO and senior management team.
- Clearly indicate what action is required by staff (e.g., staff can understand the measures and know what to fix).
- Measures that ties responsibility down to a team.
- Shows significant impact (e.g., it impacts most of the core CSFs and more than one BSC perspective).
- Encourages appropriate action in the right direction (e.g., have been tested to ensure they have a positive impact on performance, have a minimal dark side).

Task 5. Test all the KPIs in three pilots. Peter Drucker believed all testing should be performed in no less than three pilots. The KPI team would be wise to listen and act on this advice. The piloting is done to ensure that all KPIs create the desired behavioral outcomes and that there is not an unexpected consequence, a major dark side in the way the measure is performing.

BENEFITS OF THIS STEP   Organizational winning KPIs are measures that will have a profound impact on the organization, stimulating timely action and linking day-to-day activities to the strategic objectives of the organization.

Step Ten: Develop the Reporting Framework at All Levels

The reporting framework has to accommodate the requirements of different levels in the organization and the reporting frequency that supports timely decision making. A suggested framework for reporting performance indicators is set out in Exhibit 9.10.

Most KPIs should be reported each day (electronically) at 9 A.M. or, as in the case of British Airways, constantly updated 24 hours a day, 7 days a week.

In most organizations there will be another "top five" KPIs that will need to be reported at least weekly (excluding the daily KPIs identified earlier). One weekly measure that is important in most organizations is the reporting of late projects and late reports to the senior management team. Such reports will revolutionize completion in your organization.

The remaining RIs and PIs can be reported monthly along with team, department, divisional, and organizational-wide balanced-scorecard reporting. The introduction of balanced scorecards will promote more concise and prompt reporting.

The board should only receive a one-page governance dashboard on the five to eight KRIs. These KRIs cover the well-being of the organization and are not PIs or KPIs. They should cover the six balanced-scorecard perspectives, and, to do this, you may need to track up to 10 KRIs. In any one month, you will only need to report those KRIs that are telling the more important stories. It is desirable not to give the board the management balanced scorecards because their role is one of governance; giving them management information diverts them from their true role.

The reporting stage is open to procrastination, and, therefore, it is important to ensure that the just-do-it attitude is operational. It is not uncommon to find teams spending considerable time debating which colors are the most appropriate in presentations to senior management. It is important that this is not allowed to occur on the KPI project.

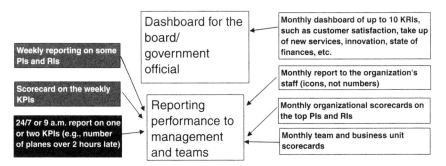

EXHIBIT 9.10   A Suggested Reporting Framework

It is recommended that the senior management team leave the design of the balanced-scorecard template to the KPI team, trusting their judgment. The senior management team should tell the KPI project team that they will be happy to live with their sculpture knowing that they can always "keep the plinth and recycle the bronze" 6 to 12 months down the road. What you are looking for is a reporting framework that covers the measures in the six balanced-scorecard perspectives. The key is to seek agreement that suggested modifications will be recorded and looked into at the end of the agreed review period. It will come as no surprise that many suggested modifications will not stand the test of time.

Some report formats are shown in Chapter 14, Reporting Performance Measures.

KEY TASKS FOR DEVELOPING THE REPORTING FRAMEWORKS AT ALL LEVELS The KPI team will need to incorporate these three tasks within the work it performs in this step:

> **Task 1. Provide appropriate training on reporting.** The project team should train the teams on how best to report their measures using a combination of the intranet, notice boards, and hard copy. There are report formats in Chapter 14.
>
> They should also give training on how to complete these reports efficiently. KPI reporting should be almost instantaneous; once appropriate systems are in place, weekly and monthly reporting should also be quick routines.
>
> A team balanced scorecard should, as a guide, be no more than half a day's preparation and be delivered to the team by the close of the first working day of the new month. Late reporting has no place in performance measurement.
>
> Staff members will need much help with maintaining a Pareto 80/20 view. There is no point spending a lot of time playing around with spreadsheets; that information will be too late to be of any use.
>
> **Task 2. Establish a suite of meaningful graphs that are easy to understand.** Although there is a vast array of graphical techniques for displaying KPI data, it is recommended that you follow the thinking of Stephen Few,[16] the world expert on data visualization. Here are some rules to follow:
>
> - *Be consistent.* It is recommended that graph standards are maintained for at least six months before updating.
> - *Show trend analysis.* Show movement over at least the past 15 to 18 months if you have a seasonal operation. Only year-to-date graphs should start off at the beginning of the year.

- *Show the range.* Show the acceptable range, which may be cascading over time, to indicate expected improvements.
- *Keep graphs simple.* Each graph should be clear even to an untrained eye (e.g., whereas waterfall, radar, and three-dimensional graphs might look nice, they can be misunderstood by staff and thus are rarely necessary).
- *Make them quick to update.* All graphs should be in a system that enables swift updating, and in some cases they should be automated to enable 24/7 analysis via the intranet. Graphs should not slow down the monthly management balanced scorecard, and the board dashboard reporting process, which should be completed by no later than day-3 post-month-end.
- *Make them accessible.* Key graphs should be accessible to all staff via the intranet.
- *Do not show a budget line.* A monthly or year-to-date budget line is an arbitrary apportionment of the annual plan number and is often done at the last minute.
- *Show key turning points.* Essential turning points on graphs should be explained by a note on the graph, and comments need to highlight major issues.
- *Insert a title that is meaningful to the reader.* For example, a title like "Return on capital employed (ROCE) is moving up well" instead of just saying "ROCE."
- *Use color wisely.* It is a good idea to use a light-yellow background and to use color to highlight what is important.
- *Use gridlines.* Four or five light-gray gridlines will enable the reader to estimate the numbers, thus eliminating the clutter of numbers within the graph columns or rows.

Task 3. Develop a hierarchy of reports to staff, management, and the board. If KPI reporting is not available 24/7 and it is not the focus of action and discussed at performance improvement meetings, attention will wane and the graphs will become symbols of frustration rather than the focus for continuous improvement.

Make sure you never give KPI reports to the board. They should receive more summarized information, as shown in the board dashboard in Chapter 14.

BENEFITS OF THIS STEP A consistent reporting regime will be developed based around decision-based reporting techniques, which will not take up too much of management's time. The reports will encourage empowered staff to undertake corrective action immediately on issues that are adversely affecting KPIs (e.g., in an airline, staff being empowered to increase the cleaning contractor's staff immediately to ensure a quicker turnaround of a late plane).

Step Eleven: Facilitate the Use of Winning KPIs

Many organizations have performed good KPI groundwork, only to have it fail or become buried when the originator leaves the organization. It is, therefore, important that the use of KPIs becomes widespread in an organization and that it is incorporated into its culture.

If the CEO, members of the senior management team, and management focus on the KPIs every day, staff will naturally follow suit. When a CEO spends about 30 minutes a day asking for explanations from managers and staff about a wayward KPI, this will soon create focus. It certainly will be seen that receiving two phone calls from the CEO is not a good career move! In other words, the CEO should walk the talk and always know where the KPIs are heading at any point during a day. Thus, on out-of-office trips, the CEO should be able to link into the intranet and obtain an update of the KPIs.

In turn, the senior management team needs to be committed to empowering staff to take immediate action; for example, Toyota empowers staff on the shop floor to stop the production line if they find any defect in a car they are working on. Resources need to be allocated so continual education and communication can be maintained. This should not just be the responsibility of the KPI project team.

The system will have failed if the review process relies on structured, regular meetings at each level where KPIs are in operation. Remember, KPIs are indicators that need monitoring, reporting, and action 24/7!

KEY TASKS FOR FACILITATING USE OF KPIS   The KPI team will need to incorporate these six tasks within the work they perform in this step:

> **Task 1. Constantly reassure the senior management team so that they are confident to empower the frontline staff.** It is essential that the members of the senior management team learn to relax their control and empower their staff. Without staff empowerment, the effectiveness of KPIs is limited, as staff members respond to management direction rather than learning to become proactive themselves.
>
> **Task 2. Roll out a road show for all staff.** The road show should be delivered in person by a skilled presenter from the project team accompanied by someone from the senior management team.

The workshop should start with an introduction from the CEO (a recorded webcast is sufficient when the CEO is not present) and a presentation on the new thinking on key performance indicators by a skilled presenter from the project team. It is essential to explain to staff:

- How the chosen KPIs are to operate.
- Who is to collect data and by when.
- The systems to be used.
- The monitoring and action to be taken by the senior management team.
- The delegated empowerment that employees have to correct situations as they arise on a 24/7 basis.

Task 3. Have relative performance measures that are compared against other organizations. Jeremy Hope and Robin Fraser, pioneers of the Beyond Budgeting methodology,[17] have pointed out how KPIs can easily end up in the trap of an annual fixed performance contract. In other words, if you set a target in the future, you will never know if it was appropriate, given the particular conditions of that time. You often end up paying incentives to management when, in fact, you have lost market share. In other words, your rising sales did not keep up with the growth rate in the marketplace.

Relative performance measures are an important addition to KPIs; for example, you may focus on all planes in the air that are flying more than two hours late 24/7, but, in addition, compare total late flights, average turnaround times, number of missing passengers, and so forth, to other airlines. This could perhaps be carried out quarterly using a benchmarking company.

Another benefit of relative measures is that they do not need alteration (e.g., if being in the top quartile or 2 percent above the norm is the relative measure, then this benchmark does not need changing).

Task 4. Ensure that there are a mix of *past, current*, and *future* performance measures. Most measures across the world are past measures. In a bid to rectify this, the terms *lead indicators* and *lag indicators* were introduced. As mentioned in the section "Lead and Lag Confusion" in Chapter 6, these terms do not work for KPIs; for example, the late-plane KPI could be called a lag indicator because it reports past events; however, while the plane is in the air and running late, it is about to create chaos for passengers, suppliers, and airline staff at the destination airport and, therefore, it is also a lead indicator.

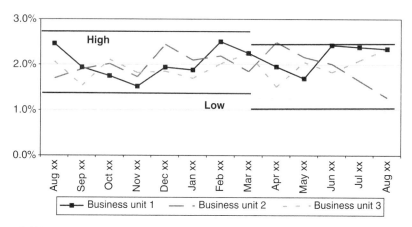

EXHIBIT 9.11   Ranging KPIs

Source: David Parmenter, *Key Performance Indicators: Developing, Implementing, and Using Winning KPIs,* 2nd ed. Copyright © 2010 by David Parmenter. Reprinted with permission of John Wiley & Sons, Inc.

> **Task 5. Set KPIs as ranges, not a single target.** An acceptable range is more beneficial than a fixed target, as a range takes into account the vagaries of the future and so is more tolerant of environmental change (e.g., a set of goalposts rather than a single thin post at the end of the playing field).
>
> It is a good idea to show the acceptable range cascading up or down over time to indicate expected improvements; see Exhibit 9.11.
>
> **Task 6. Apply the 10/80/10 rule.** Ensure that the final performance measures in use comply with the 10/80/10 rule:
>
> - Maintain up to 10 key result indicators, with only 6 to 9 shown to the board at any one time.
> - Up to 80 performance indicators and result indicators are sufficient for most organizations, especially when standard measures are used across all teams (e.g., a training-day's measure should be applied consistently with the same definition and graphical illustration across all teams).
> - Set a maximum of 10 KPIs. It is unlikely that an organization will have more than ten KPIs that fit the seven characteristics outlined in Chapter 6.

BENEFITS OF THIS STEP   The performance measures in your organization—the KRIs, RIs, PIs, and KPIs—are being applied properly and are given the opportunity to create the desired change.

Step Twelve: Refine KPIs to Maintain Their Relevance

It is essential that the use and effectiveness of KPIs be maintained. Teams will modify and change some of their KPIs and PIs as priorities change during their journey of process improvement. It is simply a case of moving on to the next priority area for improvement as the previous ones have been mastered and behavior alignment has been locked in.

Some KPIs should always be maintained because of their relevance to the organization-wide CSFs; for example, the late-plane KPI will always be used by an airline. In addition, it is likely that KPIs relating to customer focus and workplace culture will always remain in place.

Teams will also need to amend and build new measures to respond to the emergence of new CSFs. The new CSFs will be identified during quarterly rolling planning phases.

Teams should review and modify their own KPIs and PIs on a periodic basis, certainly not more frequently than every six months.

KEY TASKS FOR REFINING KPIS TO MAINTAIN THEIR RELEVANCE   The KPI team will need to incorporate these four tasks within the work it performs in this step:

Task 1. Review organization-wide CSFs at least annually. The environment in which firms operate is changing so rapidly that the requirements for survival and then prosperity can change markedly within a year. CSFs must be reviewed on a continuing planning cycle. As a better practice, it can be part of the quarterly rolling planning regime. Many of the CSFs will stay consistent for years; timely arrival and departure of planes will be a CSF as long as planes fly.

Task 2. Hold a one-day focus group revisiting the performance measures. The objectives of the workshop are to revisit the performance measures with a key group of staff and management and to learn from experience and enhance the value gained from using performance measures. A focus group needs to be selected consisting of 15 to 30 experienced staff members from the departments, teams, area offices, and head office. The staff members should include the different roles, from administrators to senior-management-team members.

On the day that the CSFs are revisited, any new CSFs will be brainstormed for new measures, and the organizational measures will be reviewed for appropriateness and completeness.

Task 3. Maintain the stakeholder consultation. Ensure that consultations with stakeholders continue to be included in the performance review process. The stakeholders will provide feedback as to whether there needs to be improvement to strategies and CSFs.

Key suppliers should be consulted, as large operational efficiency can be achieved by vertical integration of systems. For example, one wood processor has online access to a major wood merchant's stock records. The wood processor is responsible for managing stock levels and delivering the timber. They send electronic invoices, trigger electronic payment, and update the wood merchant's stock system.

Task 4. Allow team performance measures to adapt. Maintaining the team's sense of ownership of performance measures is critical and will be achieved only if employees view performance-measure information as valuable, useful, and worthwhile. As teams complete the process-improvement cycle, KPI usefulness will be tested against new challenges to the team. Team performance measures must be adapted, as required, to maintain their relevance and use.

BENEFITS OF THIS STEP   The cycle of continuous improvement in the use of KRIs, RIs, PIs, and KPIs will be locked in place.

Notes

1. Those readers who have already seen my *Key Performance Indicators: Developing, Implementing, and Using Winning KPIs* know that it is very much a how-to manual—a reference book for the KPI team. I will, as mentioned in Chapter 1, avoid going into the same detail with this chapter. For checklists and templates, refer to David Parmenter, *Key Performance Indicators: Developing, Implementing and Using Winning KPIs,* 2nd ed. (Hoboken, NJ: John Wiley & Sons, 2010), Chapter 3, Developing and Using Winning KPIs: A 12 Step Model, and Chapter 4, KPI Team Resource Kit. The templates from these two chapters can be acquired electronically from www.davidparmenter.com.
2. Ibid.
3. See draft program in Parmenter, *Key Performance Indicators.*
4. Robert S. Kaplan and David P. Norton, *The Balanced Scorecard: Translating Strategy into Action* (Cambridge, MA: Harvard Business Press, 1996).
5. Peter Drucker, *Peter Drucker on the Profession of Management* (Cambridge, MA: Harvard Business School Press, 1998)

6. Gary Hamel, *The Future of Management* (Cambridge, MA: Harvard Business Press, 2007).

7. Jack Welch and Suzy Welch, *Winning* (New York: HarperBusiness, 2005).

8. Peter Drucker *Management Challenges for the 21st Century* (New York: HarperCollins, 1999).

9. Welch and Welch, *Winning*.

10. Hamel, *Future of Management*.

11. Drucker, *Management Challenges for the 21st Century*.

12. Hamel, *Future of Management*.

13. Parmenter, *Key Performance Indicators*.

14. Ibid.

15. Hamel, *Future of Management*.

16. Stephen Few, *Show Me the Numbers: Designing Tables and Graphs to Enlighten* (Burlington, CA: Analytics Press, 2004); *Information Dashboard Design: The Effective Visual Communication of Data* (Sebastopol, CA: O'Reilly Media, 2006); *Now You See It: Simple Visualization Techniques for Quantitative Analysis* (Sebastopol, CA: Analytics Press, 2009).

17. Jeremy Hope and Robin Fraser, *Beyond Budgeting: How Managers Can Break Free from the Annual Performance Trap* (Cambridge, MA: Harvard Business Press, 2003).

CHAPTER **10**

Determining the Measures

Many performance measures are created from a flawed process. Many methodologies, including the balanced scorecard, appear to simply say the measures are a by-product of the exercise. Frequently the task of finding measures is a task carried out at the last minute by staff who do not have a clue about what is involved in finding a measure that will receive the appropriate behavioral response. As mentioned in Chapter 2, it is one of the myths of performance measurement that appropriate measures are very obvious.

There are a number of common ways to get this radically wrong:

- To be under the misconception that as long as a measure is SMART— *specific, measureable, attainable, realistic,* and *time sensitive*—it will do. This, of course, ignores the fact that the measure may not be linked to the critical success factors of the business and that its dark side may be very damaging.
- The cascading down of performance measures, where one measure is broken down into its component parts as it goes down different teams (e.g., you start with return on capital employed and then say what measures made this up, and so on down).
- Giving teams the task of finding measures without any training and placing them in the organization's balanced-scorecard application.
- Giving the task to a few accountants or performance-management specialists who complete this task in the spare moments they have.
- Tying KPIs to performance-related pay. If you do this, KPI stands for *key political indicator,* rather than *key performance indicator*. As mentioned earlier, good performance with KPIs should be seen as a "ticket to the game," a given, the reason why you are employed; thus, there is no need to incentivize them.

How to Derive Measures

The following process will help ensure you derive the most appropriate measures:

- Determine what your success factors are.
- Map the relationships to find which success factors have the most significant impact—the critical success factors.
- In work groups, brainstorm the critical success factors to find appropriate measures for the team.
- Trap all measures from the brainstorm sessions in a database, indicating the key features, such as the critical success factor, the measure influences, and measurement frequency.
- Have an experienced team member review every measure, eliminating harmful, duplicated, and unnecessary measures. All measures will have a dark side, an unintended consequence. The solution is to understand what you need to do to minimize these measures.
- Discuss measures with staff members, asking them, "If we measure XXX, what will you do?"
- Test measures in three sites to ensure they are working as anticipated.
- Roll out the measure and ensure that the CEO understands how it works and what is expected from the daily/weekly monitoring.

Brainstorming Measures

Brainstorming is a common technique used around the world, so it does not need too much explaining. I will, however, reiterate some useful rules:

- Use a mix of oracles and young guns in the brainstorming session.
- Everybody is considered an equal during the session; thus, ensure that the most senior member does not act as the facilitator as this establishes a "meeting" environment rather than a free-ranging brainstorming session.
- All ideas are treated as good ideas. There is no editing or disputing an idea. Often, the most unusual idea can give birth to a major discovery.
- When brainstorming, first pick up on some likely aspects of the critical success factor being brainstormed, as shown in Exhibit 10.1.
- With each aspect, you then commence thinking of likely measures (see Exhibit 10.2). Ask the attendees in the session:
  - "What would good performance look like?" Using their answers, ask them, "What measures would show this good performance best?"

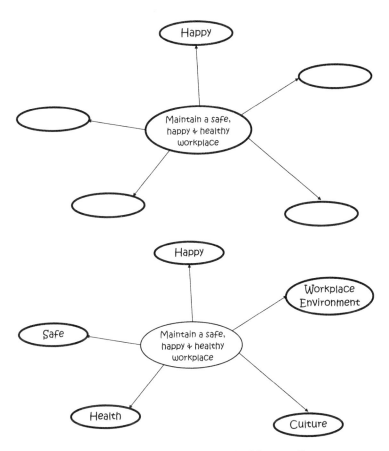

EXHIBIT 10.1   Brainstorming Measures from a Critical Success Factor

- "What would poor performance look like?" In response to their an-swers, ask them, "What measures would give advance warnings of this negative performance?"
- Before you move on, you need to ensure that you have a mix of past (P), current (C), and future (F) measures. (See Exhibit 10.2.)

Stacey Barr's PuMP

Stacey Barr is one of the world experts on performance measures. She has spent the past 15 years or so helping organizations worldwide find measures that drive performance. She has developed a methodology to

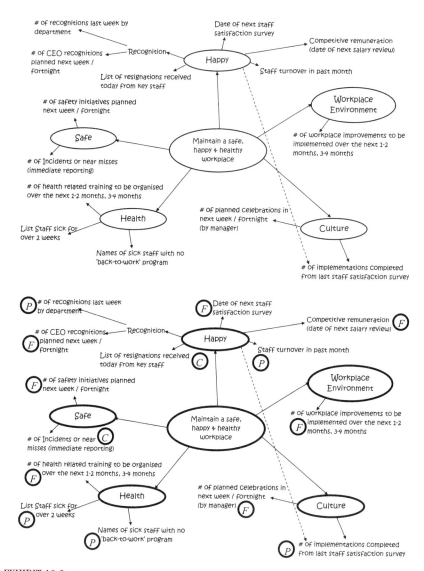

EXHIBIT 10.2   Brainstorming of Performance Measures

fill in the gap that the balanced scorecard and other methodologies have left. Barr believes that many organizations have an ad hoc approach to measuring performance and underestimate the effort and rigor needed to produce meaningful measures.

Barr has developed a successful methodology that is a step-by-step process of simple techniques and templates that create meaningful measures that drive strategic improvement. The features of the methodology include:

- **SELECT: Choose and define what is worth measuring.** Selecting what to measure means being centered on the outcomes that matter most to you and your business. Define your measures by carefully considering what form the evidence of these outcomes will take.
- **COLLECT: Gather data that have integrity.** The process of collecting data is critical to its integrity and gathering the resources is intensive. It is worth giving serious consideration to how you will accomplish collecting data, so that your data can be fit for purpose.
- **STORE: Manage the data so it is quick and easy to access.** Where and how you store your data directly determines what data you can access, when and how quickly you can access it, how easy or difficult it is to access, and how much cross-functional use you can get out of it.
- **ANALYZE: Turn the data into information.** Analysis is the process of turning raw data into information. Make sure it is the most appropriate information by adopting the simplest analytical approach that can produce the information in the form required to answer your driving questions.
- **PRESENT: Effectively communicate the information.** In communicating performance information, you are influencing which messages the audience will focus. Take care to present performance measures in ways that provide simple, relevant, trustworthy, and visual answers to their priority questions. Barr, like myself, is a fan of Stephen Few's work.
- **INTERPRET: Translate the information into implication.** Interpreting your performance measures means translating messages highlighted by performance information into conclusions about what's really going on. To turn information into implication, you must discern which messages are real messages (and not all of them are!).

Barr has called this methodology PuMP (Performance Measurement Process) and I can safely say we share the same vision, namely, organization's finding and using the measures that will make a difference when monitored by staff management and the senior management team. Visit www.staceybarr.com for more information.

Checking KPIs for Behavioral Alignment

To check the potential KPIs for appropriate behavioral alignment create a table using the headings in Exhibit 10.3 and list your top 20 performance measures. Mark the progress you have completed thus far and ensure all gaps are rectified.

EXHIBIT 10.3   Checking KPIs for Behavioral Alignment

Performance Measure	Measure Has Been Piloted to Ensure it Encourages Appropriate Action	Measure Has Been Observed and is Working Properly	Poor Performance Followed Up Immediately by GM or CEO	Performance Measure Can be Tied to a Team	Team Involved Understands the Importance of the Critical Success Factor	Support at Least Weekly During Change Process by KPI Team	Good Performance is Celebrated in the Organization
Late planes in the sky, over two hours late	✓	✓	✓	✓	✓	✓	✓
xxxx							

CHAPTER 11

Case Studies

To show how the two-day critical-success-factor workshop is run, I have provided some examples of government and non profit agencies I have worked with. I hope these examples will clarify the process set out in Chapter 7, Finding Your Organization's Success Factors.

Golf Club (Non Profit Membership Organization)

A small golf club, located in a seaside hamlet, has a membership of no more than 350 playing members. Despite the relatively small membership, this club has produced two successful professional golfers. The chairman of the golf club asked me to help the club management committee look at their operations.

Summary of Tasks Undertaken

1. Reviewed the strategic documents over the last 10 years, one of which was a very old, albeit well-thought-out, strategy paper.
2. Drafted the success factors onto a fanfold piece of paper and organized a workshop with the committee members (see Exhibit 11.1). The workshop ran for two hours and was held in the boardroom where one of the committee members worked as the CEO. His personal assistant was on hand to process the workshop output during the workshop.
3. The workshop commenced with the attendees quickly agreeing on the wording of the balanced-scorecard perspectives:
   - Satisfaction of members and visitors.
   - Satisfaction of paid and voluntary staff.
   - Finance.
   - Internal processes.
   - Learning and growth of paid and voluntary staff.
   - Environment and community.

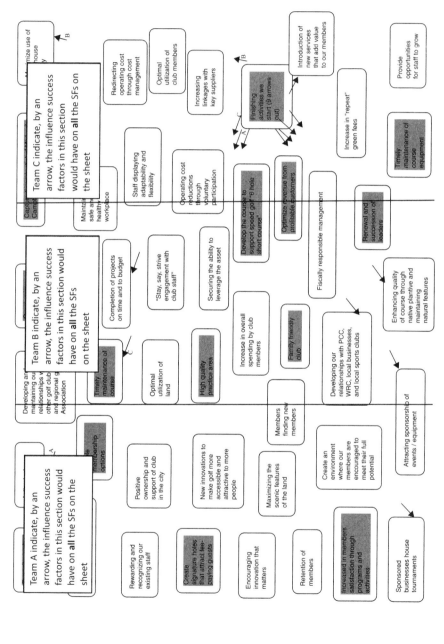

EXHIBIT 11.1 Mapping the Relationships

4. The attendees reviewed the wording of the success factors and some changes were made to the fanfold page. A secretary updated this success factor sheet while the committee members practiced the mapping of success factors of an airline, a useful training tool I have developed. These success factors are set out in Exhibit 7.8.
5. The committee members were then broken up into three teams and given one third of the fanfold page to map the relationships. (See Exhibit 11.1.)
6. The number of arrows out from each success factor were counted and the higher scoring success factors were identified.
7. At a subsequent meeting, three committee members, with a good aptitude for this exercise, were selected to reconsider the influence the top success factors had on the entire success factors on the sheet.
8. The arrows-of-influence exercise resulted in the following critical success factors being identified (number of impacts indicated in brackets):
   - Capture the potential of the XXX connection (13).
   - Family friendly club (12).
   - Growth in revenue from alternative sources (11).
   - Develop the course to support speed golf six-hole short courses (10).
   - Timely maintenance of course equipment (9).
   - Finish activities we start (9).
   - Increase in members' satisfaction through programs and activities (9).
   - Renewal and succession of leaders (8).
   - Optimize revenue from profitable members (8).
9. To ensure the critical success factors were balanced, they were mapped against the organization's balanced-scorecard perspectives. (See Exhibit 11.2.)

The performance measures were brainstormed in each of these critical success factors. These were recorded in an Excel spreadsheet (see Exhibit 11.3).

Lessons Gained

The exercise gave a better understanding of what should be focused on. However, in a club that is run by volunteer leaders, who are often active in other institutions, momentum is quickly lost. The most beneficial gain was derived from the knowledge of the critical success factors rather than from the resultant measures, which were never embedded. This process would be more beneficial with clubs who employ more than 15 paid staff.

EXHIBIT 11.2   Recording the Influence a Success Has on All Other Success Factors the Performance Measures Using a Spreadsheet

CSFs and the Number of Arrows of Influence	Satisfaction of Members and Visitors	Satisfaction of Paid and Voluntary Staff	Finance	Internal Processes	Learning and Growth of Paid and Voluntary Staff	Environment and Community
Capture the potential of the xxxx xxxx connection – 13			✓			✓
Family friendly club – 12	✓	✓	✓		✓	
Growth in revenue from alternative sources – 11			✓	✓		
Develop the course to support speed golf "6-hole short courses" – 10	✓		✓			✓
Timely maintenance of course equipment – 9	✓			✓		✓
Finish activities we start – 9	✓	✓	✓	✓	✓	✓
Increase in members satisfaction through programs and activities – 9	✓		✓	✓		✓
Renewal and succession of leaders – 8	✓			✓	✓	
Optimize revenue from profitable members – 8			✓			

Note: This showed that there was a relatively good balance with the critical success factors, as all perspectives were impacted at least twice.

Balanced-Scorecard Perspectives

MS   Satisfaction of members and visitors
SS   Satisfaction of paid and voluntary staff
F   Finance
IP   Internal Processes
LG   Learning and growth of paid and voluntary staff
EC   Environment and community

Performance Measure

KRI = financial or non financial, measured monthly
PI = non financial, measured weekly, every two weeks, monthly, quarterly
RI = financial or non financial, measured weekly, monthly, quarterly
KPI = non financial, measured daily, weekly, significant impact

| Name of Performance measure | Details about performance measure | | | | | | | Person who will monitor measure | | | | | | |
	Type of PM (KRI, PI, RI, KPI)	Person	BSC perspectives	Time zone (Past, Current, Future)	Frequency of measurement (24/7, daily, weekly, monthly)	Suggested target	Linkage to CSFs (CSFs used in brainstorming exercise)	KD	TC	Etc.	Etc.	Etc.	Etc.	Etc.
Number of press releases in pipeline to promote xxxxxx xxxxx connection	PI		EC	F	Monthly	>1	Capture the potential of the xxxx xxxxxx connection							
Number of initiatives planned to capitalize on xxxxxx xxxxx connection in next 1 to 3 months and 4 to 6 months	PI		EC	F	Monthly	>1	Capture the potential of the xxxx xxxxxx connection							
Date of opening of the first 6-hole competition at Titahi Bay	RI		MS, EC	P	Monthly	One event by 12/31/XX	Develop the course to support speed golf "6 hole short courses"							
Number of initiatives planned to capitalize on 6-hole speed golf in next 1 to 3 months and 4 to 6 months	RI		MS, EC , LG	F			Develop the course to support speed golf "6 hole short courses"							
Number of family friendly initiatives planned in next 3 months	PI		MS, EC , LG, SS	F	Monthly	>2	Family friendly Club							
Number of family friendly events held in last 3 months	RI		MS, EC,	P	Monthly	>2	Family friendly Club							
Etc.														

EXHIBIT 11.3   Recording the Performance Measures Using a Spreadsheet

Note: It is important to record the measures showing which critical success factors they relate to, the frequency of measurement (daily, weekly, monthly), and the relevant balanced-scorecard perspective(s) the measure impacts.

Surf Life Saving (Non Profit Membership Organization)

The beaches around the world are often manned by non profit organizations that undertake rescues, train children about water safety, offer sporting activities for their members, and patrol dangerous surf breaks in the summer months.

Summary of Tasks Undertaken

1. Sponsored by a national sports body that wanted to pilot the winning KPI methodology. A two-day workshop was arranged based on the workshop set out in Chapter 7.
2. Staff were requested to attend the workshop from around the country, including many experienced staff who were knowledgeable about the organization's success factors. Over half attending were volunteers.
3. Although representatives from the national sports body attended the full two-day session, the CEO from Surf Life Saving did not attend any sessions, despite the fact that a strong recommendation was made to the CEO to attend the first session of day 1 and the last session of day 2.
4. The attendees were presented with the winning KPIs methodology through a series of presentations and workshops.
5. The venue was a conference facility, and throughout the two days, the breaks and lunches were held at a local café, which ensured a break from the intensive workshops.
6. Attendees first agreed on the wording of the balanced-scorecard perspectives. As stated in Step Four in Chapter 9, this agreement was reached quickly with the knowledge that they, at some later date, could be amended to better suit the organization.
7. The names chosen reflected that the organization was made up of district offices of mainly full-time paid staff who assisted the largely volunteer surf clubs, which were based in premises on the main beaches in their area. The prospective names chosen were:
   - Financial results.
   - Satisfaction of district offices and clubs.
   - Learning and growing full-time staff members.
   - Internal processes.
   - Staff and member satisfaction.
   - Community and environment.
8. In this workshop, we used whiteboards to show the "arrows of influence" between the success factors. It worked well, even though each team had to prepare their whiteboard by writing out all the success

factors as shown in Exhibit 11.1. Time was saved by three team members writing on the whiteboard at the same time.

9. The attendees were, then, broken up into four teams of between four to five attendees with the two national body representatives split across two of the teams.

10. As shown in Exhibit 11.1, the arrows of influence, going toward another success factor were counted and a number placed in that success factor box. The success factors with the greatest sphere of influence—the success factors with more arrows of influence—were identified and called the critical success factors.

11. Due to the differences between the head office, branches, and Surf Life Saving Clubs, three sets of critical success factors were developed, although there was only a change in wording with one critical success factor (see Exhibit 11.4).

12. To ensure the critical success factors were balanced they were mapped against the organization's balanced-scorecard perspectives (see Exhibit 11.2).

EXHIBIT 11.4 Allowing Differences between Critical Success Factor Wording to Make Them More Meaningful

Organization Critical Success Factors	District Critical Success Factors	Club Critical Success Factors
Talent recruitment, retention, and succession planning (avoiding burnout)	Talent recruitment, retention, and succession planning (avoiding burnout)	Talent recruitment, retention, and succession planning (avoiding burnout)
Maintaining the positive brand (enhancing Surf Life Savings brand)	Maintaining the positive brand (enhancing SLS brand)	Maintaining the positive brand (enhancing SLS brand)
Meeting district and Club Inc. expectations in full on time (focus on top 20 clubs/2 districts)	Meeting Club Inc. expectations in full on time (focus on top 20 clubs)	Meeting members and stakeholders inc. expectations in full on time (focus on top 20 clubs/2 districts)
Diversification and growth of income streams	Diversification and growth of income streams	Diversification and growth of income streams
Meeting sponsors expectations in full on time	Meeting sponsors expectations in full on time	Meeting sponsors expectations in full on time

13. The performance measures were brainstormed in each of these critical success factors. These were recorded in an Excel spreadsheet (see Exhibit 11.3).
14. The critical success factors were ratified at a board meeting, thus permanently locking them into the organization.

Lessons Gained from Exercise

Head-office teams after the workshop commenced drafted their team scorecards; however, as weeks passed, a number of things happened:

- The CEO, who had never bought into the process, was still very distant to the process.
- The key sponsor was headhunted to another organization.
- Daily firefighting diverted the energy elsewhere, and the project lost momentum.

The exercise gave a better understanding of what should be focused on. However, the lack of adherence to the foundation stones outlined in Chapter 8 was the main reason for the project's lack of progress. (See Exhibit 11.5.)

EXHIBIT 11.5   Recording the Adherence to the Foundation Stones

Recommended Foundation Stones	Action
1. Partnership with the staff, unions, third parties	The lack of buying in by the CEO meant this foundation stone was never in place.
2. Transfer of power to the front line	Never occurred.
3. Measure and report only what matters	Never occurred.
4. KPIs are sourced the critical success factors	Only attendees to the workshop were made aware of this, so this foundation stone was not embedded.
5. Abandon processes that do not deliver	There were many activities that could have been culled that would have freed up time for this project.
6. Understand human behavior	This aspect was not given enough discussion time in the two-day workshop.
7. Organization-wide understanding of winning KPIs definition	Only attendees at the workshop were made aware of this, so this foundation stone was not embedded.

Government Department

A government department involved in community projects to integrate the feeling of togetherness in the country's population had, for some time, realized the importance of performance management and had embarked on a balanced-scorecard approach.

After making little progress, it requested assistance from me to help them embed KPIs in their organization using the winning KPI methodology.

Summary of Tasks Undertaken

1. Right from the start the CEO was right behind the project. The project leader had excellent communications skills and was well connected to the CEO.
2. A two-day workshop was arranged around the workshop discussed in Chapter 7 with the aim, not only to find the critical success factors, but also to show the team leaders how to brainstorm appropriate performance measures from the critical success factors.
3. All departmental staff members were requested to attend, with all the senior management team present. The venue was a local hotel, which ensured far greater commitment from the attendees.
4. The CEO attended the first and the last session and later admitted to regretting that he had not attended the whole two days.
5. Attendees agreed on the wording of the balanced-scorecard perspectives, which were the same as in the KPI book. The project later went back to using only four perspectives, which may turn out to be a regrettable step. (See Exhibit 11.6.)
6. The attendees in the workshop carried out the arrows-of-influence exercise as mentioned in the preceding case studies. The result was seven critical success factors. (See Exhibit 11.7.)
7. The performance measures were brain-stormed in each of these critical success factors. These were recorded in an Excel spreadsheet. (See Exhibit 11.3.)

EXHIBIT 11.6   How the Four Perspectives Evolved

Original Agreed-to Perspectives	Perspectives Used Later On
Customer	Stakeholders/customers
Financial	Resource management
Internal process	Operational excellence
Employee satisfaction	
Learning and growth	Learning and development
Environment/community	

EXHIBIT 11.7   A Government Department's Critical Success Factor

Organization Critical Success Factors

Effective community outreach and engagement.
>   Note: Effective means sufficient volume, dynamic, geared toward changing
>   aspirations of the community.
>   Outreach to be cross-sectional, that is, socioeconomic status (e.g., income, age,
>   race, new comers to the country).

Public confidence and trust in grass root leaders and in [organization name].
>   Note: Grass root leaders as the community leaders who are trained by the
>   department before they undertake their responsibilities.

Effective grass root leaders/volunteers/staff.
Enhanced partnership with groups and organizations with common interests.
An environment that encourages innovation and creativity.
Service excellence in every aspects of our interactions with residents and grass root
leaders.
A workplace that offers fulfillment, work-life balance, and job satisfaction.

Lessons Gained from Exercise

Teams now have their own scorecards and performance measures and the
accompanying critical success factors are driving performance.

The exercise gave a better understanding of what should be focused
on. However, the lack of adherence to the foundation stones outlined
in Chapter 8 was the main reason for the project's lack of progress (see
Exhibit 11.8).

Professional Accounting Body

A professional accounting body, whose CEO had been exposed to the
winning KPI methodology, held a two-day workshop in its head office,
attended by all members of the senior management team. The attendees
were given some prereading (see my KPI article, available on www.davidpar
menter.com).

Summary of Tasks Undertaken

The agenda and processes were the same in the workshop as for the government department featured earlier in this chapter.

Lessons Gained from Exercise

The professional body is still awaiting a team leader to fully implement the
project. The recruitment process has been delayed because of workload,
and the CEO moving on.

EXHIBIT 11.8   Recording the Adherence to the Foundation Stones

Recommended Foundation Stones	Action
1. Partnership with the staff, unions, third parties	While the organization has very good communication channels, it had not invited any community leaders it worked with to the workshop.
2. Transfer of power to the front line	This delegated authority had already been established.
3. Measure and report only what matters	There was a tendency to report everything. The lesson that less is better than more was not practiced.
4. KPIs are sourced from the critical success factors	Only attendees at the workshop were made aware of this, so this foundation stone was not embedded.
5. Abandon processes that do not deliver	There were many activities that could have been culled that would have freed up time for this project.
6. Understand human behavior	This aspect was not given enough discussion time in the two-day workshop.
7. Organization-wide understanding of winning KPIs definition	Only attendees at the workshop were made aware of this, so this foundation stone was not embedded.

The timing of the workshop was not right. The manager for the project should have been identified and should have attended the two-day workshop. The attendees understood the seven foundations stones and responded particularly well to Peter Drucker's abandonment foundation stone. The attendees did not take the vital step of removing the procedures and processes they had identified to abandon and, therefore, they were too tied up in the existing workflow to implement the project swiftly.

CHAPTER 12

Selling Change

M any initiatives fail, not because they were not needed or meaningful, but because the hearts and minds of the senior management team, managers, and staff had not been engaged adequately.

Selling by Emotional Drivers

Nothing was ever sold by logic! Sales are made through the use of emotional drivers (e.g., remember your last car purchase?). Many initiatives fail because we attempt to change the culture by selling using logic and issuing commands. It does not work. This project needs a public relations (PR) machine behind it. No presentation, e-mail, memo, or paper should go out unless it has been vetted by your PR expert. All your presentations should be road tested in front of the PR expert. Your PR strategy should include selling to staff, budget holders, senior management team, and the board.

I believe about two weeks of PR support would be all that is required over the life of the KPI implementation. I assure you that you will not regret this advice.

Therefore, we need to radically alter the way we pitch a sale to the senior management team and the board. We have to focus on the emotional drivers that matter to them.

Let us look at how a used car salesperson sells cars using emotional drivers.

Selling by Emotional Drivers: How a Car Sale Is Made

Three customers during the same day arrive to look at the car of the week that has been featured in the local newspaper. The first person

(Continued)

(*Continued*)

is a young information technology guru, generation Y, with the latest designer gear, baggy trousers part way down exposing a designer label on his shorts. The salesperson slowly walks up, assessing the emotional drivers of this potential buyer, looking for clues, such as clothing, the car he arrived in, and so on. The opening line could be, "I hope you have a clean license, because I will not let you out in this beast if you don't. This car has 180 BHP, a twin turbo, and corners like it is on railway tracks." SOLD.

The second person could be me, with my gray hair. The salesperson might say, "This car is five-star rated for safety, eight air bags, enough power to get you out of trouble, unbelievable braking when you have to avoid the idiots on the road, and tires that will never fail you." SOLD.

The third person is wearing designer clothing and is impeccably well groomed. He is addressed with "This car has won many awards for its design. Sit in the driver's seat and see the quality of the finish. Everything is in the right place. I assure you that every time you drive this car you will feel like a million dollars!" SOLD.

Selling the Move to Winning KPIs

We need to radically alter the way we pitch the sale of implementing winning KPIs to the senior management team and the board. We have to focus on the emotional drivers that matter to the senior management team. Start by asking these questions:

- Do we know which of our success factors are critical?
- Does the lack of alignment of daily activities to strategy concern you?
- Are you overwhelmed by too many performance measures?
- Do you enjoy sifting through information overload in your precious family time?
- Are you missing goals by taking your eye off your critical success factors?

Then, as part of the sale process, point out to the senior management team that:

- The previous performance measures have not changed anything.
- The focus on the right measures would mean the chief executive officer and senior management team would be more effective in less time, saving many long evenings/weekends of work.

- The right KPIs will link daily staff activities to the strategic objectives as they have never been linked before.
- This KPI project would start to transform the reporting into a decision-based tool with a greater focus on daily, weekly, and monthly reporting that is interesting, concise, and prompt.
- The investment of time and money in the current performance measurement system is not generating enough value (estimate on the high side—costs motivate the senior management team).

The project team needs to focus on the marketing of this new concept, budget holders will need to understand how this process is going to help them manage their business, and staff will need to understand that it is a positive experience enhancing their working life.

Many initiatives fail at this hurdle because we attempt to change the culture by selling using logic, writing reports, and issuing commands via e-mail. It does not work. This project needs a PR machine behind it. No presentation, e-mail, memo, or paper should go out unless it has been vetted by your PR expert. All your presentations should be road-tested in front of the PR expert. Your PR strategy should include selling to staff, budget holders, senior- management team, and the board.

If you were gifted at PR, you would most likely have chosen a different career. We have other gifts. If managed correctly, you will need only four to seven days of PR consultancy time. Avoid getting the PR expert caught up in lengthy meetings or writing original copy. This expert's role is to rework the output from the KPI team, working behind the scenes, often responding to e-mailed attachments once he or she has received an adequate debrief and visited the organization. This step should not be underestimated. I recommend you listen to my webcasts on www.davidparmenter.com.

CHAPTER 13

Common Critical Success Factors and Their Likely Measures for Government and Non Profit Agencies

Although organizations need to go through the processes suggested in this book, I am always asked to give examples of key performance indicators that might work in government and non profit agencies. Table 13.1 shows some *key result indicators* (KRIs), *result indicators* (RIs), *performance indicators* (PIs), and some *key performance indicators* (KPIs) that will work.

TABLE 13.1 Some KRIs, RIs, PIs, and KPIs That Work

Common CSF	KRI	RI	PI	Possible KPI
Stay, say, strive engagement with staff.	Staff satisfaction (if monitored at least three to four times a year).	Turnover of experienced staff who have been with the organization for more than three years (reported monthly).	Number of staff innovations implemented, by team (reported weekly). Staff who have been ill for over two weeks who do not have a back-to-work program (reported weekly to manager and general manager).	1. Staff who have handed in their notice today. Staff in key positions would be notified directly to the chief executive officer (CEO), other staff would be reported to the relevant general manager or senior manager. (The CEO has the opportunity to try to persuade the staff member to stay.) 2. Number of initiatives implemented after the staff-satisfaction survey (monitored weekly after survey for up to three months). 3. Teams not represented in the in-house courses to be held in the next two weeks (reported daily to CEO). 4. Accidents and breaches of safety (reported to CEO immediately). 5. New staff who have not attended an induction program within two weeks of joining (reported weekly to CEO). 6. Number of CEO recognitions in past week/past two weeks. 7. Number of CEO recognitions planned for next week/next two weeks.

Recruiting the right people all the time.	Number of staff who have left within 3 months, 6 months, and 12 months of joining organization, by division (reported quarterly).	Number of managers trained in recruiting practices (reported monthly).	1. Recruitments in progress when last interview was over two weeks ago. 2. Date of confirmed testing of candidates' capabilities (reported weekly).	1. Key position job offers that are over 48 hours old and have not yet been accepted by the chosen candidate (reported daily to CEO/general manager). 2. List of shortlisted candidates when next round of interviews has yet to be organized (reported daily).
Grow leaders who thoroughly understand the work, live the philosophy, and teach it to others.	Number of key positions with at least two protégés, by division (reported quarterly).	Number of high-performing staff, by division (reported monthly). Number of promotions for high-performing staff planned in the next three months (reported monthly).	1. Number of planned recognitions in next week/next two weeks (maintained weekly by each manager). 2. Number of planned celebrations in next week/next two weeks (maintained weekly by each manager). 3. List of high-performing staff who have been in same position for over two years (quarterly list). 4. Date of next executive course to be attended by senior management team members (monthly update).	1. Number of CEO recognitions in past week/past two weeks. 2. Number of CEO recognitions planned for next week/next two weeks.

(continued)

TABLE 13.1 (*Continued*)

Common CSF	KRI	RI	PI	Possible KPI
Grow leaders who thoroughly understand the work, live the philosophy, and teach it to others. (*continued*)	Number of managers who have attended leadership training (quarterly by manager level).	Number of managers who are scoring over XX on their leadership from the 360 feedback surveys (by manager level).	1. Date of next leadership program and the list of suggested attendees by division (reported weekly to CEO). 2. Date of next 360 feedbacks for level-1 and level-2 managers (reported monthly).	Number of vacant leadership places on in-house course (reported daily to CEO in the last three weeks before the course's scheduled date).
	Staff satisfaction with empowerment and fulfillment (assumes a survey is three to four times a year).		Date of next survey (reported monthly).	Number of initiatives implemented after the staff-satisfaction survey (monitored weekly after survey for up to three months).
	1. Percentage of level-1 and level-2 managers who have mentors (reported quarterly). 2. Percentage of high-performing staff who have a mentor. (reported quarterly).		1. Number of high-performing staff who do not have a mentor (reported weekly to general managers). 2. List of level-3 managers who do not have mentors, (reported weekly to general managers). Note: These measures would only need to be operational for a short time on a weekly basis.	List of level-1 and level-2 managers who do not have mentors, reported weekly to the CEO. This measure would only need to be operational for a short time on a weekly basis.

Innovation is a daily activity (finding better ways to do the things we do every day).	Innovations implemented over past 18 months by division.	1. Innovations that are running behind (weekly update). 2. Number of patents. 3. Date of prototype completion. 4. Date of next pilot test.	1. Number of innovations implemented last month by team (reported monthly to the CEO). 2. Date of next innovation training sessions (monthly). 3. Number of managers who have been through the innovation course (monthly). 4. Date of next innovation to our key services (monthly).	Number of innovations planned for implementation in the next 30 days, 60 days, and 90 days (reported weekly to CEO).
Abandonment: Willingness to abandon initiatives, opportunities that are not working or unlikely to succeed.	Number of abandonments over past 18 months by division (reported monthly).	Time saved each month through abandonments by team (reported monthly featuring the top-quartile performing teams in this area).	1. List of abandonments in last month by team (reported monthly). 2. Number of committees/task forces disbanded this month. 3. Number of monthly reports terminated. 4. Date of planned replacement of service that has now become outdated (monthly).	Number of abandonments to be actioned in the next 30 days, 60 days, and 90 days (reported weekly to CEO).
Making the right decisions by consensus with ready contingency plans.	Major implementations in past 18 months showing degree of success (exceeded expectations, met expectations, did not meet expectations, abandoned).	Major projects awaiting consensus sign-off (reported weekly to CEO).	1. Managers with the most success with implementations over past three years (reported quarterly to CEO).	1. Major projects awaiting decisions that are now running behind schedule (reported weekly to CEO). 2. Major projects in progress without contingency plans (reported weekly to CEO).

(continued)

TABLE 13.1 *(Continued)*

Common CSF	KRI	RI	PI	Possible KPI
Delivery in full on time, all the time, to our key customers.	Percentage of on-time in-full delivery to key customers, and to other customers. (Show past 18 months.)	Percentage of on-time in-full delivery to other customers (reported weekly to general managers).	1. Teams with the best on-time delivery record (reported weekly to general managers and all staff). 2. Calls on hold longer than XX seconds (reported immediately).	1. Emergency response time over a given duration (reported immediately to CEO). 2. Late deliveries/incomplete deliveries to key clients (reported 24/7 to CEO, general manager, and all staff). 3. Complaints from our key customers that have not been resolved within two hours (reported 24/7 to CEO and general managers).
Getting closer to our customers.	18-month trend showing take-up of new services.	Date of next outside-in activity to enhance senior-management-team understanding (e.g., CEO working undercover in customer interface frontline positions).	1. Number of initiatives implemented to improve key customer satisfaction (reported monthly). 2. List of key customers where time since last order is > X weeks (reported weekly to sales team and general managers). 3. Date of next major customer focus group (reported quarterly). 4. Date of next initiative to attract targeted noncustomers (reported quarterly).	1. Date of next visit to major customers by customer name (reported weekly to CEO and general managers). 2. Late deliveries/incomplete deliveries to our key customers (reported 24/7 to CEO, general manager, and all staff). 3. Key customer complaints not resolved within two hours (reported to CEO immediately).

We finish what we start.	Status of all major projects reported monthly.	Number of projects finished in the month.	1. Number of overdue reports/documents (reported weekly to senior management team). 2. Number of projects that are managed/staffed by contractors or consultants (reported monthly).	1. List of late projects, by manager (reported weekly to senior management team). 2. List of projects that are at risk of non completion (project is unassigned, manager has left, no progress has been made in past three months, etc.).
A bias for action.	New initiatives completed. Show past 18 months.	New initiatives that will be fully operational in the next three months by department.	1. Number of recognized mistakes highlighted last month (if the number is too low, you have an unhealthy environment). 2. Number of bureaucratic processes abandoned in the month.	1. Number of prototypes/pilots commenced in month by division. 2. Date of next new service initiative.
Breeding success.	List of key successes in the past 18 months.	New initiatives that will be fully operational in the next three months by department.	1. Number of positive press releases issued in the past 30 days/60 days (reported monthly). 2. Number of papers/radio stations who have used press release (reported monthly, by major press release).	1. Number of recognitions made last week by CEO and each member of senior management team. 2. Number of CEO recognitions planned for next week/next two weeks.

CHAPTER 14

Reporting Performance Measures

G overnment and non profit agencies, like their counterparts in the private sector, do not understand enough about the science of reporting. In addition, too many reports have been prepared monthly, which is far too late for prompt action.

We may need to report differently, depending on the reporting frequency and the intended audience. A sound knowledge about the thinking of Stephen Few is a prerequisite.

The Work of Stephen Few in Data Visualization

Data visualization is an area that is growing in importance. No longer is it appropriate for well-meaning accountants and managers to dream up report formats based on what looks good to them. There is a science behind what makes data displays work. Stephen Few is the expert in this field, having written Amazon's top three bestselling books[1] on data visualization.

Few's contribution to report design is immense. His workshops, books, white papers, and articles[2] are a must-attend/read for all those involved in reporting performance to the board, senior management, staff, and the general public. All reporting of winning KPIs and other performance measures is vastly improved if one adopts his design techniques in all forms of balanced-scorecard reporting.

He has come up with a very useful list of common pitfalls in dashboard design:

- Exceeding the boundaries of a single screen (where managers have to click on to a line to get important data).
- Supplying inadequate context for the data (he is critical of speed dials).
- Displaying excessive detail or precision (not rounding enough).
- Expressing measures indirectly (by setting the starting scale away from zero).

- Choosing inappropriate display of media (choosing the wrong graph, especially a pie chart; using a graph when a table would be better; etc.).
- Introducing meaningless variety (where there are myriad graphs on the one page, just because we can do them).
- Using poorly designed display media (lack of thought about the real issues).
- Encoding quantitative data inaccurately (by setting the starting scale away from zero).
- Arranging the data poorly (by not linking issues together, as well as not positioning graphs together that are covering the same issue).
- Failing to highlight what's important (all data competing for attention).
- Cluttering the screen with useless decoration (too many rocket scientist's toys).

Each one of these is explained in detail in Few's white paper on the topic, "Common pitfalls in dashboard design," available on www.perceptualedge .com/articles.

Reporting the KPIs to Management and Staff

Reporting measures to management needs to be timely. As mentioned previously, KPIs need to be reported 24/7, daily, or at the outside, weekly; other performance measures can be reported less frequently (monthly and quarterly).

Intraday/Daily Reporting on KPIs

The main KPIs are reported 24/7 or daily. Exhibit 14.1 shows how KPIs should be reported on the intranet. Some form of table giving the contact details, the problem, and some history of performance is required.

Another benefit of providing senior management with daily/weekly information on the key performance areas is that the month end becomes less important. One government department had a 9 o'clock news report every morning covering the processing of benefit payments by each office around the country. Regional management teams were able to compare their service levels and achievements on a daily basis.

In other words, if organizations report their KPIs on a 24/7 or daily basis, management knows intuitively whether the organization is having a good or bad month.

Late planes over 2 hours

Time:

Flight number	Statistics of last stop			Region manager's name	Current time at location	Contact details			No. of late planes over 1 hour		
	Arrival late by	Departure late by	Time added			Work	Mobile	Home	Last 30 days	30-day ave. of last 3 months	30-day ave. of last 6 months
BA1243	1:40	2:33	0:53	Pat Carruthers	18:45	xxxx	xxxxx	xxxx	4	3	4
BA1598	1:45	2:30	0:45	xxxxxxx	19:45	xxxx	xxxxx	xxxx	2	3	4
BA12	1:45	2:27	0:42	xxxxxxx	20:45	xxxx	xxxxx	xxxx	4	4	5
BA146	1:45	2:24	0:39	xxxxxxx	21:45	xxxx	xxxxx	xxxx	5	4	4
BA177	1:45	2:21	0:36	xxxxxxx	22:45	xxxx	xxxxx	xxxx	2	4	3
BA256	1:45	2:18	0:33	xxxxxxx	23:45	xxxx	xxxxx	xxxx	5	4	5
BA1249	1:45	2:15	0:30	xxxxxxx	0:45	xxxx	xxxxx	xxxx	2	4	3
Total	7 planes										

EXHIBIT 14.1 Example of a Daily KPI Report

Source: David Parmenter, *Key Performance Indicators: Developing, Implementing, and Using Winning KPIs*, 2nd ed. Copyright © 2010 by David Parmenter. Reprinted with permission of John Wiley & Sons, Inc.

Intraday Exception Reporting to the Chief Executive Officer on Human Resources Issues

It is vital that key exceptions are reported to the chief executive officer (CEO) immediately when they occur. The following issues need to be addressed in government and non profit agencies:

- All job offers that are more than two days outstanding should be personally followed up by the CEO. The lack of acceptance means, in most cases, that the candidate is still looking around. A personal call from the CEO saying "I understand Pat, that we have offered you the position of xxxxx. I believe you will succeed well in this role and I will take a personal interest in your career. What do we need to do to get your acceptance today?" could help convince the candidate to accept. This ten-minute call could well save over $20,000 of recruiting costs, a return of $120,000 per hour!
- In-house courses that are poorly attended because staff think that daily firefighting is more important. They remain caught in the "catch-22" cycle. The CEO should phone the managers who have not registered staff in the workshop and make it clear that this is not good enough.
- Staff members who have been ill for over two weeks who do not have an activated back-to-work program. The CEO should phone the HR advisers responsible for setting up the back-to-work program, visits to the company doctor, and partial return planning (e.g., a couple of half days in the office each week).
- Most CEOs treat accidents or safety breaches seriously, and, therefore, these are reported. An acceptable report-back time would be within an hour of the incident.
- The CEO should follow up on all crucial staff who have handed in their notice. This would be reported within an hour of resignation. A personal phone call may be enough to turn around the situation or, at the very least, open the door for a return in the future.

The aforementioned issues are set out in a suggested intranet-based report (see Exhibit 14.2). This report should be accessible by HR staff, the senior management team, and the CEO.

Weekly

Some KPIs need only be reported weekly. Set out in Exhibit 14.3 is an example of how they could be presented. Note that while all the KPIs will be graphed over time, at least 15 months, only the three KPIs showing a decline would be graphed. The other two KPI graphs would be maintained and used when necessary.

Position offers still outstanding

	Candidate	Contact details		Manager	Details
		home	mobile		Days outstanding
Financial Controller	Pat Curruthers	xxxxx	xxxx	Jim Curruthers	3
Store manager, Brisbane	Sam Smith	xxxxx	xxxx	Sally Smith	3

Teams not represented in the in-house courses due in next two weeks

	Manager	work	mobile	Expected numbers from team	Average training days of team in last 6 months
Team xx	Jim Curruthers	xxxxx	xxxx	3	1
Team yy	Sally Smith	xxxxx	xxxx	4	1.25
Team zz	Jim Curruthers	xxxxx	xxxx	2	1.5
Team ss	Ted Smith	xxxxx	xxxx	1	0

Staff who have been ill for over two weeks

	Manager	work	mobile	Length of illness	Back-to-work program started
xxxx xxx	Jim Curruthers	xxxxx	xxxx	10	Yes
xxx xxxxxxxxxxx	Sally Smith	xxxxx	xxxx	15	Yes
xxxxx xxxxx	Ted Smith	xxxxx	xxxx	25	No

Accidents and breaches of safety

	Manager	work	mobile	Remedial action
A. N. Other in a car crash, unhurt but needs a week recovery time	Jim Curruthers	xxxxx	xxxx	Increase participation in advanced driving courses paid by company

Staff who have handed in their notice today

	Staff member	work	mobile	Length of service	Manager
xxxx xxx	Tom Bent	xxxxx	xxxx	<1	John Bull
xxx xxxxxxxxxxx	Sally Shell	xxxxx	xxxx	<1	John Bull
xxxxx xxxxx	Ted Snell	xxxxx	xxxx	15	Sarah Marshall

EXHIBIT 14.2 Example of a Daily HR Exception Report

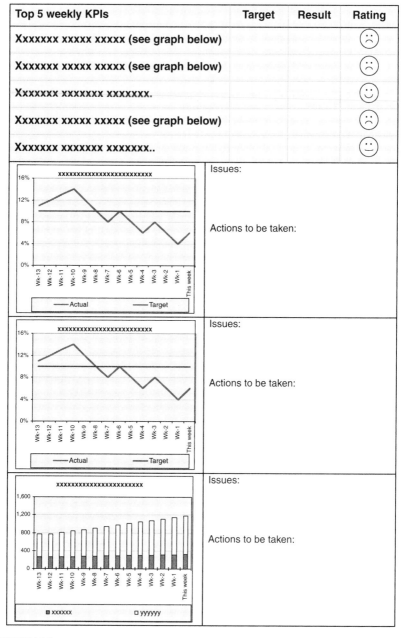

Top five KPIs
Weekly report xx xxxx 20xx

Top 5 weekly KPIs	Target	Result	Rating
Xxxxxxx xxxxx xxxxx (see graph below)			☹
Xxxxxxx xxxxx xxxxx (see graph below)			☹
Xxxxxxx xxxxxxx xxxxxxx.			☺
Xxxxxxx xxxxx xxxxx (see graph below)			☹
Xxxxxxx xxxxxxx xxxxxxx..			☺

EXHIBIT 14.3   Weekly KPI Report

Source: David Parmenter, *Key Performance Indicators: Developing, Implementing, and Using Winning KPIs,* 2nd ed. Copyright © 2010 by David Parmenter. Reprinted with permission of John Wiley & Sons, Inc.

Reporting Performance Measures to Management

Management will need some weekly reports covering *result indicators* and *performance indicators*. There thus will be a mix of financial and nonfinancial measures.

Weekly Human Resources Update to CEO

There are some HR issues that the CEO needs to focus on weekly. They are not as critical as the intraday or daily HR exceptions, and thus are not considered KPIs.

The following HR issues need to be addressed in government and non profit agencies:

- It is not uncommon for new staff to miss out on the planned induction program. This can have a negative impact on their performance over the short- to medium- term. The CEO should make it known that there is an expectation that staff will attend induction programs and that phone calls will be made to follow-up on exceptions.
- In-house courses to be held within the next two months should be highlighted weekly.
- Higher-than-average sick leave in a team may indicate a problem with leadership. The CEO should follow-up when next in the area.
- The CEO needs to keep a weekly focus on the recognitions planned for the next week or two weeks. Peters and Waterman[3] and Collins[4] have emphasized the importance of celebration as a communication tool and a way of inspiring staff to exceed normal performance benchmarks.

The suggested intranet-based report that should be accessible to the HR staff, senior management team, and CEO is shown in Exhibit 14.4.

Weekly/Monthly Updates to Management and CEO

There are endless ways these can be shown (see Exhibit 14.5), through icons, gauges, traffic lights, and so on. There are many reporting tools available that are more robust than a basic spreadsheet. It is highly likely that your organization has the license to use at least one such reporting tool.

Stephen Few has introduced a new concept that is well worth understanding—a combination of sparkline and bullet graphs (see Exhibit 14.6).

A sparkline graph looks like a line graph without the axes. Even with this truncated diagram you can still see the trend. The bullet graph shows

New staff who have not attended an induction program

	Start Date	Manager details			Staff turnover in last two years
		Name	Office	Mobile	
Alan Bevin	12/12/xx	Pat Curruthers	xxxxx	xxxx	30%
Carl Dodds	11/11/xx	Sam Smith	xxxxx	xxxx	40%

In-house training courses due in next two months

	Enrollments	Expected numbers	Date of course	Days left
First Aid	5	20	xxxxx	25
Supervisors Part 1	3	45	xxxxx	18
Leadership Paer 2	40	60	xxxxx	14
Presenting	6	20	xxxxx	15

Teams with above-average sick leave

	Days lost		
	This month	Days per employee	Avg. per month for last 3 months
Team xx	5	1.5	4
Team yy	8	2	7

CEO recognitions planned for next week

	Manager	Date
Project xx	Jim Curruthers	xxxxx
Finance team	Sally Smith	xxxxx
xxxxx xxxxx	Ted Smith	xxxxx

EXHIBIT 14.4   Example of the Weekly Human Resources Report

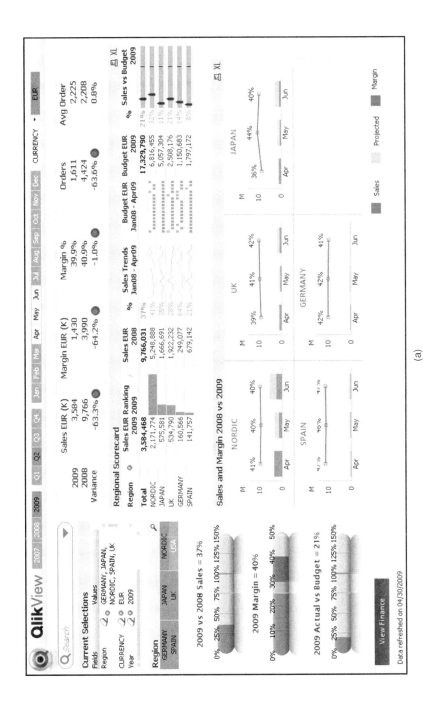

EXHIBIT 14.5   Examples of a Monthly Report to Management

Source: Inside Info; see www.insideinfo.com.au.

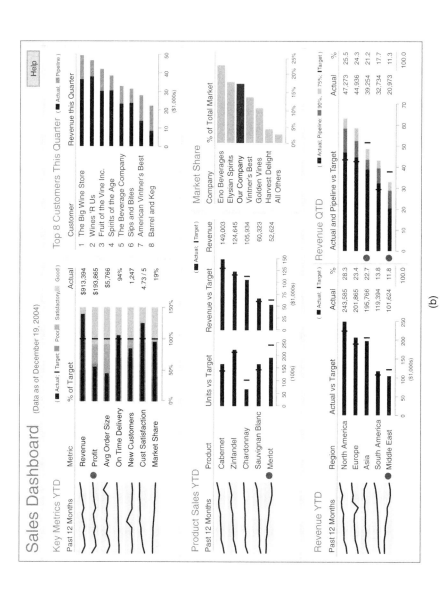

EXHIBIT 14.5 *(Continued)*

Source: Used with the permission of Stephen Few, www.perceptualedge.com.

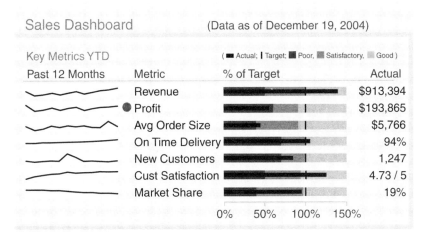

EXHIBIT 14.6 Combination of Sparklines and Bullet Graphs

Source: Stephen Few, www.perceptualedge.com.

different detail about current performance. The shades are good to poor performance, and the dark vertical line indicates the target.

Stephen Few is very cautious about the use of color. He points out that many readers will have some form of color blindness. In Exhibit 14.5, the only use of color would be red bullet points indicating the exceptions that need investigation and follow-up.

Reporting Performance Measures to Staff

It is a good idea to have some form of monthly icon report for staff. If this report happens to be left on a bus, it would not be damaging to the organization if it found its way to a competitor. Icon reports are ideal because they tell you what is good, what is adequate, and what needs to be improved without giving away core data. Exhibit 14.7 is an example of an icon staff report that covers the critical success factors and reminds staff about the strategies.

Reporting Performance Measures to the Board

Government and non profit agencies need to report to a board, a council, or an elected government official. To simplify, let's call the reporting body a board.

Progress Report to Staff - For our Operations Throughout September 20XX

Our mission	To provide energy at the right price at the right time
Our vision for next five years	To be the preferred energy provider in the xxx
Our strategies (what we are doing to achieve our vision)	1. Acquiring profitable customers 2. Increase cost efficiencies 3. Innovation through our people 4. Using best business practices

What we have to do well every day - our Critical Success Factors (CSFs)	Our performance measures in the CSFs		Actual	Target
Delivery in full on time to key customers (KC)	On time deliveries to key customers (KC)		98%	99%
	Goods rejected by KC due to quality defects		3%	4%
We are warriors against waste	Wastage reduction programs started in month		0	2
	Waste reduced from existing programs		9%	10%
We finish what we start	Number of late projects		5	15
	Number of project finishes in month by due date		9	10
We are a learning organization	Staff training hours this month		150	220
	Staff with mentors		35	80
We grow leaders	Leaders appointed from within last month		4	2
	Managers in leadership programs		9	10
Attracting new profitable customers	Orders from new customers		3	10
	Positive feedback from new customers		3	2
Innovation is a daily activity	Ideas adopted last month		9	20
	Ideas for implementation within 3 months		20	50
We are respected in the communities we work in	Community participation by employees in month		30	20
	New initiatives planned for community, next 3 months		3	2
Increase in repeat business from key customers (KC)	Order book from key customers		$320,000	$400,000
	Number of product developments in progress		3	2

Yellow (acceptable)
Red (poor)
Green (good)

EXHIBIT 14.7 Example of a Monthly Report to the Organization's Staff

Source: David Parmenter, *Winning CFOs: Implementing and Applying Better Practices*, Copyright © 2011 by David Parmenter. Reprinted with permission of John Wiley & Sons, Inc.

In most organizations that have boards, there is a major conflict of interest over what information is appropriate for the board to receive. Because the board's role is clearly one of governance and not of management, it is totally inappropriate to be providing the board with KPIs. As mentioned in Chapter 2, it is a myth that a balanced scorecard can report progress to both management and the board.

To me, KPIs are the very heart of management. Used properly, many of them are monitored 24/7 or at least weekly; they are certainly not measures to be reported monthly or bimonthly to the board.

We need indicators of overall performance that need only be reviewed on a monthly or bimonthly basis. These measures need to tell the story about whether the ocean liner is being steered in the right direction at the right speed, whether the customers and staff are happy, and whether we are acting in a responsible way by being environmentally friendly.

These measures are called key result indicators (KRIs). Typically a board would need to see between 6 and 12 graphs covering the critical success factors and all six balanced-scorecard perspectives. To help teams, I thought I would give some examples of good KRIs that you might want to use. These measures work particularly well in helping the board focus on strategic, rather that management, issues, and they will support management in their thrust to move board meetings away from the monthly cycle. These KRIs are best reported in a dashboard.

A dashboard should be a one-page display (see Exhibit 14.8) with the graphs, summary financials, and commentary all appearing on the page.

A good dashboard, with the KRIs going in the right direction, will give confidence to the board that management knows what it is doing and that the ocean liner is being steered in the right direction. Then, management can concentrate on what they do best, focusing on the horizon, checking for icebergs from the first-class lounge, instead of parking themselves on the bridge and getting in the way of the captain (who is trying to perform important day-to-day duties). Ten examples of KRI dashboard graphs for a board can be found in Exhibit 14.9.

There are some key points that need to be understood about the graphs in Exhibit 14.9, including:

- The rules of Stephen Few covered in this chapter need to be understood and applied.
- The guidelines in Task 2: Establish a Suite of Meaningful Graphs That Are Easy to Understand, from Step Ten in Chapter 9, should also be applied.
- As already mentioned you will need to maintain somewhere between 6 and 12 graphs. From experience, you will only need to report the six to nine measures most relevant to the board.

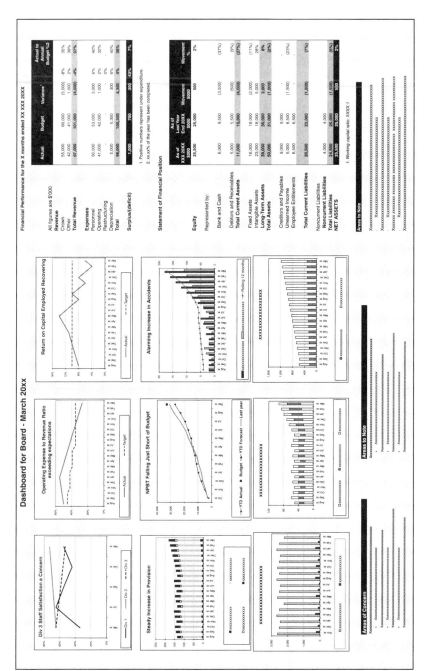

EXHIBIT 14.8 Board Dashboard on a Large (A3/U.S. Fanfold) Page

Source: David Parmenter, *Winning CFOs: Implementing and Applying Better Practices*, Copyright © 2011 by David Parmenter. Reprinted with permission of John Wiley & Sons, Inc.

Staff satisfaction:

No different or less important than customers. As one person said, happy staff make happy customers that make a happy bottom line. If you believe in this connection, run a survey now. A staff satisfaction survey need not cost the earth and should never cover all staff; instead it should be replaced by a rolling survey. See article "How You Can Seek Staff Opinion for Less than $6,000" on www.davidparmenter.com.

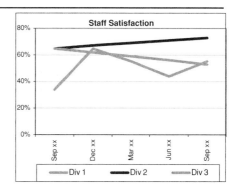

Expenses to revenue as a ratio:

The board should be interested in how effective the organization has been in utilizing technology and continuous improvement to ensure cost of operations is tracking well against revenue.

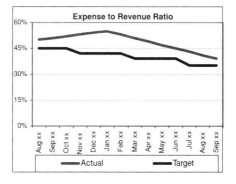

Customer satisfaction:

This needs to be measured at least every three months. By using statistical samples and focusing on your top 10 to 20 percent of customers (the ones who are generating most if not all of your bottom line), you can keep this process from being overly expensive. If you think once a year is adequate for customer satisfaction, stick to running a sports club as you are not safe in the public or private sector.

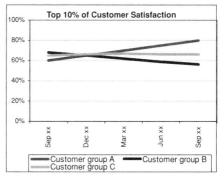

EXHIBIT 14.9   Key Result Indicators for a Board

Source: David Parmenter, *Winning CFOs: Implementing and Applying Better Practices,* Copyright © 2011 by David Parmenter. Reprinted with permission of John Wiley & Sons, Inc.

Value of new business:

All government and non profit agencies need to focus on the growth of their new services. It is important to monitor the pickup of this new business, especially among the top 10 to 20 percent of customers.

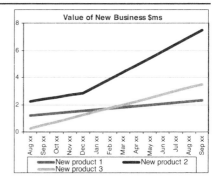

Net profit before tax (NPBT):

This graph, while designed for the private sector, can be modified to show how the agency's expenditure is tracking against its funding. This graph will include the most recent forecast, which should be updated on a quarterly basis.

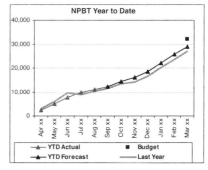

Health and Safety:

All boards are interested in this area, as the well-being of staff is a much higher priority these days.

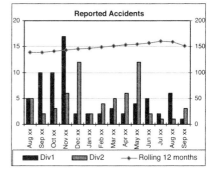

Return on Capital Employed:

The old stalwart of reporting in the private sector will apply to a small number of agencies who have capital. Most agencies will instead show more analysis on potential funding shortfalls.

EXHIBIT 14.9   (*Continued*)

Cash Flow:
This would be
   projected out
   at least six
   months forward.

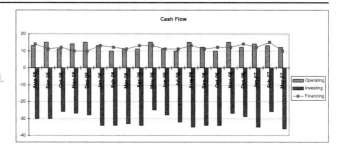

Capacity:
This monitors the capacity of key
   equipment. It would go
   forward at least 6 to 12 months.
   The board needs to be aware of
   capacity limitations, and such a
   graph will help focus it on new
   capital expenditure requirements.

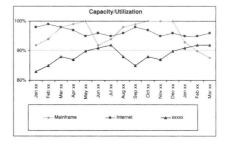

Operational Efficiency:
Some agencies, such as hospitals,
   will need to measure the
   operational efficiency of key
   units (e.g., operating theatres).

EXHIBIT 14.9   *(Continued)*

Reporting Team Performance Measures

Set out in Exhibits 14.10 and 14.11 are examples of the weekly and monthly
reporting a team would do to monitor its own performance. The examples
shown are in Excel, a useful template tool until a more robust and integrated
solution is found.

The weekly report tracks those measures too important to leave until
the end of the month.

Team reports should be communicated only to the team members until they are proud enough to report their performance to the rest of the
organization on the intranet.

EXHIBIT 14.10   Example of a Weekly Team-Progress Update

Weekly Progress Update

	Week-2	Week-1	Target (mth)
1. Proactive visits to managers	0	1	6
2. Number of staff recognitions made	0	0	6
3. Projects in progress	7	7	<8
4. Reports/documents still in draft mode	12	15	<5
5. Initiatives underway based on satisfaction survey	0	0	5 by 6/30/xx

Source: David Parmenter, *Winning CFOs: Implementing and Applying Better Practices,* Copyright © 2011 by David Parmenter. Reprinted with permission of John Wiley & Sons, Inc.

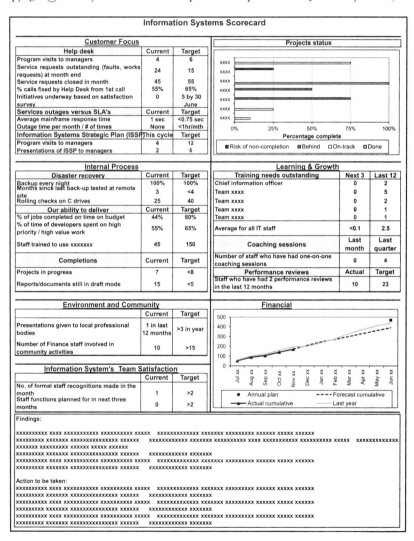

EXHIBIT 14.11   Example of an IS Monthly Team Balanced Scorecard

Source: David Parmenter, *Winning CFOs: Implementing and Applying Better Practices,* Copyright © 2011 by David Parmenter. Reprinted with permission of John Wiley & Sons, Inc.

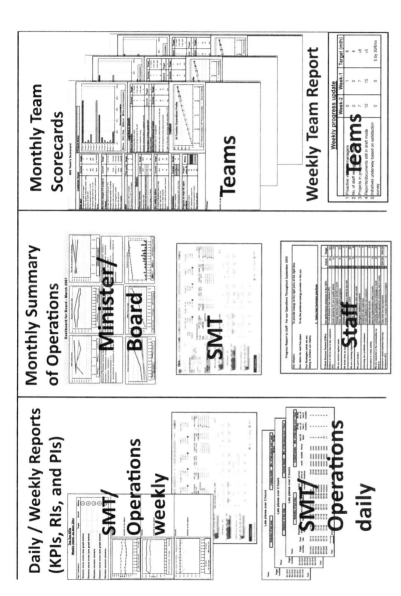

EXHIBIT 14.12 Performance Reporting Portfolio

Source: David Parmenter, *Winning CFOs: Implementing and Applying Better Practices,* Copyright © 2011 by David Parmenter. Reprinted with permission of John Wiley & Sons, Inc.

How the Reporting of Performance Measures Fits Together

Exhibit 14.12 shows how the reporting of performance measures should work in a private, public, or not for profit organization.

The important reports are the daily and weekly reports shown in the left-hand column. These are seen by the senior management team and the relevant operational staff. Some of these would be intranet-based, being updated 24/7 (e.g., late planes in the sky).

At month's end, summary information would be given to:

- The board, to help them understand the operations and general progress within the critical success factors.
- The staff, to give feedback on their efforts in progress with the critical success factors.
- The management, summarizing progress in the critical success factors, which will have been monitored in the daily and weekly reports, and other success factors that are monitored only monthly.

In the right-hand column of Exhibit 14.12, we show that teams will be monitoring performance through their scorecards. If a team is involved with a KPI, they would also be monitoring the KPI reporting shown in the left-hand column.

Notes

1. Stephen Few, *Information Dashboard Design: The Effective Communication of Data* (Sebastopol, CA: O'Reilly Media 2006); *Show Me the Numbers: Designing Tables and Graphs to Enlighten* (Burlington, CA: Analytics Press, 2004); *Now You See It: Simple Visualization Techniques for Quantitative Analysis* (Burlington, CA: Analytics Press, 2009).
2. Articles can be found at www.perceptualedge.com/articles.
3. Thomas J. Peters and Robert H. Waterman, *In Search of Excellence: Lessons from America's Best Run Companies* (New York: Harper & Row, 1982).
4. Jim Collins, *Good to Great: Why Some Companies Make the Leap and Others Don't* (New York: HarperBusiness, 2001).

Epilogue: Resources

Although it would be very gratifying to think that this book could provide you with everything you need to implement winning KPIs successfully, I can safely say, with years of experience behind me and a few grey hairs to add to the mix, this is not possible.

The following references, covering books, webcasts, and third parties, will also assist you in creating winning KPIs.

I would recommend that you:

- Access my book *Key Performance Indicators: Developing, Implementing, and Using Winning KPIs,* 2nd ed. (Hoboken, NJ: John Wiley & Sons, 2010), because I have not included all the details in this book so as to avoid repetition.
- Listen to my webcasts on KPIs, which have been recorded by various providers (see my webcast section on www.davidparmenter.com).
- Engage an in-house or external public relations expert to help sell the concept of working with your organization's critical success factors and winning KPIs.
- Deliver a PowerPoint presentation to the senior management team to get them to buy into your KPI/balanced-scorecard project.
- Subscribe to my latest thoughts (www.davidparmenter.com) to receive free access to templates.
- Link with an external expert who can contribute to brainstorming sessions designed to ascertain the critical success factors for your organization.
- Hold a focus group workshop (see Chapter 9) to brainstorm the future "new look" balanced-scorecard process:
  - Sell the need for change.
  - Build a case for change.
  - Design the new approach.
  - Ask for their advice and help.

Key Reference Books

To enable you to improve access to KPIs I have listed some books that will help you with this project. Read them and leave them in an accessible area as a reference guide and a required read for all new team members.

Paul R. Niven, *Balanced Scorecard: Step-by-Step for Government and Nonprofit Agencies* (Hoboken, NJ: John Wiley & Sons, 2008).

This book is a masterpiece and my personal copy has earmarked pages, which is a sure sign of how useful I think it is. I have highlighted the main places to visit in Table E.1.

Stephen Few, *Information Dashboard Design: The Effective Visual Communication of Data* (Sebastopol, CA: O'Reilly Media, 2006).

This book is a classic. It will help you make a major step forward in data visualization—the way you report information to management and staff. Everybody involved in the KPI project should have to read the book as prerequisite to joining the team. It should then be on the project team's bookshelf.

Robert S. Kaplan and David P. Norton, *The Balanced Scorecard: Translating Strategy into Action* (Cambridge, MA: Harvard Business Press, 1996).

This book is a masterpiece. It is the original book that catapulted the balanced-scorecard journey in the first place. Although I do not agree with all of the content in the book, it should be read by the KPI team so that they can draw their own conclusions. Chapter 12 and the Appendix should be reread many times. There are also some very useful illustrations throughout the book.

Key Reference Web Sites

Stacey Barr's www.staceybarr.com. As previously mentioned, Stacey Barr is one of the world experts on performance measures. She has developed a methodology to fill in the gap that the balanced scorecard and other methodologies have left. Visit her site and attend one of her webcasts—or even better, attend one of her workshops, which she delivers in a number of locations around the world.

Stephen Few's Perceptual Edge web site, www.perceptualedge.com. Few writers can really dominate a space, and Few stands head and shoulders above everybody in the data-visualization genre. His three books are masterpieces. His web site is full of excellent white papers and articles. I would recommend subscribing to his blog and accessing some of his white papers, such as:

- "Common Pitfalls of Dashboard Design"
- "Dashboard Design for Real-Time Situation Awareness"
- "With Dashboards, Formatting and Layout Definitely Matter"

TABLE E.1   Outline of Paul Niven's *Balanced Scorecard*

Chapter 1 Introduction to the Balanced Scorecard	A very useful chapter. I have identified some sections in particular for special attention.
▪ Strategy execution is everything	A must-read.
▪ The balanced scorecard as a communication tool: Strategy maps	A good overview. Make your own mind up about whether you consider strategy mapping a useful process.
▪ Creating objectives for the four perspectives of a strategy map	I like to use the words *success factors* rather than *objectives.*
Chapter 2 Adapting the Balanced Scorecard to Fit the Public and Nonprofit Sector	A very useful chapter. I have identified some sections in particular for special attention.
▪ Adapting the balanced scorecard	A good section on the importance of mission.
▪ Importance of cause and effect	It is important to understand the balanced-scorecard viewpoint, which is very well explained in this book. Although strategy maps may be a good communication tool, they can be dangerous if they are the source of measures.
▪ Benefits of using a balanced scorecard	A must-read section, it will help with your sale process.
Chapter 3 Before You Begin	I would encourage you to read this large chapter in its entirety.
Chapter 4 Training and Communication Planning for the Balanced Scorecard	Read this entire chapter.
Chapter 5 Mission, Values, and Vision	Simply the best summary written anywhere of this aspect of the balanced scorecard. Encourage everybody on the senior management team to read this chapter.
Chapter 6 Strategy: The Core of Every Balanced Scorecard	I would read Jack Welch's chapter on strategy in *Winning*[1] first before digesting this version.
Chapter 7 Strategy Maps	I have expressed my views in Chapters 2 and 7. Determine which approach you want to adopt and then implement.

(continued)

TABLE E.1   (*Continued*)

Chapter 8 Performance Measures, Targets, and Initiatives	This is where I digress from Niven's work. Understand the contrast between my Chapter 6 on KPIs and Niven's Chapter 8 and draw your own conclusions.
Chapter 9 Creating Alignment by Cascading the Balanced Scorecard	I think cascading measures down in the classical balanced scorecard method as explained here will not move you toward achieving your optimal goal. I would prefer you to follow the method in this book.
Chapter 10 Linking Resource Allocation to the Balanced Scorecard	Read my section on quarterly rolling planning in Appendix C first. Also, refer to Jeremy Hope's *Beyond Budgeting*.[2]
Chapter 11 Reporting Results	A very useful analysis of software selection. It should be read in conjunction with Stephen Few's books which are covered in more detail later in this section. Niven also points out the importance of well-structured meeting protocol. See www.actionmeetings.com. This is the best template for running meetings that I have come across.
Chapter 12 The City of Charlotte: A Balanced Scorecard Success Story	Useful for the project KPI project team

Few holds workshops around the world. Make sure you view his web site to find the workshop nearest to you. You will not regret attending one of his workshops.

Dean Spitzer has a web site that contains useful articles, presentations, extracts of Spitzer's book *Transforming Performance Measurement*, and transcripts of interviews with Spitzer. Visit www.deanspitzer.com/resources /performance-assessment-resources.html

David Parmenter's www.davidparmenter.com. On my web site, I have placed some complementary electronic resources that will be helpful to readers of this book and my *Key Performance Indicators* book. In addition to these free resources, there are other electronic materials available for a fee:

- All the templates from this book.
- All the templates from the *Key Performance Indicators* book.
- White papers on a variety of topics.

Notes

1. Jack Welch and Suzy Welch, *Winning* (New York: HarperBusiness, 2005).

2. Jeremy Hope and Robin Fraser, *Beyond Budgeting: How Managers Can Break Free from the Annual Performance Trap* (Cambridge, MA: Harvard Business Press, 2003).

Foundation Stones of
Performance-Related
Pay Schemes*

Performance-related pay is broken both within the private sector and government and non profit agencies. Companies give away billions of dollars each year in bonuses based on methodologies to which little thought has been applied. Who are the performance bonus experts? What qualifications do they possess to work in this important area other than prior experience in creating the mayhem we currently have?

When one looks at their skill base, you wonder how they attracted an audience in the first place. In the private sector, some of the foolishness is breathtaking. Which bright spark advised the hedge funds to pay a $1 billion bonus to one fund manager who created a paper gain that never turned into cash? These schemes were flawed from the start; "super profits" were being paid out, there was no allowance made for the cost of capital, and the bonus scheme was only "high–side" focused.

There are a number of foundation stones that need to be laid down and never undermined when designing performance-related pay schemes (schemes) that make sense and will move the organization in the right direction. The foundation stones relevant to government and non profit agencies include the following:

- Schemes need to be based on a relative measure rather than on a fixed annual performance contract.
- Any at-risk portion of salary should be separate from the scheme.

---

*This appendix is extracted with permission from David Parmenter, *The Leading-Edge Manager's Guide to Success: Strategies and Better Practices* (Hoboken, NJ: John Wiley & Sons, 2011).

- Schemes should be linked to a "balanced" performance.
- All schemes should be tested to minimize risk of being "gamed" by participants in the scheme.
- Schemes should not be linked to KPIs.
- Schemes need to be communicated to staff using public relations experts.
- Schemes should be tested on past results.

Base the Performance-Related Pay Schemes on a Relative Measure

Most bonuses fail at this first hurdle. Jeremy Hope and Robin Fraser,[1] pioneers of the Beyond Budgeting methodology, have pointed out the trap of an annual fixed performance contract. If you set a target in the future, you will never know if it was appropriate, given the particular conditions of that time. You often end up paying incentives to management when, in fact, their performance was substandard; for example, in the private sector, if rising sales did not keep up with the market growth rate.

Relative-performance targets measures involve comparing performance to the marketplace. Thus, the financial institutions that are making super profits out of this artificial lower-interest-rate environment would have a higher benchmark set retrospectively, when the actual impact is known. As Jeremy Hope says, "Not setting a target beforehand is not a problem as long as staff are given regular updates as to how they are progressing against the market." He argues that if you do not know how hard you have to work to get a maximum bonus, you will work as hard as you can.

At-Risk Portion of Salary Separate From the Scheme

Any at-risk portion of salary should be separate from the performance-related pay scheme. The at-risk portion of the salary should be paid when the expected profits figure has been met (see Exhibit A.1). Note that, as already mentioned, this target will be set as a relative measure, set retrospectively, when actual information is known.

When the relative target has been met or exceeded, the "at-risk" portion of the salary will be paid. The surplus over the relative measure will then create a bonus pool for a further payment, which will be calculated, taking into account the adjustments already discussed.

Linked to a Balanced Performance

Performance-related pay schemes should be linked to a "balanced" performance. The balanced scorecard has been used, I would argue, largely

EXHIBIT A.1   At-Risk Component of Salary

	Remuneration		
	Mgr 1	Mgr 2	Mgr 3
Base salary, paid monthly	48,000	64,000	80,000
At-risk salary (bonus is paid separately)	12,000	16,000	20,000
Salary package	60,000	80,000	100,000
Relative measure, set retrospectively	not met	met	exceeded
Percentage of at-risk salary paid	40%	100%	100%
At-risk salary paid	4,800	16,000	20,000
Share of bonus pool	nil	5,000	10,000
Total period-end payout	4,800	21,000	30,000

Source: David Parmenter, *The Leading-Edge Manager's Guide to Success: Strategies and Better Practices,* Copyright © 2011 by David Parmenter. Reprinted with permission of John Wiley & Sons, Inc.

unsuccessfully, as a vehicle to pay performance. Schemes using a balanced scorecard are often flawed on a number of counts:

- The balanced scorecard is often based on only four perspectives, ignoring the important environment-and-community and staff-satisfaction perspectives.
- The measures chosen are open to debate and manipulation.
- There is seldom a link to progress in the organization's critical success factors.
- Weighting of measures leads to crazy performance agreements such as those shown in Exhibit A.2.

An alternative would be to link the scheme to the organization's critical success factors. See an example of an airline scheme in Exhibit A.3.

In this exhibit, all teams have the same weighting for the financial results. Some readers will feel this is too low. However, when you do more research on the balanced-scorecard philosophy, you will understand that the greatest impact to the bottom line, over the medium- and long-term, will be in the organization's critical success factors.

The operational team, at one of the airports, has a major focus on timely arrival and departure of planes. You could argue that this should have a higher weighting such as 30 percent. However, this team does impact in many other critical success factors. This team clearly impacts the timely maintenance of planes by making them available on time; and impacts the satisfaction of our first class, business class, and gold-card- holder passengers. The public's perception of the airline is reflected in the interaction between staff and the public, along with press releases and the timeliness of planes.

EXHIBIT A.2   Performance-Related Pay System That Will Never Work

Category	Perspective Weighting	Measure	Measure Weighting
Financial	60%	EVA	25%
		Unit profit	20%
		Market growth	15%
Customer	20%	Customer satisfaction survey	10%
		Dealer satisfaction survey	10%
Internal	10%	Above-average rank on process industry quality survey	5%
		Decrease in dealer delivery cycle time	5%
Innovation and learning	10%	Suggestions/employee	5%
		Satisfaction survey	5%

Source: International Institute of Management. David Parmenter, *The Leading-Edge Manager's Guide to Success: Strategies and Better Practices,* Copyright © 2011 by David Parmenter. Reprinted with permission of John Wiley & Sons, Inc.

EXHIBIT A.3   How the Performance-Related Bonus Would Differ across Teams (Airline)

	Operational Team	Public Relations Team	Maintenance Team	Accountants
Financial performance	30%	30%	30%	30%
In the critical success factors (CSFs)				
Timely departure and arrival of planes	20%	0%	20%	0%
Timely maintenance of planes	10%	0%	30%	0%
Retention of key customers	10%	0%	0%	0%
Positive public perception of organization—being a preferred airline	10%	30%	0%	0%
"Stay, say, strive engagement with staff"	10%	20%	10%	20%
Encouraging innovation that matters	10%	20%	10%	20%
Accurate, timely information that helps decisions	0%	0%	0%	30%

Source: David Parmenter, *The Leading-Edge Manager's Guide to Success: Strategies and Better Practices,* Copyright © 2011 by David Parmenter. Reprinted with permission of John Wiley & Sons, Inc.

Ensuring that staff members are listened to, are engaged successfully, and are constantly striving to do things better (Toyota's *Kaizen*) is reflected in the weighting of "stay, say, strive" as well as the catchphrase "encouraging innovation that matters." There is no weighting for "accurate timely information that helps decisions" because other teams such as IT and accounting are more responsible for this, and I want to avoid using precise percentages such as 7 percent or 8 percent, which tend to give the impression that a performance pay scheme can be a science-based instrument.

The public relations team has a major focus of creating positive spin to the public and to the staff. All great leaders focus in this area (a superb example is Sir Richard Branson). The weights for the public relations team will focus them in the key areas that they can contribute. By having innovation success stories and recognition celebrations, staff will want to focus in this important area of constant improvement, which has been demonstrated so well in Toyota over the past couple of decades.

The maintenance and accounting teams' focus is narrower. The accounting team has a higher weighting on "stay, say, strive" and "encouraging innovation that matters" to help focus their attention in these important areas. This will improve performance and benefit all the other teams they impact through their work.

Test to Minimize Risk of Being a Gaming Risk

All performance-related pay schemes should be tested to minimize the risk of being manipulated by participants in the scheme. All schemes in which money is at stake will be gamed. Staff will find ways to maximize the payment by undertaking actions that may well be not in the general interest of the organization.

The testing of the new scheme should include:

- Rework bonuses paid to about five individuals over the last five years to see what would have been paid under the new scheme and compare against actual payments made.
- Consult with a cross-section of staff and ask them "What actions would you undertake if this scheme was in place?"
- Discuss effective best-practices with your peers in other companies. This will help move the industry standard while avoiding the implementation of a scheme that failed elsewhere.

Schemes Should Not Be Linked to KPIs

Performance-related pay schemes should not be linked to KPIs. KPIs are a special performance tool, and it is imperative that these are not included in any performance related pay discussions. KPIs, as defined in Chapter 6, are too important to be gamed by individuals and teams to maximize bonuses. Performance with KPIs should be considered a "ticket to the game."

Although KPIs will show how teams are performing 24/7, daily, or weekly, it is essential to leave the KPIs uncorrupted by performance-related pay. As mentioned in Chapter 2, it is a myth that by tying KPIs to pay, you will increase performance. You will merely increase the manipulation of these important measures, undermining them so much that they will become *Key Political Indicators*.

Certainly most teams will have some useful monthly summary measures, results indicators that will help teams track performance and be the basis of any performance bonus scheme.

Schemes Need to Be Communicated

Performance-related pay schemes need to be communicated to staff using public relations experts. All changes to such a fundamental issue as performance-related pay need to be sold through the emotional drivers of the audience. With a PRPS, this will require different presentations when selling the change to the board, chief executive officer (CEO), senior management team, and management and staff. They all have different emotional drivers.

As mentioned in Chapter 12, many change initiatives fail at this hurdle because we attempt to change the culture by using logic, writing reports, and issuing commands via e-mail. It does not work. The new performance-related pay scheme needs a public relations machine behind it. No presentation, e-mail, memo, or paper should go out unless it has been vetted by your public relations expert. In addition you should "road-test" the delivery of all of your presentations in front of the public relations expert before going live.

Schemes Should Be Tested on Past Results

Performance-related pay schemes should be road-tested on the last complete business cycle. When you think you have a good scheme, test it on the results of the last full business cycle, the period between the last two recessions. View the extent of the bonus on the net profit.

You need to appraise the scheme with the same care and attention you would apply to a major fixed asset investment. See Exhibit A.4 for an example of this test.

EXHIBIT A.4   Testing the Performance Scheme on Past Results

	1991	1992	1993	1994	1995	1996	1997	1998	1999	2000
Annual profits (excluding all cost of capital charges)	180	180	200	220	240	350	370	390	410	450
Removal of accounting entries (30)			(30)							
Super profits clawback	(30)	(30)	(30)	(32)	(35)	(10)	(20)	(30)	(30)	(40)
Full cost of capital						(60)	(62)	(62)	(75)	(75)
Adjusted profit	150	150	140	188	205	280	288	298	305	335
Expected profit based on market share	140	140	140	160	180	260	260	265	280	290
Profits subject to bonus pool	10	10	0	28	25	20	28	33	25	45
Percentage of pool (33% in this example)	**3**	**3**	**0**	**9**	**8**	**7**	**9**	**11**	**8**	**15**

	2001	2002	2003	2004	2005	2006	2007	2008	2009	Last Year
Annual profits (excluding all cost of capital charges)	(240)	(60)	290	310	460	520	210	(700)	(125)	200
Removal of accounting entries			(20)		(40)	(40)				
Super profits clawback					(20)	(30)				
Full cost of capital	(25)	(28)	(40)	(42)	(65)	(70)	(30)	(30)	(35)	(30)
Adjusted profit	(265)	(88)	230	268	335	380	180	(730)	(160)	170
Expected profit based on market share			190	220	300	350	170			160
Profits subject to bonus pool			40	48	35	30	10			10
Percentage of pool (33% in this example)	**0**	**0**	**13**	**16**	**12**	**10**	**3**	**0**	**0**	**3**

Source: David Parmenter, *The Leading-Edge Manager's Guide to Success: Strategies and Better Practices*, Copyright © 2011 by David Parmenter. Reprinted with permission of John Wiley & Sons, Inc.

Additional Foundation Stones for Schemes in the Private Sector

For readers who are in the private sector, I have included some more foundations stones that are relevant to any performance-related pay scheme you are planning to put in place in your organization. The foundation stones include the following:

- Super-profits should be excluded from schemes.
- Schemes should be free of profit-enhancing adjustments.
- Take into account the full cost of capital.
- Avoid any linkage to the share price.
- Avoid having deferral provisions.

Super-Profits Should Be Excluded from Schemes

Super-profits should be excluded from performance-related pay schemes and retained to cover possible losses in the future. In boom times, annual performance targets give away too much. These "super-profit" years come around infrequently and are needed to finance the dark times of a recession. Yet, what do our remuneration experts advise? A package that includes a substantial slice of these super-profits, but no sharing in any downside. This downside, of course, is borne solely by the shareholder.

There needs to be recognition that the boom times have little or no correlation to the impact of the teams. The organization was always going to achieve this, no matter who was working for the firm. As Exhibit A.5 shows, if an organization is to survive, super-profits need to be retained. If you look at Toyota's great years, the percentage paid to the executives was a fraction of that paid to the executives in Detroit who had underperformed.

This removal of super-profits has a number of benefits:

- It avoids the need to have a deferral scheme for all unrealized gains.
- It is defensible and understandable to employees.
- It can be calculated by reference to the market conditions relevant in the year. When the market has become substantially larger, with all the main players reporting a great year, we can attribute a certain amount of period-end performance as super-profits.

When designing a bonus scheme, the super-profits component should be removed from the calculation rather than used to create a windfall gain to all those in the bonus scheme. If a bonus pool has maxed out, then staff

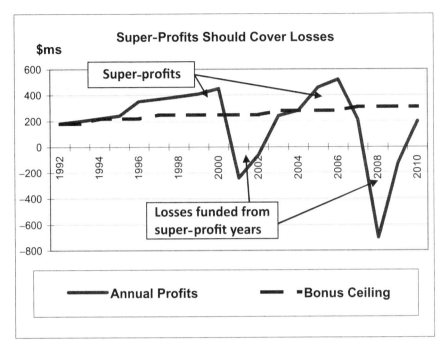

EXHIBIT A.5   Retention of Super-Profits

Source: David Parmenter, *The Leading-Edge Manager's Guide to Success: Strategies and Better Practices,* Copyright © 2011 by David Parmenter. Reprinted with permission of John Wiley & Sons, Inc.

would rather play golf than go hard to win further business. The ceiling in Exhibit A.5 is shown for illustration purposes only.

Schemes Should Be Free of Profit-Enhancing Adjustments

The profits included in a performance-related pay schemes should be free of all major profit-enhancing accounting adjustments. Many banks will be making super-profits from 2010 to 2012, because part of the massive write-downs will be written back as some monies from defaulted loans will be recovered. This will happen as sure as night will follow day.

I recall a classic case where a merciless CEO was rewarded solely on a successful sale of a publicly owned bank. The loan book was written down to such an extent that the purchasing bank merely had to realize these write-downs to report a profit in the first year that equated to nearly the full purchase price.

This activity is no different from many other white-collar crimes that occur under the eyes of poorly performing directors.

One simple step you can take is to eliminate all short-term accounting adjustments from the bonus scheme profit pool of senior management and the CEO. These eliminations should include:

- Recovery of written-off debt.
- Profit on sale of assets.

The aim is to avoid the situation in which management, in a bad year, will take a massive hit to their loan book so they can feather their nest on the recovery. This type of activity will be alive and well around the globe.

These adjustments do not have to be made for the loan team's bonus calculations. We still want them motivated to turn around nonperforming loans.

Schemes Should Take into Account the Full Cost of Capital

The full cost of capital should be taken into account when calculating any bonus pool. A trader can only trade in the vast sums involved because they have a bank's balance sheet behind them. If this was not so, then the traders could operate at home and be among the many solo traders who also play in the market. These individuals cannot hope to make as much profit because of the much smaller positions their personal cash resources facilitate.

Each department in a bank should have a cost of capital, which takes into account the full risks involved. In today's unusual environment, the cost of capital should be based on a five-year average cost of debt and a risk weighting associated with the risks involved. With the losses that bank shareholders have had to endure, the cost of capital should be set, in some "higher-risk departments, as high as 25 percent.

With the current artificially low base rate, a fool could run a bank and make a huge bottom line. All banks should, thus, be adjusting their cost of capital based on a five-year average in their schemes.

Avoid Any Linkage to the Share Price

Performance-related pay schemes should avoid any linkage to share price movements. No bonus should be pegged to the stock market price, as the stock market price does not reflect the contribution that staff, management, and the CEO have made.

Only a fool believes that the current share price reflects the long-term value of an organization. Just because a buyer, who is often ill-informed, wants to pay a certain sum for a "packet" of shares does not mean the total shareholding is worth that amount.

Providing share options is also giving away too much of shareholders' wealth in a frequently disguised way.

Avoid Having Deferral Provisions

The treatment of unrealized gains is a sensitive issue. Some performance-related pay schemes include deferral provisions in an attempt to avoid paying out bonuses on unrealized gains that may never materialize. The question is whether the cure is worse than the ailment. The issue comes back to the impact on human behavior.

Already, some banks have adopted a deferral mechanism on unrealized gains. While this is understandable, we need to consider the likely impacts:

- We do not want all stocks sold and bought back the next day as a window dressing exercise that dealers/brokers could easily arrange with each other.
- The financial sector is driven by individuals who worship the monetary unit, rather than any other benevolent force. This is a fact of life. A deferral system will be very difficult for them to accept.
- Staff will worry about their share of the pool when they leave. The last situation you want is a team leaving so they can cash up their deferral pool while it is doing well.
- Dead wood may wish to hang around for future pay days out of their deferred bonus scheme.

Although some sectors may be able to successfully establish a deferral scheme, the financial sector is fraught with difficulties. It would be better to focus on the other foundation stones, especially the removal of super-profits.

Note

1. Jeremy Hope and Robin Fraser, *Beyond Budgeting: How Managers Can Break Free from the Annual Performance Trap* (Cambridge, MA: Harvard Business Press, 2003).

Effective Recruiting—Getting the Right People on the Bus

Effective recruiting is so fundamental to performance measurement that I would argue that, if you have the wrong staff on board, you will never get your measures to work.

To assist you with recruiting, I have set out some guidelines on recruiting that were originally covered in *The Leading-Edge Manager's Guide to Success*.[1]

Understand That Time Spent Recruiting Is the Most Valuable Time

Far too often, when managers look at their calendars, they throw up their hands when they realize that they have another recruitment interview to do. It is the last thing they need at this point in time. In reality, recruitment should be seen as the most important thing a manager does, for the following reasons:

- Recruiting properly is like putting a fence on the top of a cliff: it prevents casualties. As Jim Collins, of *Good to Great* fame, says, "You need to get the right people on the bus."[2]
- You can recruit for technical skills and improve skill levels through training, but you cannot change a person's values. If an individual's values are different from those of the organization, you will always have conflict.
- Better recruits will lead to more internal promotion, saving cost and maintaining institutional knowledge.

To have an excellent team, it is essential to start with the best resources available. There are still too many staff selections made via an antiquated interview process accompanied by some cursory reference checking. The result is a high failure rate among new staff. Greater effort needs to be put into the selection process through the adoption of recruiting techniques as discussed in the following paragraphs.

Management guru Peter Drucker once observed General Motors' top committee spending hours discussing the promotion of one employee. On questioning management about the effectiveness of this task, the reply from the chief executive officer (CEO) was, "If we didn't spend four hours placing a man and placing him right, we'd spend four hundred hours cleaning up after our mistake."[3]

Look for Values and Fit Before Focusing on Expertise

The common recruiting failure is placing too much focus on expertise and experience. When you come across a seemingly perfect fit with a candidate, it is all too easy to brush aside all the warning signals and rush into signing him or her up.

In every workshop, I ask the same question: "Who here has made a recruiting decision they have lived to regret?" Every manager raises a hand. As I get older and hopefully wiser, I have realized the importance of an organization understanding its ideology.

Jim Collins points out the importance of organizations having a core ideology which he defines very succinctly in the following formula:

Core ideology = Core values + Purpose

There are some very good examples of built-to-last organizations' core values and purpose statements (mission statements) in Chapter 3 of his book *Built to Last* that are well worth reading.[4]

Recruiting will never be successful if the recruiters do not have a shared understanding of the organization's core values and purpose. The primary objective should always be to weed out candidates who do not share the same values and who will not buy into the organization's purpose. This takes time, using processes far wider-ranging than the recruitment interview. This chapter explains some of these techniques.

It is far wiser to recruit someone slightly less experienced who is clearly able and has a close fit with the organization's core ideology than to recruit an expert who will not fit from day one.

Cathay Pacific Recruitment

Cathay Pacific constantly seeks frontline staff who were born with the desire to serve. They firmly believe that you cannot train staff to be as good at serving as Cathay Pacific requires—they have to be born that way.

In order to sort the wheat from the chaff, all frontline applicants have to go through an arduous recruitment process consisting of five interviews that often takes about three months to complete. Only applicants who are committed to joining Cathay Pacific get over this hurdle. During these interviews, management is looking for the traits they need. The investment in the front end pays off with a quicker and more successful training process and one of the lowest staff turnover ratios in the industry.

Peter Drucker's Five-Step Process

Management guru Peter Drucker, on observing great leaders, noted that there were five steps to achieving sound recruitment:

Step 1. Understand the job so you have a better chance of getting a good fit.

Step 2. Consider three to five people to maximize your chances of getting the best fit.

Step 3. Study candidates' performance records to find their strengths so that you can ascertain whether these strengths are right for the job.

Step 4. Talk to each shortlisted candidate's previous bosses and colleagues to ascertain the candidate's values, team playing ability, and whether they would employ them again if they had the opportunity.

Step 5. Once the employment decision is made, make sure the appointee understands the assignment.

14 Great Questions to Help Get Select "A" Players

Dr. Richard Ford has written a first-rate article[5] on how to hire the "A" players. From his piece, and the sage advice from Peter Drucker and Jack Welch, I have developed some interview questions for you.

1. Why did you leave your last job? Or, why do you want to leave your current job? Jack Welch says that you should ask the five whys. To each answer, then ask "Why was that?"

2. What have been your greatest achievements?

3. What has been the hardest decision you have had to make that may have made you unpopular?

4. What are your strengths?

5. What sorts of things irritate and frustrate you most, and how do you express your emotions when frustrated?

6. When was the last time you celebrated team members?

7. What will reference checks disclose about your personal operating style and how will your style affect other team members?

8. How do you plan to grow and stretch yourself in the next five years?

9. What would your colleagues say is the best thing about you?

10. Give examples of your commitment to innovation.

11. Tell me about a time when you had to persuade people to do something they did not want to do. What happened?

12. When I call your last boss, how will he/she rate your performance on a scale from 0 to 10 and why?

13. How would your colleagues describe your team-playing abilities?

14. Why do you want this job?

Use Simulation Exercises and Psychometric Testing

The basic interview is a totally flawed tool; we tend to warm to those candidates who are similar to us. Clever interviewees realize this and will mimic back to us what we want to hear. Situation, role-playing, or scenario exercises are thus becoming more common in the recruitment process in an effort to find out more about the candidates. It is now quite common for report writing and presentation exercises to be set during the final interview round for the more senior roles.

Many organizations that I have surveyed report that they have been burned by recruiting staff who describe themselves as competent on an important skill, only to find out otherwise.

Psychometric tests, especially arithmetical and verbal reasoning, are found to be valuable predictors and should be used when sorting out which of the short-listed candidates you will offer the position. High scores in these two tests are seen as a sign of a superior performer.

One organization comments on the usefulness of a simple scenario exercise as part of the recruitment process, with the candidate and the panel playing their respective roles. The organization says that it is not hard to set up and yet helps significantly in the selection process. Candidates are given only 15 minutes notice of what the scenario is going to be.

Involve Your Team in the Final Selection Process

Far too often, a new staff member is soon found to be deficient in a key process in which he or she previously claimed a level of expertise. This is a shame, as a brief exposure to the team during a casual walk could have exposed a potentially serious weakness in the candidate's skill base.

It is a good idea to have staff on the team somehow involved in the final selection from the short list of candidates. This does not need to be too complex. A meeting over an afternoon cup of coffee can give the staff a chance to subtly quiz candidates on their expert knowledge.

One technology team had interviewed an impressive candidate and duly short-listed him. In the second round of interviews, they found that the candidate, though a certified Microsoft engineer, had little or no practical experience. This was discovered by the team members when they gave him a tour of the team's IT equipment.

Ask Your Top Employees for Referrals

One high-performance manager asks the team members if they know a person who would fit in the team before she advertises a position. Often this has proved successful in saving hours of sifting through complete unknowns.

Google is famous for its referral recruiting. Staff members who recommend candidates are rewarded for their efforts if and when their contact becomes an employee.

Reference Checks: The Do's and Don'ts

A reference check has little or no validity unless it is from a person known to your organization or a past employer whom you can rely on. Random references, especially if they are received attached to the resume, should be treated with caution. At the very least, you should phone more than one of their previous managers and ask questions about the candidate. Here are some suggestions:

- How would you rate XXX's performance on a 0 to 10 scale and why?
- What were XXX's team-playing abilities like?
- How would you describe the values that XXX displayed during his/her employment with your organization?
- Would you employ XXX again if you had the opportunity?

One important government organization asks all short-listed candidates to find a referee who is known by the organization. If none can be found, they ignore this step. Naturally, this would count against an applicant. They believe a reference is worth getting only if it can be relied upon. They know that a referee, who is aware of the organization, how it operates, and its values and staff would be unlikely to give an unreliable reference if he wants to retain his relationship with the organization.

A common mistake is not to verify the candidate's academic record. Papers are littered with cases where high-profile appointments have been made and the appointee has falsely claimed to have a PhD or master's degree, only to be discovered when poor performance brings these claims into question. Always check against the university records for all senior appointments.

Notes

1. This appendix is extracted with permission from David Parmenter, *The Leading-Edge Manager's Guide to Success: Strategies and Better Practices* (Hoboken, NJ: John Wiley & Sons, 2011).
2. Jim Collins, *Good to Great: Why Some Companies Make the Leap . . . and Others Don't* (New York: HarperBusiness, 2001).
3. Peter Drucker, *Adventures of a Bystander* (New York: John Wiley & Sons, 1997).
4. Jim Collins and Jerry Porras, *Built to Last: Successful Habits of Visionary Companies* (New York: HarperBusiness, 1994).
5. Richard G. Ford, "How to Hire the 'A' Players," *Finance & Management* ICAEW, March 2010.

The Public Sector Can Abandon the Flawed Budget Process

Companies, governments, and non profit agencies worldwide are beginning to recognize that existing budget processes are not satisfactory. These methods have been used since the Romans planned and estimated their invasion of Northern Europe! The budget process is often seen as a hindrance rather than a benefit to management. Jack Welch summed it up perfectly when he said, "the budgeting process at most companies has to be the most ineffective practice in management. It sucks the energy, time, fun, and big dreams out of an organization. It brings out the most unproductive behaviors in an organization, from sandbagging to settling for mediocrity."[1] Chapter 12 in his book *Winning*, "Budgeting—Reinventing the Ritual," is a must-read.

Example: Road Construction Company

A managing director of a large New Zealand road construction company told me the group has never had an annual planning process. He said if the group could predict when it was going to be sunny and when it was going to rain, annual planning would be useful.

The business encompasses concrete, transport (local and rural), fuel distribution, and road construction. The group has around 1,000 staff and a constant profit growth—the envy of many larger organizations.

The company monitors key ratios and has different league tables depending on the size of operations so the group companies

(continued)

(Continued)

can compare performance with each other. The ratios they monitor include:

- Return per kilometer (km): revenue and cost per km.
- Margin per liter.
- Delivery cost per liter.
- Concrete cost per cubic meter.
- Cubic meter delivered by pay hour.

Providing operations are working within set ranges, operational managers have a high degree of autonomy. If, for example, a unit hits a problem constructing a road, the head office would be informed immediately through the daily ratios and would investigate how the manager intended to get around the issue.

In a month of favorable weather, management would expect all companies to be performing well, the ratios in the zone, and results tracking well against prior months' activity. Any exceptions would be spotted in the daily and weekly ratios and performance measures and investigated.

In my discussions with government and non profit agencies, a common misunderstanding has emerged: "this beyond budgeting model cannot work with an annual appropriation process." The good news is that it can in a modified format.

The Flawed Budgeting Process

The budgeting process that underpins the annual appropriation process is flawed. It takes too long, is not focused on performance drivers, is not linked to strategic outcomes or critical success factors, leads to dysfunctional behavior, builds silos, and is a major barrier to success. The answer is to throw the budget process out, not the annual appropriation or planning processes. The solution is to separate out the three processes: the appropriation, the annual plan, and the monthly budgets.

A sporting game analogy can be used to explain the folly of the monthly budget, as shown in Exhibit C.1. Imagine a game where you have to get a ball from your end of the field to the other end and place it between two goalposts. The annual plan is the establishment of goalposts at the end of the field, and the budget process is where we set 12 ten-yard lines to report

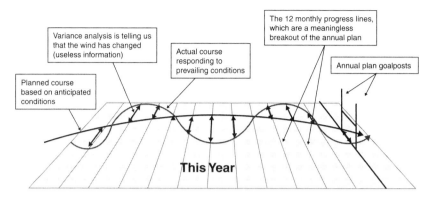

EXHIBIT C.1   Annual Plan Analogy

Source: David Parmenter, *Winning CFOs: Implementing and Applying Better Practices,* Copyright © 2011 by David Parmenter. Reprinted with permission of John Wiley & Sons, Inc.

against. The problem is that the ten-yard lines (the monthly budgets) are wrong as soon as the year has started. When there is stoppage, the coach comes on the field and asks, "Why are you here? You should have been over there." The reply from the team is "The ball is over here." This progress reporting is as useful as our monthly variance commentary.

Instead of setting monthly budgets during the annual planning process, we should report against more recent targets derived from the quarterly rolling forecasting process. This process will give us the monthly targets for the next quarter. It is important to realize that monthly targets are not set any farther out than the upcoming quarter. In fact, information for quarters 3, 4, 5, and 6 are set only quarterly. In other words, we patiently wait until the relevant quarter is upon us before putting the budget holders' estimates in the reporting tool.

Quarterly Rolling Forecasting and Planning

The quarterly forecasting process is where management sets out the required expenditure for the next 18 months. Many government and non profit agencies are currently using views of the future to control expenditure, but in reality, they are flawed from the start because they often feature some or all of the following:

■ Due to poor tools and expediency, the forecaster (budget holder or analyst in finance) uses the budgets of the remaining months as a guide to future expenditure.

- Forecasts do not involve the budget holders because it would be a nightmare to consolidate budget holder forecasts in a bottom-up process in the existing Excel models.
- Forecasts are done monthly, an unnecessary time frame creating much number noise.
- Forecasts only go up to year's end, even though the new financial year may be starting in four weeks time.

Each quarter, before approving these estimates, management sees the bigger picture six quarters out. As you can see from Exhibit C.2, the annual plan falls short of one of these quarterly forecasts. All subsequent forecasts, while firming up the short-term numbers for the next three months, also update the annual forecast. Budget holders are encouraged to spend half the time getting the detail of the next three months right because these will become targets, on agreement, and they should spend the rest of their time on the next five quarters. Each quarter forecast is never a cold start because they have reviewed the forthcoming quarter a number of times. Provided you have appropriate forecasting software, management can do their forecasts very quickly; one airline even does this in three days. The overall time spent in the four forecasts, one of which is a two-week annual plan, is no more, and in many cases much less, than the typical annual planning and budget process.

December: We forecast out to year's end, with monthly numbers, the remaining in quarterly breaks. Budget holders obtain approval to spend January to March numbers subject to their forecast still going through the goal posts. The budget holders, at the same time, forecast next year's numbers for the first time. Budget holders are aware of the baseline, and the first cut

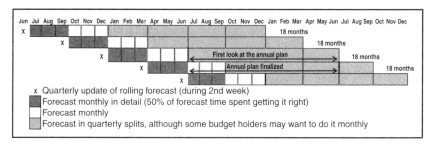

EXHIBIT C.2 How the Rolling Forecast Works for a Government and Non Profit Agency (June to year-end)

Source: David Parmenter, *Winning CFOs: Implementing and Applying Better Practices,* Copyright © 2011 by David Parmenter. Reprinted with permission of John Wiley & Sons, Inc.

is reasonably close. This is a precursor to the annual plan. This forecast is stored in the planning tool.

March: We reforecast to year's end and the first quarter of next year with monthly numbers, the remaining period in quarterly breaks. Budget holders obtain approval to spend April to June numbers. The budget holders, at the same time, revisit the forecast of next year's numbers and fine-tune them for the annual plan. Budget holders know that they will not be getting an annual lump-sum funding for their annual plan. The number they supply is for guidance only.

For the annual plan, budget holders will be forecasting their expense codes using an annual number and in quarterly lots for the significant accounts, such as personnel costs. Management reviews the annual plan for next year and ensures that all numbers are broken down into quarterly lots, and this is stored in a new field in the planning tool called "March xx [year] forecast." This is the second look at the next year, so the managers have a better understanding. On an ongoing basis, you would only need a two-week period to complete this process provided you followed the process set out in Exhibit C.3.

June: We can reforecast the end of June numbers, and we should be able to eliminate the frantic activity that is normally associated with the spend-or-lose-it mentality. Budget holders are now also required to forecast the first six months of next year, monthly and then quarterly, for the remaining period. Budget holders obtain approval to spend July to September numbers, provided their forecast once again passes through the annual goalposts. This is stored in a new field in the general ledger called "June xx [year] forecast." This updated process should only take one elapsed week.

September: We re-forecast the next six months in monthly numbers, and then quarterly for the remaining nine-month period of the next fiscal year. Budget holders obtain approval to spend October to December numbers. This is stored in a new field in the general ledger called "September xx [year] forecast." This updated process should only take one elapsed week.

You will find that the four cycles take about five to six weeks, once management is fully conversant with the new forecasting system and processes.

The key is to fund budget holders on a rolling quarter-by-quarter basis through a quarterly rolling forecasting process. In this process, the organization is aware that you need $1 million, and we can fund it, but the organization asks, "How much do you need in the next three months?" It will come as no surprise that when a budget holder only needs to look three months ahead, the cost estimates are much more precise—say, in this case, $225,000—and management becomes very accountable about progress (see Exhibit C.4). This process means that the approval process by the senior management team will be quicker because the senior-management

EXHIBIT C.3 Timeline for the Fourth Quarter Forecast (which Generates the Annual Plan)

	Prior Work			10 Working Days										
Process =>	Budget prework	Meeting with divisional heads (DHs)	Present budget workshop	1	2	3	4	5	Weekend	6	7	8	9	10
Activities by team =>														
Strategic Planning			Attend	BHs prepare and load their forecast			First look at numbers	Rework some budgets		Submissions by BHs to budget committee			Present final annual plan	Final alterations and finishing off documentation
Strategic Planning			Attend				Reviewing to ensure linkage to plan and advising of any discrepancies						Attend	
SMT	Set assumptions	One-to-one with the finance team	Give presentation to BHs				First look at numbers			Review submissions, all day long			Hear presentation and give instructions for final changes	
Finance Team	Prepare system, presentation, calculate known costs, overheads, personnel costs, etc.	One-to-one with DHs	Give presentation to BHs	Help BHs with budget plans (extended team)			Questions and answers	Help BHs		Further questions and answers			Complete preparation and deliver annual plan presentation	Complete documentation
Budget Holders			Attend	Prepare budget			Alter numbers after feedback	Attend		Present plan to SMT when called			Document and file all calculations	

Source: David Parmenter, *Winning CFOs: Implementing and Applying Better Practices*, Copyright © 2011 by David Parmenter. Reprinted with permission of John Wiley & Sons, Inc.

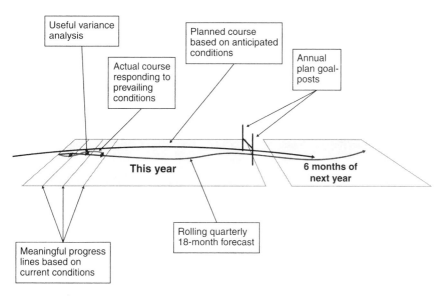

EXHIBIT C.4 Quarterly Rolling Plan Analogy

Source: David Parmenter, *Winning CFOs: Implementing and Applying Better Practices,* Copyright © 2011 by David Parmenter. Reprinted with permission of John Wiley & Sons, Inc.

team can adjust the quarter-by-quarter allocations as the conditions and environment dictate.

Some public-sector organization have recognized the folly of giving a budget holder the right to spend an annual sum, while saying that, if you get it wrong, there will be no more money. By forcing budget holders to second-guess their needs in this inflexible regime, you enforce a defensive behavior, a stockpiling mentality. In other words, you guarantee dysfunctional behavior from day one! This process, therefore, highlights "free funds" for new projects earlier on in the financial year.

> The quarterly rolling funding process has a lot in common with the handling of a nine-year-old's birthday cake. A clever parent says to Johnny, "Here is the first slice. If you finish that slice and you are not going green around the gills and want more, I will give you a second slice." Instead, what we do in the annual planning process is divide the cake up and portion all of it to the budget holders. Like nine-year-olds,
>
> *(continued)*

> (*Continued*)
>
> budget holders lick the edges of their cake so that, even if they do not need all of it, nobody else can have it. Why not, like the clever parent, give the manager what they need for the first three months and then say, "What do you need for the next three months and so on?" Each time, we can apportion the amount that is appropriate for the trading conditions at that time.

An additional benefit is the freeing up of funds for new initiatives that the budget holder could not have anticipated at the time of the budget round. It is a comment that is heard frequently from budget holders: "I cannot undertake that initiative, though we should, because I did not include it in my budget." In the new regime, the budget holder would say, "I will put it in my next update, and if funds are available, I am sure I will get the go-ahead."

If significant underfunding is being forecast due to changes in major assumptions, this can be communicated earlier to treasury and the appropriate mechanisms followed.

This more flexible environment, as long as it is communicated clearly and frequently to budget holders, will ensure good buy-in.

Thus, the budget process should be replaced with a new target-setting process that comes out of a quarterly rolling forecast process. Let us now look at how it can work in more detail.

Quarterly Rolling Funding in Government and Non Profit Agencies

The key features of a quarterly rolling funding process for government and non profit agencies would include:

- The annual appropriation is underpinned by a bottom-up quarterly rolling forecasting regime.
- Budget holders provide an annual plan but are not assigned these funds; this is done on a quarter-by-quarter basis.
- Monthly reporting is more meaningful because it measures performance against the most recent forecast and not against a monthly split of the original annual plan.
- Each subsequent forecast is still expected to put the ball through the posts at the end of the field (year end annual plan), the difference being that the ball carries on to the next pitch (into next year). For example, budget holders always looking forward 18 months.

- Forecasting is carried out on an appropriate planning tool that can handle a bottom-up forecast once a quarter. Excel is not, and has never been, an appropriate tool for a vital company system.
- Benchmarking and trend analysis is used to provide better relative measures to monitor progress.
- The monthly cash-flow projections to the central government treasury team will be generated from the forecasting tool as well.

Forecasting the Truth

A forecasting process should also bring more realistic forecasts, so long as you do not shoot the messenger. Hope[2] pointed out the necessity to ensure honesty with forecasts. It is important to give the best estimates no matter how unsavory they may be.

More Meaningful Monthly Reporting

We now report monthly progress differently, as shown in Exhibit C.5. We no longer want to compare actual against a flawed monthly budget. Instead, we compare last month's actual against the most recent forecast. The year-to-date (YTD) actual is no longer compared against a YTD budget. Instead, YTD progress is evaluated alongside progress against the year-end forecast and the accompanying trend graphs. Now trend analysis is much more the focus.

The forecasted year-end numbers are now more prominent and are moved to where the YTD numbers traditionally are placed. Commentary is much more targeted because there is no place for the explain-it-all-away timing difference comment as the forecast is updated quarterly.

Most planning tools can store a number of forecasts, and they can also be manipulated to hold monthly, quarterly, and yearly numbers. To support this new process we need to erase the word "budget" and replace it with "forecast," "target," or "expected actual."

Throw Out the Excel Forecasting Model

Forecasting requires a good robust tool, not an in-house solution built by some innovative accountant who has since left the organization, leaving no one who can understand what was designed. If your forecasting experts have not already up-skilled in this area, they will need to do so immediately.

Acquiring a planning tool is the first main step forward. This is particularly important because, in my view, there is no room for top-top forecasts,

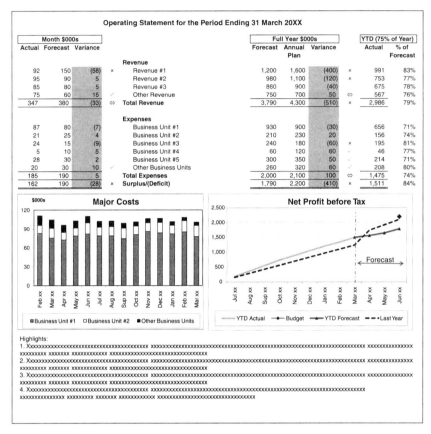

EXHIBIT C.5   Business Unit Reporting Against Latest Forecast Instead of a Budget

Source: David Parmenter, *Winning CFOs: Implementing and Applying Better Practices,* Copyright © 2011 by David Parmenter. Reprinted with permission of John Wiley & Sons, Inc.

where management prepares it without consultation from budget holders. Top-top forecasts exist only because organizations use Excel, a nightmare for a bottom-up process. To do bottom-up forecasting every quarter, you need a robust planning tool.

Benchmarking Is Now Reborn

Benchmarking becomes more important as progress is compared against best in class, both internally and externally for teams and divisions. A budget holder will never know in advance what a good result is in reality because conditions and what other teams manage are the determining factors. Although many public-sector organizations benchmark, they may not be linking them into performance agreements.

Benchmarks must also be seen in a wider context, because many public-sector activities are the same as those in, say, the service sector; hence benchmarks should not be limited merely to the public sector.

The importance of relative measures was summed up nicely by Hope and Fraser,[3] who use an analogy that I particularly like:

> *Golfers keep their own score. There is a transparency, everybody knows each other's score. No one cheats on the course or misrepresents their score. To do so would bring disgrace and an abrupt end to their membership. Nor do golfers need anyone telling them what score to aim for. They already know their ranking whether it be a club or international competition. They know their handicap and what they have to do to improve relative to their peers. Their performance is continuously measured after each event and their aim is continuous improvement.*

Why Removing the Word *Budget* Is Important

The word *budget* in core government should solely apply to the national government's annual budget. The phrase *budgeting process* should go for all the reasons already stated.

We would now have:

- A budget (for the government).
- An annual plan.
- An annual appropriation from parliament.
- An internal quarterly funding model of budget holders.
- Performance targets that are from the quarterly rolling forecasts. All monthly reports would refer to targets, revised annual forecast, and annual plan (see Exhibit C.5).

The First Steps to Take

I recommend the following steps to get you started on this important journey of replacing the annual planning process:

- Listen to Jeremy Hope on YouTube, especially to his broadcasts on "Reinventing the CFO."
- Obtain Hope and Fraser's *Harvard Business Review* paper[4] and *Beyond Budgeting* book.[5]

- Consider joining the Beyond Budgeting round table. See www.bbrt.org.
- Access the "How to Implement Quarterly Rolling Forecasting and Planning" white paper (www.davidparmenter.com).
- Circulate Chapter 12 in Jack Welch's book *Winning*,[6] "Budgeting–Reinventing the Ritual," to the board and the senior management team.

Notes

1. Jack Welch with Suzy Welch, *Winning* (New York: HarperBusiness, 2005).
2. Jeremy Hope, *Reinventing the CFO: How Financial Managers Can Transform Their Roles and Add Greater Value* (Cambridge, MA: Harvard Business Press, 2006).
3. Jeremy Hope and Robin Fraser, *Beyond Budgeting: How Managers Can Break Free from the Annual Performance Trap* (Cambridge, MA: Harvard Business Press, 2003).
4. Jeremy Hope and Robin Fraser, "Who Needs Budgets?" *Harvard Business Review*, Volume 81, issue 2 (February 2003), pp 108–115.
5. Hope and Fraser, *Beyond Budgeting: How Managers Can Break Free from the Annual Performance Trap*.
6. Jack Welch with Suzy Welch, *Winning*.

Jack Welch's Strategy Slides

Great management writers, such as Jim Collins, Tom Peters, Robert Waterman, and Jack Welch have all pointed out that prominent organizations are not great because they have the largest strategic plan. In fact, it is quite the reverse; the poor-performing organizations are the ones that spend the most time in strategy and the dreaded annual planning process.

Jack Welch, in his book *Winning*,[1] professes that strategy should be able to fit on five slides. Although this may not be achievable, the points he makes that should be covered could certainly fit within 10 slides. I have set out my interpretation of his slides and also include the thoughts from Jim Collins.

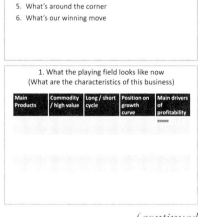

(*continued*)

1. What the playing field looks like now (strengths and weakness of competitors)

Competitor	Their strengths	Their weaknesses
Competitor #1	xxxxxxxxxxxx	xxxxxxxxxxxx
Competitor #2		

2. What have the competition been up to (main customers and new entrants)

Main Competitors	Innovations in last year	Any game breakers	Revenue Estimate last 12 months
Competitor #1			
Competitor #2			

New Entrants	Innovations in last year	Any game breakers	Revenue Estimate last 12 months
New entrant #1			
New entrant #2			

2. What have the competition been up to (main customers and new entrants)

Main Competitors	Innovations in last year	Any game breakers	Revenue Estimate last 12 months
Competitor #1			
Competitor #2			

New Entrants	Innovations in last year	Any game breakers	Revenue Estimate last 12 months
New entrant #1			
New entrant #2			

3. What have we been up to in the last year

Key product	Innovations	Changes in sales force	Gain / Loss in competitiveness	Product sales in last 12 months
Key Product #1				

- Company purchased xxxxxxx

4. What is our hedgehog

The area where these three spheres share is your 'Hedgehog' your reliable, robust and safe place to be.

4. Increase the momentum of your flywheel

- Good to great organizations focus on their flywheel increasing its momentum until it is almost effortless

5. What's around the corner

- Competitor actions that could adversely affect us:
  - xxxxxxxxx xxxxxxxxxx xxxxxx xxxxxxxxxx
  - xxxxxxxx xxxxxxxxx xxxxx xxxxxxxxxxx
- New 'game changing' technologies
  - xxxxxxxxx xxxxxx xxxxxxx xxxxxxxxx
  - xxxxxxx xxxxxxxxxxxxx
- Possible M&A deals that could adversely affect us
  - xxxxxxxxxx xxxxxxxx xxxxxx xxxxxxxxx
  - xxxxxx xxxx xxxxxxxxxx xxxx xxxxxxxxxx

6. What's our winning move

- Actions we can do to build a bigger hedgehog
  - xxxxxxxxx xxxxxxxxxx xxxxxx xxxxxxxxx
  - xxxxxxxx xxxxxxxxx xxxxx xxxxxxxxxxx
- How we can change the playing field
  - xxxxxxxxx xxxxxxxxxx xxxxxx xxxxxxxxx
  - xxxxxxxx xxxxxxxxx xxxxx xxxxxxxxxxx
- Changes to increase key customer retention
  - xxxxxxxxx xxxxxxxxxx xxxxxx xxxxxxxxx
  - xxxxxxxx xxxxxxxxx xxxxx xxxxxxxxxxx

Note

1. Jack Welch with Suzy Welch, *Winning* (Cambridge, MA: HarperBusiness, 2005).

Suggested Success Factors for Government and Non Profit Agencies

To assist agencies, I have set out some success factors indicating their influence over the balanced-scorecard perspectives. To aid organizations, I have also shortlisted potential critical success factors. However, you do need to perform the fine-tuning of the success factor wording and then the mapping exercise to ascertain whether these are, in fact, the critical success factors for your organization. See Chapter 7 for the details of this process.

As you will notice, success factors can often impact more than one perspective.

The agencies covered include the following:

- Hospital
- School/university
- Local municipality
- Police force
- Armed forces
- Development bank
- Tax collecting agency
- Professional body
- Government department

Note that success factors often affect more than one perspective.

Success Factors for a Hospital by Balanced-Scorecard Perspective	Environment and Community	Internal Process	Finance	Customer	Innovation and Learning	Staff Satisfaction
Common Critical Success Factors						
Stay, say, strive engagement with staff	Y	Y	Y	Y	Y	Y
Recruit the right people all the time	Y	Y	Y	Y	Y	Y
Develop exceptional people and teams who follow our organization's philosophy		Y	Y	Y	Y	Y
Grow leaders who thoroughly understand the work, live the philosophy, and teach it to others	Y		Y		Y	Y
Innovation is a daily activity (finding better ways to do the things we do every day)		Y	Y	Y	Y	Y
Willingness to abandon initiatives and opportunities that are not working or are unlikely to succeed		Y	Y	Y	Y	Y
Make decisions slowly by consensus, thoroughly considering all options; implement decisions rapidly (a Toyota principle)		Y	Y	Y	Y	Y
Delivery in full, on time, all the time to our critical patients		Y		Y		Y
Other Success Factors with an Environment-and-Community Focus						
Be seen in the community as an employer of first choice (attracting quality staff to the organization)	Y					Y
Support educational institutions (who are source of new employees)	Y					Y
Encourage voluntary assistance by staff to the local community	Y					Y
Support minorities through employment	Y					Y

Recognition in community for environmental endeavors	Y					Y
Good working relationships with key community organizations	Y					Y
Support local businesses (percent of purchases to have local content)	Y					Y
Enhanced community interaction (favorable reputation in the community)	Y					Y

Other Success Factors with an Internal-Process Focus

Maintain leadership in specific disciplines	Y	Y				Y
Respect your extended network of partners and suppliers by challenging them and helping them improve	Y	Y		Y		Y
Completion of projects on time and to budget		Y	Y			
A culture of getting quality right the first time		Y				
Use visual controls so problems are seen		Y		Y		
Optimize reliable, thoroughly tested technology that serves our staff, patients, suppliers, and processes	Y	Y	Y	Y		Y
Timely, accurate, decision-based information		Y				
We finish what we start		Y			Y	Y
We administer change-management processes successfully		Y			Y	Y
Paperless information flow with our key suppliers		Y		Y		

Other Success Factors with a Finance Focus

Cost reduction/increasing employee productivity		Y			Y	Y
Improve risk management (better forecasting, contingency planning, etc.)		Y			Y	Y
Fiscally responsible management, by all managers		Y			Y	
Prioritize all activities that will speed up cash collection from patients		Y			Y	

Success Factors for a Hospital by Balanced-Scorecard Perspective	Environment and Community	Internal Process	Finance	Customer	Innovation and Learning	Staff Satisfaction
Other Success Factors with a Customer Focus						
Get the right service in the right place at the right time		Y	Y	Y	Y	Y
Improve turnaround time from first visit to treatment of designated patients		Y		Y	Y	
Identify and introduce new treatments in ____ (specify areas)	Y		Y	Y	Y	Y
New and innovative low-cost patient-care services				Y	Y	Y
Seek excellence in every aspect of our patient interaction		Y	Y	Y	Y	Y
Other Success Factors with an Innovation-and-Learning Focus						
Create an environment in which our people are encouraged to meet their full potential		Y	Y	Y	Y	Y
Be a learning organization through relentless reflection and continuous improvement		Y	Y	Y	Y	Y
Go and see for yourself to thoroughly understand the situation (a Toyota principle)		Y			Y	Y
Increase adaptability and flexibility of staff		Y	Y		Y	Y
Increase empowerment (delegated decision making)		Y		Y	Y	Y
Other Success Factors with a Staff-Satisfaction Focus						
Reward and recognize our staff			Y		Y	Y
Support balance in work and home life (respect different working styles/working hours)		Y			Y	Y
Promoting open decision making		Y			Y	Y
We see celebrating success as a priority						Y
A pleasant and healthy physical work environment for all staff						Y

Success Factors for a School/University by Balanced-Scorecard Perspective	Environment and Community	Internal Process	Finance	Customer	Innovation and Learning	Staff Satisfaction
Common Critical Success Factors						
Stay, say, strive engagement with staff	Y	Y	Y	Y	Y	Y
Recruit the right people all the time	Y	Y	Y	Y	Y	Y
Develop exceptional people and teams who follow our organization's philosophy		Y	Y	Y	Y	Y
Grow leaders who thoroughly understand the work, live the philosophy, and teach it to others	Y	Y	Y	Y	Y	Y
Innovation is a daily activity (finding better ways to do the things we do every day)		Y	Y	Y	Y	Y
Willingness to abandon initiatives and opportunities that are not working or are unlikely to succeed		Y	Y	Y	Y	Y
Make decisions slowly by consensus, thoroughly considering all options; implement decisions rapidly (a Toyota principle)		Y	Y	Y	Y	Y
Delivery in full, on time, all the time to our students (and their parents—for schools)		Y		Y		Y
Other Success Factors with an Environment-and-Community Focus						
Be seen in the community as an employer of first choice (attracting quality staff to the organization)	Y					Y
Encourage voluntary assistance by staff to the local community	Y					Y
Support minorities through employment	Y					Y
Good working relationships with key community organizations	Y					Y
Support local businesses (percent of purchases to have local content)	Y					Y
Enhanced community interaction (favorable reputation in the community)	Y					Y

Success Factors for a School/University by Balanced-Scorecard Perspective	Environment and Community	Internal Process	Finance	Customer	Innovation and Learning	Staff Satisfaction
Environmentally friendly culture and reputation (use of environmentally friendly materials)	Y			Y		Y
Other Success Factors with an Internal-Process Focus						
Leadership in xxxxxxxxxx disciplines	Y	Y		Y	Y	Y
A culture of getting quality right the first time		Y			Y	Y
Use visual controls so problems are seen		Y		Y	Y	Y
Optimize reliable, thoroughly tested technology that serves our staff, students, suppliers, and processes	Y	Y	Y	Y	Y	Y
Timely, accurate, decision-based information		Y	Y			
We finish what we start		Y	Y			
We administer change-management processes successfully		Y	Y		Y	Y
Paperless information flow with our key suppliers, students, and parents		Y	Y	Y	Y	
Other Success Factors with a Finance Focus						
Cost reduction/increasing employee productivity		Y	Y		Y	Y
Improve risk management (better forecasting, broaden revenue base, increase brand awareness, etc.)		Y	Y		Y	Y
Active interface with alumni (past students)			Y	Y		Y
Fiscally responsible management, by all managers		Y	Y		Y	
Prioritize all activities that will speed up cash collection from students/parents		Y	Y		Y	
Other Success Factors with a Customer Focus						
Get the right course in the right place at the right time (new services that add value to our students)		Y	Y	Y	Y	Y
Improve turnaround time from student application to decision on acceptance/rejection		Y		Y	Y	

Encourage our students to be active advocates for our institution	Y	Y			Y
Identify and capture the potential of new and emerging courses	Y	Y	Y		Y
New and innovative low-cost access channels for learning		Y	Y	Y	Y
Seek excellence in every aspect of our student interaction		Y	Y		Y
Acquisition of new students		Y	Y		Y
Other Success Factors with an Innovation-and-Learning Focus					
Create an environment in which our staff are encouraged to meet their full potential		Y	Y	Y	Y
Be a learning organization through relentless reflection and continuous improvement		Y	Y	Y	Y
Go and see for yourself to thoroughly understand the situation (a Toyota principle)		Y		Y	Y
Increase adaptability and flexibility of staff		Y	Y	Y	Y
Increase empowerment (delegated decision making)		Y		Y	Y
Other Success Factors with a Staff-Satisfaction Focus					
Reward and recognize our staff		Y			Y
Support balance in work and home life (respect different working styles/working hours)			Y	Y	Y
Promoting open decision making		Y			Y
We see celebrating success as a priority					Y
A pleasant and healthy physical work environment for all staff			Y		Y

Success Factors for a Local Municipality by Balanced-Scorecard Perspective	Environment and Community	Internal Process	Finance	Customer	Innovation and Learning	Staff Satisfaction
Common Critical Success Factors						
Stay, say, strive engagement with staff	Y	Y	Y	Y	Y	Y
Recruit the right people all the time	Y	Y	Y	Y	Y	Y
Develop exceptional people and teams who follow our organization's philosophy		Y	Y	Y	Y	Y
Grow leaders who thoroughly understand the work, live the philosophy, and teach it to others	Y		Y		Y	Y
Innovation is a daily activity (finding better ways to do the things we do every day)		Y	Y	Y	Y	Y
Willingness to abandon initiatives and opportunities that are not working or are unlikely to succeed		Y	Y	Y	Y	Y
Make decisions slowly by consensus, thoroughly considering all options; implement decisions rapidly (a Toyota principle)		Y	Y	Y	Y	Y
Delivery in full, on time, all the time to our rate payers and community		Y	Y	Y		Y
Other Success Factors with an Environment-and-Community Focus						
Be seen in the community as an employer of "first choice" (attracting quality staff to the organization)	Y					Y
Encourage voluntary assistance by staff to the local community	Y					Y
Support minorities through employment	Y					Y
Good working relationships with key community organizations	Y					Y

Success Factor				
Support local businesses (percent of purchases to have local content)	Y			Y
Enhanced community interaction (favorable reputation in the community)	Y			Y
Environmentally friendly culture and reputation (use of environmentally friendly materials)	Y		Y	Y
Other Success Factors with an Internal-Process Focus				
Completion of projects on time and on budget		Y		
A culture of getting quality right the first time		Y		Y
Use visual controls so problems are seen		Y	Y	Y
Optimize reliable, thoroughly tested technology that serves our staff, customers, suppliers, and processes	Y	Y	Y	Y
Timely, accurate, decision-based information		Y		
We finish what we start		Y		Y
We administer change-management processes successfully		Y		Y
Paperless information flow with both our key suppliers and rate payers		Y	Y	
Other Success Factors with a Finance Focus				
Cost reduction/increasing employee productivity		Y		Y
Improve risk management (better forecasting, broaden revenue base, contingency planning, etc.)		Y		Y
Optimize working capital (optimize stock levels and minimize debtors)		Y		
Fiscally responsible management, by all managers		Y		
Other Success Factors with a Customer Focus				
Get the right service in the right place at the right time (new services that add value to our rate payers)		Y		Y

Success Factors for a Local Municipality by Balanced-Scorecard Perspective	Environment and Community	Internal Process	Finance	Customer	Innovation and Learning	Staff Satisfaction
Improve turnaround time from service request to delivery for our rate payers/customers		Y		Y	Y	
New and innovative low-cost access channels for our services		Y		Y	Y	Y
Seek excellence in every aspect of our customer interaction			Y	Y	Y	Y
Other Success Factors with an Innovation-and-Learning Focus						
Create an environment in which our people are encouraged to meet their full potential		Y	Y	Y	Y	Y
Be a learning organization through relentless reflection and continuous improvement		Y	Y	Y	Y	Y
Go and see for yourself to thoroughly understand the situation (a Toyota principle)		Y			Y	Y
Increase adaptability and flexibility of staff		Y	Y	Y	Y	Y
Improved alignment of individual and organizational goals		Y			Y	Y
Increasing empowerment (delegated decision making)		Y		Y	Y	Y
Other Success Factors with a Staff-Satisfaction Focus						
Reward and recognize our staff			Y			Y
Support balance in work and home life (respect different working styles/working hours)		Y			Y	Y
Promoting open decision making		Y			Y	
We see celebrating success as a priority						Y
A pleasant and healthy physical work environment for all staff						Y

Success Factors for a Police Force by Balanced-Scorecard Perspective	Environment and Community	Internal Process	Finance	Customer	Innovation and Learning	Staff Satisfaction
Common Critical Success Factors						
Stay, say, strive engagement with staff	Y	Y	Y	Y	Y	Y
Recruit the right people all the time	Y	Y	Y	Y	Y	Y
Develop exceptional people and teams who follow our organization's philosophy		Y	Y	Y	Y	Y
Grow leaders who thoroughly understand the work, live the philosophy, and teach it to others	Y		Y		Y	Y
Innovation is a daily activity (finding better ways to do the things we do every day)		Y	Y	Y	Y	Y
Willingness to abandon initiatives and opportunities that are not working or are unlikely to succeed		Y	Y	Y	Y	Y
Make decisions slowly by consensus, thoroughly considering all options; implement decisions rapidly (a Toyota principle)		Y	Y	Y	Y	Y
Delivery in full on time, all the time to the community we serve		Y		Y		Y
Other Success Factors with an Environment-and-Community Focus						
Be seen in the community as an employer of first choice (attracting quality staff to the organization)	Y					Y
Encourage voluntary assistance by staff to the local community	Y					Y
Support minorities through employment	Y					Y
Good working relationships with key community organizations	Y					Y

Success Factors for a Police Force by Balanced-Scorecard Perspective	Environment and Community	Internal Process	Finance	Customer	Innovation and Learning	Staff Satisfaction
Support local businesses (percent of purchases to have local content)	Y					Y
Enhanced community interaction (favorable reputation in the community)	Y					Y
Environmentally friendly culture and reputation (use of environmentally friendly materials)	Y			Y		Y
Other Success Factors with an Internal-Process Focus						
Completion of projects on time and on budget		Y	Y			
A culture of getting quality right the first time		Y			Y	Y
Use visual controls so problems are seen		Y		Y	Y	Y
Optimize reliable, thoroughly tested technology that serves our staff, the public, suppliers, and processes	Y	Y	Y	Y	Y	Y
Timely, accurate, decision-based information		Y	Y			
We finish what we start		Y	Y		Y	Y
We administer change-management processes successfully		Y	Y		Y	Y
Paperless information flow with both our key suppliers and stakeholders		Y	Y	Y	Y	
Other Success Factors with a Finance Focus						
Cost reduction/increasing employee productivity		Y	Y		Y	Y
Improved risk management (better forecasting, contingency planning, etc.)		Y	Y		Y	Y
Fiscally responsible management, by all managers		Y	Y		Y	
Maximize effectiveness of roistering to minimize penalty overtime payments		Y	Y		Y	Y

Other Success Factors with a Customer Focus (can be included in Environment and Community)

Getting the right service in the right place at the right time (new services that reduce crime)	Y	Y	Y
Improve response to urgent callouts	Y	Y	
New and innovative low-cost access channels for policing services	Y	Y	Y
Seeking excellence in every aspect of our public interface	Y	Y	Y

Other Success Factors with an Innovation-and-Learning Focus

Create an environment in which our people are encouraged to meet their full potential	Y	Y	Y
Be a learning organization through relentless reflection and continuous improvement	Y	Y	Y
Go and see for yourself to thoroughly understand the situation (a Toyota principle)	Y	Y	Y
Increase adaptability and flexibility of staff	Y	Y	Y
Improve alignment of individual and organizational goals	Y	Y	Y
Increase empowerment (delegated decision making)	Y	Y	Y

Other Success Factors with a Staff-Satisfaction Focus

Reward and recognize our staff	Y		Y
Supporting balance in working and home life (respect different working styles/working hours)	Y	Y	Y
Promote open decision making	Y	Y	Y
We see celebrating success as a priority			Y
A pleasant and healthy work environment for all staff (status of police stations etc.)			Y

Success Factors for the Armed Forces by Balanced-Scorecard Perspective	Environment and Community	Internal Process	Finance	Stakeholder	Innovation and Learning	Staff Satisfaction
Common Critical Success Factors						
Stay, say, strive engagement with staff	Y	Y	Y	Y	Y	Y
Recruit the right people all the time	Y	Y	Y	Y	Y	Y
Develop exceptional people and teams who follow our organization's philosophy		Y	Y	Y	Y	Y
Grow leaders who thoroughly understand the work, live the philosophy, and teach it to others	Y		Y		Y	Y
Innovation is a daily activity (finding better ways to do the things we do every day)		Y	Y	Y	Y	Y
Willingness to abandon initiatives and opportunities that are not working or are unlikely to succeed		Y	Y	Y	Y	Y
Make decisions slowly by consensus, thoroughly considering all options; implement decisions rapidly (a Toyota principle)		Y	Y	Y	Y	Y
Delivery in full, on time, all the time (this could be reworded to better reflect the forces activities)		Y		Y		Y
Other Success Factors with an Environment-and-Community Focus						
Be seen in the community as an employer of first choice (attracting quality staff to the organization)	Y					Y
Support minorities through employment	Y					
Good working relationships with key community organizations	Y					Y
Support local businesses (percent of purchases to have local content)	Y					Y

Enhanced community interaction (favorable reputation in the community)	Y				Y
Environmentally friendly culture and reputation (use of environmentally friendly materials)	Y		Y		Y
Other Success Factors with an Internal-Process Focus					
Respect your extended network of partners and suppliers by challenging them and helping them improve	Y	Y		Y	Y
Completion of projects on time and on budget		Y			
A culture of getting quality right the first time		Y		Y	Y
Use visual controls so problems are seen		Y	Y	Y	Y
Optimize reliable, thoroughly tested technology that serves our staff, customers, suppliers, and processes	Y	Y	Y	Y	Y
Timely, accurate, decision-based information		Y			
We finish what we start		Y		Y	Y
We administer change-management processes successfully		Y		Y	Y
Paperless information flow with our key suppliers		Y	Y	Y	
Other Success Factors with a Finance Focus					
Optimize supply contracts on a price/quality basis		Y		Y	Y
Optimize stock levels		Y		Y	Y
Fiscally responsible management, by all managers		Y		Y	
Other Success Factors with a Stakeholder Focus					
Getting the right troops in the right place at the right time, with the right equipment		Y	Y	Y	Y

Other Success Factors with an Innovation-and-Learning Focus

Success Factors for the Armed Forces by Balanced-Scorecard Perspective	Environment and Community	Internal Process	Finance	Stakeholder	Innovation and Learning	Staff Satisfaction
Other Success Factors with an Innovation-and-Learning Focus						
Create an environment where the troops are encouraged to meet their full potential		Y	Y	Y	Y	Y
Be a learning organization through relentless reflection and continuous improvement		Y	Y	Y	Y	Y
Go and see for yourself to thoroughly understand the situation (a Toyota principle)		Y			Y	Y
Increasing adaptability and flexibility of staff		Y	Y		Y	Y
Improved alignment of individual and organizational goals		Y			Y	Y
Increasing empowerment (delegated decision making)		Y	Y		Y	Y
Other Success Factors with a Staff-Satisfaction Focus						
Equip our troops with training and equipment so they can perform to the best of their ability		Y			Y	Y
Reward and recognize our troops			Y			Y
Support balance in working and home life (respect different working styles/working hours)		Y			Y	Y
Promote open decision making		Y			Y	Y
We see celebrating success as a priority						Y
A pleasant and healthy physical work environment for the troops and support staff						Y

Success Factors of a Development Bank by Balanced-Scorecard Perspective	Environment and Community	Internal Process	Finance	Customer	Innovation and Learning	Staff Satisfaction
Common Critical Success Factors						
Stay, say, strive engagement with staff	Y	Y	Y	Y	Y	Y
Recruit the right people all the time	Y	Y	Y	Y	Y	Y
Develop exceptional people and teams who follow our organization's philosophy		Y	Y	Y	Y	Y
Grow leaders who thoroughly understand the work, live the philosophy, and teach it to others	Y		Y		Y	Y
Innovation is a daily activity (finding better ways to do the things we do every day)		Y	Y		Y	Y
Willingness to abandon initiatives and opportunities that are not working or are unlikely to succeed		Y	Y		Y	Y
Make decisions slowly by consensus, thoroughly considering all options; implement decisions rapidly (a Toyota principle)		Y	Y		Y	Y
Delivery in full, on time, all the time to our customers		Y		Y		Y
Other Success Factors with an Environment-and-Community Focus						
Be seen in the community as an employer of first choice (attracting quality staff to the organization)	Y				Y	
Encourage voluntary assistance by staff to the local community	Y					Y
Good working relationships with key community organizations	Y				Y	
Enhanced community interaction (favorable reputation in the community)	Y					Y

Success Factors of a Development Bank by Balanced-Scorecard Perspective	Environment and Community	Internal Process	Finance	Customer	Innovation and Learning	Staff Satisfaction
Environmentally friendly culture and reputation (use of environmentally friendly materials)	Y			Y		Y
Other Success Factors with an Internal-Process Focus						
Collaboration with the extended network of regional bankers	Y	Y			Y	Y
A culture of getting quality right the first time		Y			Y	Y
Get loan-application completed in full and make a funding decision on a timely basis		Y		Y	Y	Y
Optimize reliable, thoroughly tested technology that serves our staff, customers, and processes	Y	Y	Y	Y	Y	Y
Timely, accurate, information on loan-payment defaults		Y	Y			
We finish what we start		Y	Y		Y	
Paperless information flow with key suppliers and key lenders and borrowers		Y	Y	Y	Y	Y
Other Success Factors with a Finance Focus						
Improve risk management (better loan portfolio, increase brand awareness, etc.)		Y	Y		Y	Y
Increase repeat business from first-time-borrowing businesses			Y	Y		Y
Prioritizing all activities that will speed up cash collection of major accounts		Y	Y		Y	
Other Success Factors with a Customer Focus						
Get the right service in the right place at the right time (new services that add value to our key borrowing groups)		Y	Y	Y	Y	Y

Success Factor					
Improve turnaround time from application and approval for our key borrowing groups	Y			Y	Y
Our key borrowers being active advocates for our business	Y	Y	Y	Y	Y
New and innovative low-cost access channels for our services	Y		Y	Y	Y
Seek excellence in every aspect of our customer interaction		Y	Y	Y	Y
Acquisition of borrowers in our target areas	Y	Y	Y	Y	Y
Other Success Factors with an Innovation-and-Learning Focus					
Create an environment in which our people are encouraged to meet their full potential	Y	Y	Y	Y	Y
Being a learning organization through relentless reflection and continuous improvement	Y	Y	Y	Y	Y
Go and see for yourself to thoroughly understand the situation (a Toyota principle)	Y			Y	Y
Increasing adaptability and flexibility of staff	Y	Y	Y	Y	Y
Increasing empowerment (delegated decision making)	Y	Y	Y	Y	Y
Other Success Factors with a Staff-Satisfaction Focus					
Reward and recognize our staff	Y				Y
Support balance in work and home life (respect different working styles/working hours)	Y			Y	Y
Promote open decision making	Y			Y	Y
We see celebrating success as a priority					Y
A pleasant and healthy physical work environment for all staff					Y

Success Factors by a Tax-Collecting Agency by Balanced-Scorecard Perspective	Environment and Community	Internal Process	Finance	Customer	Innovation and Learning	Staff Satisfaction
Common Critical Success Factors						
Stay, say, strive engagement with staff	Y	Y	Y	Y	Y	Y
Recruit the right people all the time	Y	Y	Y	Y	Y	Y
Develop exceptional people and teams who follow our organization's philosophy		Y	Y	Y	Y	Y
Grow leaders who thoroughly understand the work, live the philosophy, and teach it to others	Y		Y		Y	Y
Innovation is a daily activity (finding better ways to do the things we do every day)		Y	Y	Y	Y	Y
Willingness to abandon initiatives and opportunities that are not working or are unlikely to succeed		Y	Y	Y	Y	Y
Make decisions slowly by consensus, thoroughly considering all options; implement decisions rapidly (a Toyota principle)		Y	Y	Y	Y	Y
Delivery in full, on time, all the time to tax payers		Y		Y		
Other Success Factors with an Environment-and-Community Focus						
Be seen in the community as an employer of first choice (attracting quality staff to the organization)	Y					Y
Support educational institutions (who are source of new employees)	Y					Y
Encourage voluntary assistance by staff to the local community	Y					Y
Supporting minorities through employment	Y					Y
Good working relationships with key community organizations	Y					Y

	1	2	3	4
Support local businesses (percent of purchases to have local content)	Y			Y
Enhanced community interaction (favorable reputation in the community)	Y			Y
Environmentally friendly culture and reputation (use of environmentally friendly materials)	Y	Y		Y
Other Success Factors with an Internal-Process Focus				
Respect your extended network of partners and suppliers by challenging them and helping them improve	Y		Y	Y
Completion of projects on time and on budget			Y	
A culture of getting quality right the first time			Y	Y
Use visual controls so problems are seen		Y	Y	Y
Optimize reliable, thoroughly tested technology that serves our staff, tax payers, suppliers, and processes	Y	Y	Y	Y
Timely, accurate, decision-based information			Y	
We finish what we start			Y	Y
We administer change-management processes successfully			Y	Y
Paperless information flow with our key suppliers		Y	Y	
Other Success Factors with a Finance Focus				
Cost reduction/increasing employee productivity			Y	Y
Improve risk management (better forecasting, broaden revenue base, increase brand awareness, etc.)			Y	Y
Fiscally responsible management, by all managers			Y	Y
Prioritize all activities that will speed up collection of taxation			Y	Y

Success Factors by a Tax-Collecting Agency by Balanced-Scorecard Perspective	Environment and Community	Internal Process	Finance	Customer	Innovation and Learning	Staff Satisfaction
Other Success Factors with a Customer Focus						
Improve turnaround time from tax payer enquiry to resolution		Y		Y	Y	
New and innovative low-cost access channels for our tax payers		Y		Y	Y	Y
Seek excellence in every aspect of our tax payer interaction			Y	Y	Y	Y
Other Success Factors with an Innovation-and-Learning Focus						
Create an environment in which our people are encouraged to meet their full potential		Y	Y	Y	Y	Y
Be a learning organization through relentless reflection and continuous improvement		Y	Y	Y	Y	Y
Go and see for yourself to thoroughly understand the situation (a Toyota principle)		Y			Y	Y
Increase adaptability and flexibility of staff		Y	Y	Y	Y	Y
Improve alignment of individual and organizational goals		Y			Y	Y
Increase empowerment (delegated decision making)		Y		Y	Y	Y
Other Success Factors with a Staff-Satisfaction Focus						
Rewarding and recognizing our staff			Y			Y
Support balance in work and home life (respect different working styles/working hours)		Y			Y	Y
Promoting open decision making		Y			Y	Y
We see celebrating success as a priority						Y
A pleasant and healthy physical work environment for all staff						Y

Success Factors for a Professional Body by Balanced-Scorecard Perspective	Environment and Community	Internal Process	Finance	Members	Innovation and Learning	Staff Satisfaction
Common Critical Success Factors						
Seamless interdepartmental communications and feedback	Y	Y		Y	Y	Y
Find better ways to do the things we do every day		Y	Y	Y	Y	Y
Create an environment in which our people are encouraged to meet their full potential		Y	Y	Y	Y	Y
Increase adaptability and flexibility of staff		Y	Y	Y	Y	Y
Increase empowerment (delegated decision making)		Y		Y	Y	Y
Stay, say, strive engagement with staff	Y	Y	Y	Y	Y	Y
We administer change-management processes successfully		Y	Y		Y	Y
Increase employee productivity		Y	Y	Y	Y	Y
Electronic correspondence with key stakeholders and members		Y	Y	Y	Y	Y
Our members are active advocates for the profession	Y		Y	Y		Y
Bringing leading thinkers to present courses to our members	Y		Y	Y		
Other Success Factors with an Environment-and-Community Focus						
Be seen in the community as an employer of first choice	Y					Y
Attract the right students into the profession	Y					
Increased dialogue with news media to highlight our statutory roles, missions, values, and distinctive brand of the "Success Ingredient"	Y			Y		Y

Success Factors for a Professional Body by Balanced-Scorecard Perspective	Environment and Community	Internal Process	Finance	Members	Innovation and Learning	Staff Satisfaction
Get member volunteers to provide community services	Y					Y
Be a preferred profession for undergraduates	Y					
Public recognition and support from government, legislative, and regulatory authorities	Y					Y
Good working relationships with key stakeholder organizations	Y					Y
Leadership in setting international standards and practices with our affiliated institutions	Y			Y		Y
Maintain mutual recognition agreements and relationship with the international affiliated professional bodies	Y			Y		Y
Other Success Factors with an Internal-Process Focus						
Willingness to abandon initiatives and opportunities that are not working or unlikely to succeed		Y	Y	Y	Y	Y
Make decisions slowly by consensus, thoroughly considering all options; implement decisions rapidly (a Toyota principle)		Y	Y	Y	Y	Y
Completion of projects on time and to budget		Y	Y			
Timely, accurate, decision-based information		Y	Y			
We finish what we start		Y	Y		Y	Y
Enhancing operational efficiency (e.g., reducing cost per transaction)		Y	Y		Y	Y

Other Success Factors with a Finance Focus

Success Factor					
Retain members by offering them services they value			Y		Y	Y
Continual growth with the qualifications program					Y	
Increase in activity by members with the organization's services			Y		Y	Y
Increased interaction with members (leading to increasing retention of membership)			Y		Y	Y
Fiscally responsible management, by all managers			Y	Y		
Other Success Factors with a Member Focus						
Delivery in full, on time, all the time to our members			Y		Y	Y
Increased interface with our members			Y	Y	Y	Y
Improve turnaround time from request to service delivery for our key members			Y	Y	Y	Y
Mobility of members qualifications around the world	Y		Y	Y	Y	Y
New and innovative qualifications that demonstrate our thought leadership				Y	Y	Y
New and innovative services across all our various sector groups			Y	Y	Y	Y
Active _____ (target group) membership through attractive offerings of training, networking, career enhancement			Y		Y	
Proactive advocacy on behalf of our members	Y				Y	
Retention of xxxxxxx members (class of members who are leaving)			Y	Y	Y	

267

Success Factors for a Professional Body by Balanced-Scorecard Perspective	Environment and Community	Internal Process	Finance	Members	Innovation and Learning	Staff Satisfaction
Other Success Factors with an Innovation-and-Learning Focus						
Improve alignment of individual and organizational goals		Y			Y	Y
Encourage our people to take up ownership and use their initiative		Y			Y	Y
Other Success Factors with a Staff-Satisfaction Focus						
Reward\ and recognize our existing staff			Y		Y	Y
Recruit\ the right people all the time	Y	Y	Y	Y	Y	Y
Develop exceptional people and teams who follow our organization's philosophy		Y	Y	Y	Y	Y
Support\ balance in work and home life		Y			Y	Y
Continuous-learning environment	Y		Y		Y	Y
Promote open decision making		Y			Y	Y
Increase recognition throughout the organization (e.g., recognition being a daily activity for managers and staff, celebrating success, etc.)						Y
A pleasant physical work environment for all staff						Y

Success Factors for a Government Department by Balanced-Scorecard Perspective	Environment and Community	Internal Process	Finance	Customer	Innovation and Learning	Staff Satisfaction
Critical success factors						
Effective community outreach and engagement	Y				Y	Y
Public confidence and trust in our organization	Y				Y	Y
Enhanced partnership with groups and organizations with common interests	Y	Y				Y
An environment that encourages innovation and creativity (finding better ways to do the things we do every day)		Y	Y	Y	Y	Y
Service excellence in every aspects of our interactions with the public	Y	Y			Y	Y
A workplace that offers fulfillment, work-life balance, and job satisfaction		Y			Y	Y
Other Success Factors with an Environment-and-Community Focus						
Be seen in the community as an employer of first choice (attracting quality staff to the organization)	Y					Y
Encourage voluntary assistance by staff to the local community	Y					Y
Support minorities through employment	Y					Y
Good working relationships with key community organizations	Y					Y
Enhance community interaction (favorable reputation in the community)	Y					Y
Environmentally friendly culture and reputation (use of environmentally friendly materials)	Y			Y		Y

Other Success Factors with an Internal-Process Focus

Success Factors for a Government Department by Balanced-Scorecard Perspective	Environment and Community	Internal Process	Finance	Customer	Innovation and Learning	Staff Satisfaction
Willingness to abandon initiatives and opportunities that are not working or are unlikely to succeed		Y	Y	Y	Y	Y
Make decisions slowly, by consensus, thoroughly considering all options; implement decisions rapidly (Toyota)		Y	Y	Y	Y	Y
Delivery in full, on time, all the time to our key customers		Y		Y		Y
Recruiting the right people all the time	Y	Y	Y	Y	Y	Y
Respect your extended network of partners and suppliers by challenging them and helping them improve	Y	Y			Y	Y
Completion of projects on time and on budget		Y	Y			
A culture of getting quality right the first time		Y			Y	Y
Use visual controls so problems are seen		Y		Y	Y	Y
Optimize reliable, thoroughly tested technology that serves our staff, the public, suppliers and processes	Y	Y	Y	Y	Y	Y
Timely, accurate, decision-based information		Y	Y			
We finish what we start		Y	Y		Y	Y
We administer change-management processes successfully		Y	Y		Y	Y

Success Factor					
Paperless information flow with our key suppliers	Y	Y	Y		
Other Success Factors with a Finance Focus					
Cost reduction/increasing employee productivity	Y		Y	Y	
Improved risk management (better forecasting, broaden revenue base, etc.)	Y		Y	Y	
Increase repeat business from key customers (only relevant for government agencies that collect fees from the public)	Y	Y		Y	
Minimize debtors	Y		Y		
Fiscally responsible management, by all managers	Y		Y		
Prioritize all activities that will speed up cash collection of major accounts	Y		Y		
Other Success Factors with a Customer Focus					
Improve turnaround time from order to delivery for our key customers	Y	Y	Y		
Our key customers being active advocates for our operations	Y	Y		Y	Y
Identify and capture the potential of new and emerging markets	Y	Y	Y	Y	Y
New and innovative low-cost access channels for our services	Y	Y		Y	
Seek excellence in every aspect of our customer interaction	Y	Y	Y	Y	

271

Success Factors for a Government Department by Balanced-Scorecard Perspective	Environment and Community	Internal Process	Finance	Customer	Innovation and Learning	Staff Satisfaction
Other Success Factors with an Innovation-and-Learning Focus						
Develop exceptional people and teams who follow our organization's philosophy		Y	Y	Y	Y	Y
Grow leaders who thoroughly understand the work, live the philosophy, and teach it to others	Y		Y		Y	Y
Create an environment where our people are encouraged to meet their full potential		Y	Y	Y	Y	Y
Be a learning organization through relentless reflection and continuous improvement		Y	Y	Y	Y	Y
Go and see for yourself to thoroughly understand the situation (a Toyota principle)		Y			Y	Y
Increase adaptability and flexibility of staff		Y	Y		Y	Y
Improve alignment of individual and organizational goals		Y			Y	Y
Increase empowerment (delegated decision making)		Y		Y	Y	Y
Other Success Factors with a Staff-Satisfaction Focus						
Stay, say, strive engagement with staff	Y	Y	Y	Y	Y	Y
Reward and recognize our staff			Y			Y
Support balance in work and home life (respect different working styles/working hours)		Y			Y	Y
Promote open decision making		Y			Y	Y
We see celebrating success as a priority						Y
A pleasant and healthy physical work environment for all staff					Y	Y

List of Performance Measures Suitable for Government and Non Profit Agencies

The key performance indicator (KPI) team will have gathered and recorded performance measures from information gained from discussions held with senior management, revisiting company archives, reviewing monthly reports and external research. In addition, teams will, during brainstorming sessions, come up with performance measures they wish to use.

These identified performance measures need to be recorded, collated, and modified in a database that is available to all staff. This database will have a read-only facility for all employees. Amendment is permitted only by team coordinators (restricted to their area) and the KPI team (unlimited restriction).

Table F.1 is a list of performance measures to help start this process off. It will be a valuable resource when looking at performance measures during brainstorming sessions. (You can acquire this database electronically from www.davidparmenter.com for a small fee).

It is advisable not to provide attendees with this list of performance measures until they have participated in some brainstorming sessions and come up with measures themselves. Introducing this list too early will lead to a narrowing of potential performance measures.

Some of the performance measures in this list will be performance indicators (PIs), result indicators (RIs), KPIs, and key result indicators (KRIs). It is up to the KPI project team to ascertain in which of the four categories the final set of performance measures should be placed.

TABLE F.1   Performance Measures to Begin a Database

Performance Measure	Frequency of Measure	Time Zone (Past, Current, Future)	Balanced-Scorecard Perspective(s)
List of key customers for whom time since last order is > xx weeks	Weekly	Past	CF
Date of last contact with customer with current major projects (list by major projects only)	Monthly	Past	CF
Date when remedial work is planned to be completed (major projects only)	Weekly	Future	CF
Quality problems detected during product audits	When audits performed	Past	CF
Number of initiatives completed from the recent customer-satisfaction survey	Weekly for three months post-survey	Past	CF
Abandon rate at call center (caller gives up)	Daily	Current	CF, IP
Calls answered first time (not having to be transferred to another party)	Daily and in some cases 24/7	Current	CF
Calls on hold longer than xx seconds	Daily and in some cases 24/7	Current	CF
Complaints from our key customers that have not been resolved within 2 hours, reported to chief executive officer (CEO) and general managers	24/7	Current	CF
Unresolved complaints—from other customers (not key customers)	Weekly	Past	CF
Complaints not resolved during first phone call by customer	Daily	Current	CF
Initiatives completed from last corporate office satisfaction survey (e.g., HR team)	Weekly for three months post-survey	Past	CF

Measure	Frequency	Timeframe	Perspective
The time elapsed between quality assurance failures	Weekly	Past	CF
Times during day when line at serving counter is over xx minutes long	Daily	Current	CF
Date of next outside-in activity to enhance senior management team understanding	Monthly	Future	CF
Date of next major customer focus group	Quarterly	Future	CF
Date of next initiative to attract targeted noncustomers	Quarterly	Future	CF
Key customers service requests outstanding for more than 48 hours, reported to the general manager	24/7	Current	CF
Number of applicants for each advertised position	Quarterly	Past	ES
Candidates who have not yet accepted their job offer	Daily	Future	ES, IP
Expressions of interest from candidates who have not been responded to within 24 hours of receipt of interest	Daily	Current	ES
Percentage of staff working flexible hours	Monthly	Past	ES
Analysis of absenteeism	Monthly	Past	ES
Employee complaint resolution timelines and effectiveness	Monthly	Past	ES
Number of initiatives implemented after staff satisfaction survey	Weekly for four months post-employee survey	Past	ES
Date of next staff survey	Monthly	Future	ES
Number of CEO recognitions in past week/two weeks	Weekly	Past	ES
Number of CEO recognitions planned for next week/two weeks	Weekly	Future	ES
Number of planned recognitions in next week/two weeks by each manager	Weekly	Future	ES
Number of planned celebrations in next week/two weeks by each manager	Weekly	Future	ES

(continued)

TABLE F.1 *(Continued)*

Performance Measure	Frequency of Measure	Time Zone (Past, Current, Future)	Balanced-Scorecard Perspective(s)
List of high performing staff who have been in same position for over two years	Quarterly	Past	ES
Staff satisfaction with empowerment and fulfillment (assumes a survey is done three to four times a year)	Every employee survey	Past	ES
Staff who have handed in their notice today. Staff in vital positions would be notified directly to the CEO, other staff would be reported to the relevant general manager or senior manager. (The CEO has the opportunity to try to persuade the staff member to stay)	24/7	Current	ES
Number of potential recruits that come from employee referrals	Quarterly	Past	ES
Feedback on recruitment (survey of all new employees)	Every employee survey	Past	ES
Satisfaction with a balanced working and nonworking life (from staff survey)	Every employee survey	Past	ES
Attendance numbers for social club functions—by function in last quarter	Quarterly	Past	ES
Length of service of staff who have left (by bands less than 1 year, 2 to 5 years, 6 to 10 years, etc.)	Monthly	Past	ES

Description	Frequency	Time	Category
Turnover of experienced staff who have been with the organization for more than three years	Monthly	Past	ES
Number of staff members who have left within 3 months, 6 months, and 12 months of joining organization by division	Quarterly	Past	ES
Number of managers trained in recruiting practices	Monthly	Past	ES
Managers who have recruited staff who have left within 12 months of joining	Monthly	Past	ES
Recruitments in progress for which last interview was over two weeks ago	Weekly	Past	ES
Date of confirmed testing of candidates' capabilities (to avoid delays in testing that would delay recruiting)	Weekly	Past	ES
Key position job offers issued to candidates that are outstanding over 48 hours (report daily, all key position offers to CEO/general manager)	Daily	Current	ES
List of shortlisted candidates for whom next round of interviews has yet to be scheduled	Daily	Future	ES
Community/environmental satisfaction rating from external survey	Periodic survey	Past	E and C
Volunteers recruited in month	Monthly	Past	E and C
Volunteers resigned in month	Monthly	Past	E and C
Energy consumed by department	Daily/Weekly	Past	E and C
Percentage of recycled material used as consumables	Weekly	Past	E and C
Percentage of waste generated from consumables and is later recycled	Weekly	Past	E and C
Number of employees involved in community activities	Quarterly	Past	E and C
Donations to the community	Quarterly	Past	E and C

(continued)

TABLE F.1 *(Continued)*

Performance Measure	Frequency of Measure	Time Zone (Past, Current, Future)	Balanced-Scorecard Perspective(s)
Percentage of staff who are local residents	Quarterly	Past	E and C
Entries to environment/community awards to be completed in next three months	Monthly	Future	E and C
Number of environmental complaints received in a week	Weekly	Past	E and C
Number of external charity volunteers trained by company staff	Quarterly	Past	E and C
Number of employees involved in up-skilling local community organizations	Quarterly	Past	E and C
Number of media coverage events planned for next month, months 2 to 3, months 4 to 6	Monthly	Future	E and C
Number of positive press releases issued to the press in past 30 days/60 days	Monthly	Past	E and C
Number of positive press releases printed in the newspapers in past 30 days/60 days.	Monthly	Past	E and C
Number of papers/radio stations who have used key press release	Monthly	Past	E and C
Number of photos in papers last month, months 2 to 3, and months 4 to 6	Monthly	Past	E and C
Number of sponsorship projects in past 12 months by company	Quarterly	Past	E and C
Number of students recruited for holiday work	Quarterly	Past	E and C
Number of students who have been offered holiday work for the next holiday period	Quarterly	Future	E and C

Measure	Frequency		Category
Debtors over 30 days/60 days/90 days	Weekly	Past	F
Average number of days of usage by the major stock items	Monthly	Past	F
Days of purchases in accounts payable	Quarterly	Past	F
Net deficit/surplus by major department	Monthly	Past	F
Debt-to-tax payers' funds (equity) ratio	Monthly	Past	F
IT expense as a percentage of total administrative expense	Quarterly	Past	F
Total headquarters costs/employee (total organization's staff)	Monthly	Past	F
Status on the major top 10 capital expenditure (CAPEX) projects	Monthly	Past	F
Percentage of accounts payable invoices processed within the week of receipt	Monthly	Past	IP
Number of post-project reviews outstanding (major projects only)	Weekly	Past	IP
Number of registered patents	Quarterly	Past	IP
Number of overdue reports/documents	Weekly	Past	IP
Number of projects that are managed/staffed by contractors or consultants	Monthly	Past	IP
List of late projects by manager, reported weekly to the senior management team	Weekly	Past	IP
List of projects that are at risk of non-completion (unassigned, manager has left, no progress made in past three months, etc.)	Weekly	Past	IP
Number of committees/task forces that have not generated any substantive action within the past six weeks, reported to the CEO	Weekly	Past	IP

(continued)

TABLE F.1 (*Continued*)

Performance Measure	Frequency of Measure	Time Zone (Past, Current, Future)	Balanced-Scorecard Perspective(s)
Number of recognized mistakes highlighted last month (Note: if this number is too low, you have an unhealthy environment)	Monthly	Past	IP
Number of bureaucratic processes abandoned in month	Monthly	Past	IP and ES
List of consumable items where last consumption was over 6 months ago	Monthly	Past	IP
Availability of the major services we offer—average waiting time for service	Weekly	Past	IP
Percentage of on-time in-full delivery of service over 18 months	Monthly	Past	IP and CF
Teams with the best on-time delivery record, reported to the general managers and made available to all the staff in the organization	Weekly	Past	IP and CF
Emergency calls on hold longer than xx seconds notified to the CEO	24/7	Current	IP, CF, E, and C
Emergency response time when it is over a given duration (reported immediately to the CEO)	24/7	Current	IP, E, and C
Late deliveries/incomplete deliveries to our key customers, reported 24/7 to CEO, general manager, all staff	24/7	Current	IP
Number of improvements made to existing services	Monthly	Past	IP
Number of service improvements to be implemented in next 30 days, 60 days, and 90 days	Weekly	Future	IP
Number of hours system unavailable in month during office hours (list top ten worst offenders)	Monthly	Past	IP

Measure	Frequency	Time	Type
Percentage of products for which the first design of a device fully met the customer's functional specification	Monthly	Past	IP
Expected launch dates of top five next new services	Weekly	Future	IP
Service launches behind schedule	Weekly	Future	IP
Dollars saved by employee suggestions	Quarterly	Past	IP
Percentage of payments (excluding payroll) where the right amount was paid and on time	Monthly	Past	IP
Percentage of payroll payments where right amount was paid and on time	Monthly	Past	IP
Percentage of payments made by electronic funds transfer (include direct debits processed by suppliers)	Monthly	Past	IP
Percentage of requests for help fixed by Help Desk during the first phone call	Monthly	Past	IP
Percent of time IT program developers have spent on programming (excludes administrative time, etc.)	Monthly	Past	IP
Percentage spent of this year's technology capital expenditure	Monthly	Past	IP
List of top 20 capital expenditure projects running behind schedule	Weekly	Past	IP
Accidents and breaches of safety, reported to the CEO immediately	24/7	Past	IP
Date of prototype completion	Monthly	Future	IP
Average mainframe response time	Weekly	Past	IP
Percentage of staff, who have been absent for more than three weeks, who have a back-to-work program	Weekly	Past	IP
Percentage of days where key systems were backed-up at night this week	Weekly	Past	IP

(continued)

TABLE F.1 *(Continued)*

Performance Measure	Frequency of Measure	Time Zone (Past, Current, Future)	Balanced-Scorecard Perspective(s)
Date of last back-up test at remote site	Monthly	Past	IP
Business development expense/administrative expense	Monthly	Past	IP
Completion of projects on time and on budget (percent or dollar of total projects)	Monthly	Past	IP
Number of current users of xxx system	Monthly	Past	IP
Faults or service requests closed in month	Monthly	Past	IP
IT capacity of top five systems	Monthly	Past	IP
Percentage of key work carried out by contractors	Monthly	Past	IP
Last update of each team intranet page	Monthly	Past	IP
Lost time injury frequency	Weekly	Past	IP
Number of manual transactions converted to automated electronic feed	Monthly	Past	IP
Time taken from month's end to get the monthly finance report to the CEO	Monthly	Past	IP
Time taken from month's end to get the monthly report to budget holders	Monthly	Past	IP
Number of accounts payable invoices paid late	Monthly	Past	IP
Number of customer calls in test week (e.g., third week of month)	Monthly	Past	IP

Number of strategic supply relationships	Monthly	Past	IP
Number of systems that have been integrated with other company systems	Quarterly	Past	IP
Number of progress payments due that have not yet been invoiced	Monthly	Past	IP
Number of management team meetings last week (or number of management meeting planned for next week)	Weekly	Future	IP
Number of IT contractors as a percentage of IT employees	Quarterly	Past	IP
Number of critical assets in a catastrophic state	Monthly	Past	IP
Time delay between major event happening and it being reported to the senior management team (integrity gap)	Daily	Current	IP
Number of employees in organization	Monthly	Past	IP
Number of projects finished in the month	Monthly	Past	IP
Number of staff trained in first aid	Quarterly	Past	IP
Number of times xxx scheduled slipped in month	Monthly	Past	IP
New initiatives that will be fully operational in the next three months, by department	Monthly	Future	IP
Number of policy and procedures sections updated this month	Monthly	Past	IP
Percent of operational purchases from certified vendors	Monthly	Past	IP
Percent of positive feedback from employees after attending meetings (every meeting rated via intranet)	Monthly	Past	IP

(continued)

TABLE F.1 *(Continued)*

Performance Measure	Frequency of Measure	Time Zone (Past, Current, Future)	Balanced-Scorecard Perspective(s)
Product changes to correct design deficiencies	Quarterly	Past	IP
Safety measures—accidents, days lost by reason	Monthly	Past	IP
Number of staff who have attended the stress management course	Monthly	Past	IP
Staff with >30 days leave owing	Monthly	Past	IP
Staff who have been ill for over two weeks who *do not* have a back to work program, reported to the relevant manager and the senior management team	Weekly	Past	IP
Stakeholder feedback (on activities, working style, and communication)	When survey is performed	Past	IP
Number of protégés for each key position	Quarterly	Past	IP
Time spent by team on quality improvement activities	Monthly	Past	IP
Visits to managers planned next week, next two weeks	Monthly	Future	IP
Average emergency response time	Weekly	Past	IP
Number of quality improvement milestones implemented in month	Monthly	Past	IP
Programming changes to off-the-shelf applications by reason	Monthly	Past	IP
Engineering changes after design completion	Monthly	Past	IP
Improvement in productivity (percent)	Weekly	Past	IP
Number of improvements to products in month	Monthly	Past	IP
Number of processes made foolproof	Quarterly	Past	IP

	Frequency	Time	Code
Unplanned versus planned maintenance	Monthly	Past	IP
Waste—all forms: scrap, rejects, underutilized capacity, idle time, downtime, excess production, and so on	Weekly	Past	IP
Number of innovations planned for implementation in next 30 days, 60 days, and 90 days, reported to the CEO	Weekly	Future	I and L
Major implementations in past 18 months showing degree of success (exceeded expectations, met expectations, less than expectations, abandoned)	Quarterly	Past	I and L
Major projects awaiting consensus and sign-off, reported to the CEO	Weekly	Past	I and L
Managers demonstrating the most success with implementations over past three years, reported to the CEO	Quarterly	Past	I and L
Major projects in progress without contingency plans	Weekly	Past	I and L
Innovations that are running behind	Weekly	Past	I and L
Date of pilot completion	Weekly	Past	I and L
Date of next pilot test	Weekly	Future	I and L
Number of innovations implemented last month by team, reported to the CEO	Monthly	Past	I and L

(continued)

TABLE F.1 *(Continued)*

Performance Measure	Frequency of Measure	Time Zone (Past, Current, Future)	Balanced-Scorecard Perspective(s)
Date of next innovation training sessions	Monthly	Future	I and L
Number of managers who have been through the innovation course	Monthly	Past	I and L
Date of next innovation to our key services	Monthly	Future	I and L
Number of prototypes/pilots commenced in month by division	Monthly	Past	I and L
Date of next new service initiative	Monthly	Future	I and L
Number of crucial positions with at least two protégés by division	Quarterly	Past	I and L
Time saved each month through abandonments by team (reported monthly, featuring the top quartile performing teams in this area)	Monthly	Past	I and L
List of abandonments in last month by team (reported monthly)	Monthly	Past	I and L
Number of committees/task forces disbanded this month	Monthly	Past	I and L
Last meaningful action implemented by each standing committee	Monthly	Past	I and L
Number of monthly reports terminated	Monthly	Past	I and L
Date of planned replacement of service that has now become outdated	Monthly	Future	I and L

Number of abandonments to be actioned in the next 30 days, 60 days, and 90 days, reported to the CEO	Weekly	Future	I and L
Number of high performing staff by division	Monthly	Past	I and L
Number of promotions for high performing staff planned in the next three months	Monthly	Future	I and L
Date of next executive course to be attended by senior management-team member (monthly update)	Monthly	Future	I and L
Number of managers who have attended leadership training (quarterly by manager level)	Quarterly	Past	I and L
Number of managers who are scoring over xx on their leadership on the 360 feedback surveys (by manager level)	Post-survey	Past	I and L
Date of next leadership program and the list of suggested attendees by division (report weekly to CEO)	Weekly	Future	I and L
Date of next 360 feedbacks for level-1 and level-2 managers	Monthly	Future	I and L
Number of vacant leaderships places on in-house course (reported daily to the CEO in last three weeks before the course)	Daily	Current	I and L
Percentage of customer-facing employees having on-line access to information about customers (effective communication of accurate information to employee)	Monthly	Past	I and L
Percentage of employees below age xx	Quarterly	Past	I and L
Percentage of employees who interact with customers	Monthly	Past	I and L
Percentage of employees with tertiary education	Quarterly	Past	I and L

(continued)

TABLE F.1 *(Continued)*

Performance Measure	Frequency of Measure	Time Zone (Past, Current, Future)	Balanced-Scorecard Perspective(s)
Percentage of managers with satisfactory IT literacy	Monthly	Past	I and L
Percentage of staff who joined less than three months ago who have had a postemployment interview	Monthly	Past	I and L
Percentage of performance reviews completed on time	Monthly	Past	I and L
Percentage of level-1 and level-2 managers who have mentors	Quarterly	Past	I and L
Number of high-performing staff who do not have a mentor	Weekly	Past	I and L
List of level-3 managers who do not have mentors	Weekly	Past	I and L
List of level-1 and level-2 managers who do not have mentors, reported weekly to the CEO	Weekly	Past	I and L
Percentage of staff performance reviews completed	Monthly	Past	I and L
Percentage of contractors to total staff	Quarterly	Past	I and L
Annual average of training days by team	Monthly	Past	I and L
Average employee years of service with company	Quarterly	Past	I and L
Training expense/payroll cost	Quarterly	Past	I and L
Number of employees certified for skilled job functions or positions	Quarterly	Past	I and L
Number of employees complying with their development plan	Quarterly	Past	I and L
Number of employees terminated for performance or other issues	Monthly	Past	I and L

Number of employees who have improved skills during last six months	Six-monthly	Past	I and L
Number of employees with delegated spending authority	Quarterly	Past	I and L
Number of employees attending sponsor courses to increase reading and math skills	Quarterly	Past	I and L
Investment in new product support and training	Quarterly	Past	I and L
Number of leadership initiatives targeted to rising stars to be completed next month, months 2 and 3, and months 4 to 6	Monthly	Future	I and L
Number of managers who have had performance-management training	Monthly	Past	I and L
Number of positions where needs assessment gap has not been performed for position	Quarterly	Past	I and L
Number of current users of X system	Quarterly	Past	I and L
Number of staff members trained to use X system	Quarterly	Past	I and L
Number of in-house training courses planned for next month, months 2 and 3, and months 4 to 6	Quarterly	Future	I and L
Number of internal promotions in the last quarter	Monthly	Past	I and L
Number of staff who have agreed-upon development plans	Quarterly	Past	I and L
Number of teams with a balanced scorecard	Monthly	Past	I and L
Number of training hours—booked for next month, months 2 and 3, and months 4 to 6—in both external and internal courses, by team	Monthly	Future	I and L

(continued)

TABLE F.1 (*Continued*)

Performance Measure	Frequency of Measure	Time Zone (Past, Current, Future)	Balanced-Scorecard Perspective(s)
Number of training hours—booked for months 1 to 3 and months 4 to 6—for the senior management team	Monthly	Future	I and L
Number of contractors who have been employed for over three months	Quarterly	Future	I and L
Number of internal applications for job applications closed in month	Monthly	Future	I and L
Number of level-1 and level-2 managers who were promoted internally	Quarterly	Future	I and L
New staff who have not attended an induction program, within two weeks of joining (to be reported to the CEO)	Weekly	Past	I and L
Percentage of managers who are women	Quarterly	Past	I and L
Percentage of teams having team meetings once a week	Monthly	Past	I and L
Percentage of cross-trained personnel per team	Quarterly	Past	I and L
Teams not represented in the in-house courses to be held in the next two weeks. Report daily to the CEO	Daily	Future	I and L

Staff who have verbal feedback about performance every month	Quarterly	Past	I and L
Average number of innovations per employee per 12 months, by team	Quarterly	Past	I and L
Ratio of implementations to suggestions made	Quarterly	Past	I and L
Total hours employees spend in mentoring	Quarterly	Past	I and L
Training days this month	Monthly	Past	I and L
Turnover of female staff	Quarterly	Past	I and L
Turnover of staff by ethnicity	Quarterly	Past	I and L
Number of staff who are aware of new initiatives	Monthly	Past	I and L
Number of teams who have undertaken internal user satisfaction surveys in past six months	Monthly	Past	I and L
Percentage of staff meeting continuing professional development requirements	Quarterly	Past	I and L
Number of research papers generated	Quarterly	Past	I and L

The recommended category headings for a performance measures database are set out in Chapter 9.

Key for Database

CF: Customer Focus
E and C: Environment and Community
ES: Employee Satisfaction
F: Finance
IP: Internal Process
I and L: Innovation and Learning

Past Measure: All measures measuring past activity. (Note: Yesterday's activity is considered a current measure.)

Current Measure: Yesterday's or today's activity.

Future Measure: Measure of an event that is to occur in the future (date of next meeting with key client, date of next staff survey, date of next in-house leadership course, etc.).

Presenting the Critical Success Factors to the Board/ Government Official

I have attached a draft presentation that all readers of this book can access electronically, free of charge, from my web site.

Critical Success Factors
Presentation to the Board on xx/xx/20xx

Presented by: xxxxx

CSF Program Overview	Setting the context of the KPI project.
<ul><li>CSF and Balanced Scorecard concept was started in 20xx</li><li>The program involves developing CSFs for XXXXXX and for all its important business lines and support functions</li><li>The program will finally result in having online dashboards for XXXXXX and its business lines by First/Second Quarter of XXXX</li><li>Focusing on KPIs will help XXXXXX staff to focus on the daily activities that are critical to the business</li></ul>	

CSF Program Objectives	These objectives may be usable in your organization.
<ul><li>To capture XXXXXX's critical success factors (CSFs)</li><li>To develop KPIs that will focus staff and management, daily, on what matters</li><li>Help senior management and business line heads use daily KPI flash reports and weekly/monthly progress update dashboards</li><li>Enable management and business line heads to monitor the health of their line functions and respond to deviations</li><li>To align daily activities in the business to organization's future strategy</li></ul>	

Critical Success Factors - Evolution

Discussing the evolution of working with the critical success factors

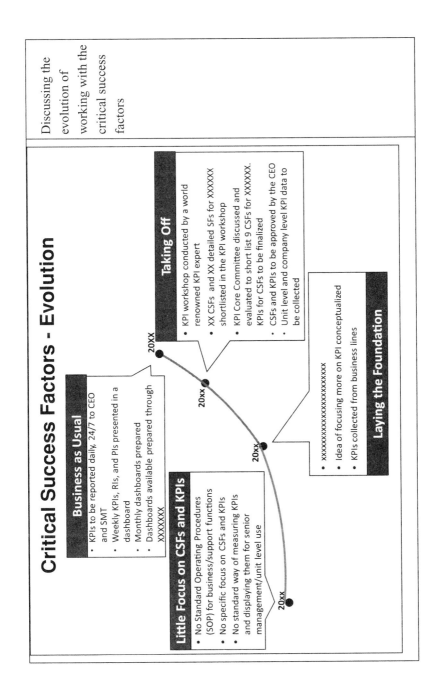

Business as Usual

- KPIs to be reported daily, 24/7 to CEO and SMT
- Weekly KPIs, RIs, and PIs presented in a dashboard
- Monthly dashboards prepared
- Dashboards available prepared through XXXXXXX

Taking Off

- KPI workshop conducted by a world renowned KPI expert
- XX CSFs and XX detailed SFs for XXXXXX shortlisted in the KPI workshop
- KPI Core Committee discussed and evaluated to short list 9 CSFs for XXXXXX. KPIs for CSFs to be finalized
- CSFs and KPIs to be approved by the CEO
- Unit level and company level KPI data to be collected

Little Focus on CSFs and KPIs

- No Standard Operating Procedures (SOP) for business/support functions
- No specific focus on CSFs and KPIs
- No standard way of measuring KPIs and displaying them for senior management/unit level use

Laying the Foundation

- xxxxxxxxxxxxxxxxxxxxxxx
- Idea of focusing more on KPI conceptualized
- KPIs collected from business lines

20XX

20xx

20xx

20xx

Critical Success Factors

CSF Name

xxxxxxxxxxxxxxxxxxxxxxxxxxxxxxxxxxxxxxxxxxxxxxxxxxx

xxxxxxxxxxxxxxxxxxxxxxxxxxxxxxxxxxxxxxxxxxxxxxxx

xxxxxxxxxxxxxxxxxxxxxxxxxx

xxxxxxxxxxxxxxxxxxxxxxxxxxxxxxxxxxxxxxxxxxxxxxxxxxxxx xxxxxxx

xxxxxxxxxxxxxxxxxxxxxxxxxxxxxxxxxxxxxxxxxxxxxx

The top 5 CSFs

xxxxxxxxxxxxxxxxxxxxxxxxxxxxxxxxxxxxxxxxxxxxxx

xxxxxxxxxxxxxxxxxxxxxxxxxxxxxxxxxxxxxxxxxxxxxxxxxxxxxx

xxxxxxxxxxxxxxxxxxxxxxxxxxxxxxxxxxxxxxxxxxxxxxxxxxxxxx xxxxxxxxx

xxxxxxxxxxxxxxxxxxxxxxxxxxxxxxxxxxxxxxxxxxxxxxxxxxxxxx xxxxxxxxxx

You would typically have between 7 and 12 critical success factors at first. It is worth separating out those that scored very high such as the top five critical success factors.

Mapping Criteria for KPI / PI / KRI / RI

Explaining the difference between the four measures.

KPI

- Measured daily/weekly
- Nonfinancial measures (not expressed in dollars, yen, pounds)
- Indicates where the action should be
- Tells you what to do to increase performance dramatically

KRI

- Measured monthly/quarterly/yearly
- Can be a financial/nonfinancial measure
- Indicates results rather than actions
- Reported as a way of trend/graph

PI

- Measured daily/weekly/monthly
- Nonfinancial measure (not expressed in dollar format)
- Focuses on a specific activity/team

RI

- Measured daily/weekly/monthly
- Can be a financial/nonfinancial measure
- Indicates results rather than actions
- Indicates results of more than one team

An organization should not exceed 10 KRIs, 80 PIs/RIs, and 10 KPIs

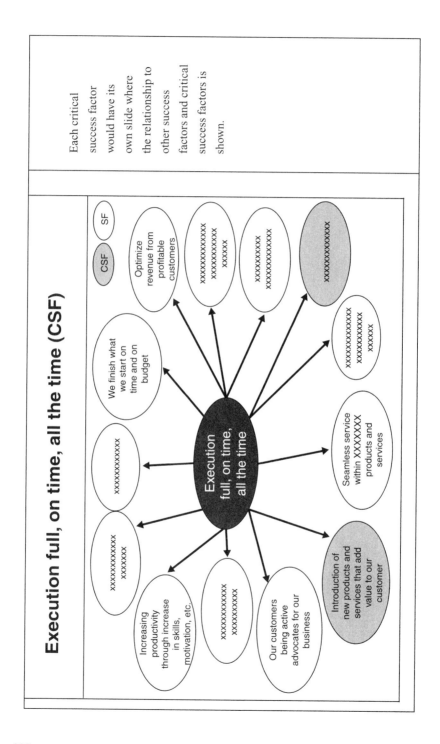

298

Innovation is a daily activity (CSF)

Each critical success factor would have its own slide where the relevant measures are outlined.

KPI	PIs	RIs	KRIs
Number of innovations planned in the next 30, 60, 90 days	1. Number of innovations last month by team 2. Date of next innovation training session	1. Innovations that are running behind schedule 2. Date of prototype completion	Innovations implemented in the last 18 months by division
xxxxxxxxxxxxx	1. Xxxxxxxxxxxxxxx 2. Xxxxxxxxxxxxxxx 3. xxxxxxxxxxxxxx	1. Xxxxxxxxxxxxx 2. xxxxxxxxxxxxxx	xxxxxxxxxxxxxx

(one slide per CSF)

Process to discuss these CSFs with staff

The critical success factors will need to be discussed with staff and their importance explained.

- Discuss communication with union reps xx Jan
- Deadline date for final presentation
- Pilot presentation to a small group xx Feb
- Dates of roll-out of presentations to all staff
  - xx March Division A
  - xx March Division B
  - xx March Division C
- Preparation of video for overseas staff xx April
- xxxxxxxxxxxxxxxxxxxxxxxxxxxxxx

The ramifications on existing performance measurement

- Abandonment of process, reports, measures
  - xxx process
  - xxx process
  - xxx report
  - xxx measures
- Moratorium on all new measures outside of KPI project
- Greater focus on unintended consequences (the dark side of performance measures)
- xxxxxxxxxxxxxxxxxxxxxxx

To make room for this project, other performance-management activities will need to be abandoned.

Visit Chapter 2 to understand the significance of this.

Permission to proceed to next stage

- Selection of the KPI team by xx Jan
- Contract external facilitator to mentor KPI project team by xx Jan
- Backfill KPI staff so they can be full-time on KPI project by xx Feb
- Complete training of KPI team xx Feb
- xxxxxxxxxxxxxxxxxxxxxxxxxxx
- xxxxxxxxxxxxxxxxxxxxxxxxxxx

The last slide is to obtain approval of the board for:

- Critical success factors
- The appointment of the project team
- The commitment of resources

Main Differences between the Balanced-Scorecard and Winning-KPIs Methodologies

R ight from the start, organizations around the world were quick to see the benefits of a balanced-scorecard approach, and many organizations initiated projects. The groundbreaking work of Kaplan and Norton[1] brought to management's attention the fact that strategy had to be balanced, needed to be implemented, and performance should be measured using a more holistic approach.

Unfortunately, many balanced-scorecard initiatives have failed. So how do you adapt and apply a balanced-scorecard approach and get it right the first time? We need to place sturdier support underneath the balanced-scorecard platform, as set out in Exhibit H.1.

These four supports have been discussed at great length in Chapters 1, 2, 3, 7, and 9.

Main Differences in the Two Methodologies

The balanced scorecard will be with us for centuries to come. We just need to make it work better. I see my methodology *underpinning* the work of Kaplan and Norton rather than undermining it.

There are some important differences that need to be understood. The winning-KPIs methodology states that:

- The primary role of performance measures is to help the workforce focus on the *critical success factors* of the business, day-in and day-out. Kaplan and Norton see the primary purpose of performance measures as the need to monitor the implementation of strategic initiatives.

Giving the balanced scorecard some support

EXHIBIT H.1   Four Supports to the Balanced Scorecard

- You need to know your organization's critical success factors because these are the crux to finding the KPIs. However, Kaplan and Norton do not mention critical success factors in their work.
- *All* KPIs are all non financial, measured frequently, have five other characteristics, and thus, are rare, with fewer than 10 in a business. Measures that are not KPIs are either result indicators, key result indicators, or performance indicators. Kaplan and Norton see all measures as KPIs.
- You find your critical success factors through mapping the relationships of the organization's success factors ignoring any attempt to place these success factors into balanced-scorecard perspectives. By contrast, Kaplan and Norton focus on a strategic mapping process where strategic objectives and success factors neatly fit into a balanced-scorecard perspective—a process that is stimulating to intellectuals, but of little practical use to the workforce in managing their daily activities.
- An organization needs to look at six perspectives, adding "environment and community" and "employee satisfaction" to the standard four perspectives of Kaplan and Norton.
- The balanced scorecard's perspectives are seen as a guiding force ensuring you have balance; the critical success factors and KPIs are seen as transcending more than one balanced-scorecard perspective. In fact, the "timely arrival and departure of planes" critical success factor of an airline impacts all six perspectives. Kaplan and Norton see the perspectives as firm boundaries into which you can slot strategic objectives neatly. Strategic objectives are seen as a succinct statement describing what an organization needs to do well (success factors) in each of the four perspectives in order to implement the strategy.

EXHIBIT H.2   Differences between the Balanced-Scorecard and Winning-KPIs Methodologies

Winning-KPIs Methodology	Balanced-Scorecard Methodology
Emphasizes the importance of implementing strategy in a balanced way. Total agreement with Kaplan and Norton	Emphasizes the importance of implementing strategy in a balanced way
Strategy mapping is seen as an intellectual process with questionable value. This is replaced with relationship mapping of success factors with multiple relationships.	Based around strategy mapping where success factors neatly fit into an individual balanced-scorecard perspective
Knowing one's critical success factors is seen as fundamental to knowing what to measure	Critical success factors not addressed in their work
Performance measures are brainstormed from the critical success factors	Performance measures are brainstormed from strategic initiatives
Six balanced-scorecard perspectives through the addition of "staff satisfaction" and "environment and community" perspectives	Four balanced-scorecard perspectives
KPIs have seven characteristics and are thus rare. Other measures are either result indicators, key result indicators, or performance indicators	Key performance indicators not defined. All measures are called KPIs and therefore seen as important to the organization
Less than 10 KPIs in a business	Many KPIs in a business
Measures seen as either looking at the past, the here and now, or the future	Performance measures are either lead/lag KPIs
A philosophy that says it can be implemented by an in-house team	An approach that is largely consultant based, requiring much intellectual rigor
No applications required. At some stage a reporting tool will be needed to monitor and report on measures.	A myriad of balanced-scorecard applications that support the strategy mapping and cascading performance measures leading to hundreds of performance measures without any linkage to the organization's critical success factors.
The KPI book is a tool kit for implementation, containing checklists, agendas for workshops, a framework for a database, report formats, and guidance notes on all twelve steps.	The balanced-scorecard books are largely an academic-based approach with few implementation-based tools provided. There is an implicit suggestion that you will require a consultant to implement the measures.

■   The process of finding the right performance measures can be done in-house, whereas the balanced-scorecard approach, due to its complexity, is frequently led by consultants and has created a major industry of providers of software and balanced-scorecard consultants.

The differences between the two approaches are summarized in Exhibit H.2.

Note

1. Robert S. Kaplan and David P. Norton, *The Balanced Scorecard: Translating Strategy into Action* (Cambridge, MA: Harvard Business Press, 1996).

Index